# SUBURBAN SLUMS

*BILLY JOE is a Hero and Role Model for everyone who thinks they cannot change their life. Billy Joe has overcome odds that would have crushed most people's spirit, but she has shown us that anything is possible if we believe in ourselves and work hard. This book will be an inspiration to everyone who reads it. I am very fortunate to have the honor of being her friend for the past 34 years.*

*Lori (Lena)*


This book is highly engaging in that we are transported into an almost alien world of a little girl who is brutalized by her mother and then because of this situation, moved into the drug underworld of Detroit. This woman has had more experiences and close calls than any soldier in battle. And then one cannot be more touched by her enlightenment, redemption, and turn-around in her life towards the good. In a sense, this is a firsthand account, and historical novel, which catches a part of the Detroit underworld of the 70s and 80s that most people only know sparingly from the cop shows. This will keep you captivated!

W. L. Wheeler


*When I started to read the book I could not put it down. This is a true story of one woman's life. Billy Joe found her in the midst of a real life nightmare. Not only has she survived her lonely and non-conventional childhood, her teenage drug years, her failed relationships, her young motherhood, her years behind bars, she has now become a very accomplished, proud, hard-working woman. Billy Joe has made her life a testimony to overcoming nightmares. This book will inspire all who read it. It gives us proof that we can survive. Billy Joe is now using every day of her life to inspire and help others to survive.—Kimberley*

# SUBURBAN SLUMS

## THE SECRET LIFE OF ONE WOMAN

# BILLY JOE

iUniverse, Inc.
Bloomington

**Suburban Slums**
The Secret Life of One Woman

iUniverse books may be ordered through booksellers or by contacting:

iUniverse
1663 Liberty Drive
Bloomington, IN 47403
www.iuniverse.com
1-800-Authors (1-800-288-4677)

ISBN: 978-1-4759-7715-8 (sc)
ISBN: 978-1-4759-7717-2 (hc)
ISBN: 978-1-4759-7716-5 (ebk)

Library of Congress Control Number: 2013903329

Printed in the United States of America

iUniverse rev. date: 02/23/2013

# PREFACE

This book is a true chronicle recording a roller-coaster of events of a young girl who was brought up by a mentally ill mother and then enchanted with a Sicilian gangster who was 29 years her senior. Her life was entwined around the street life of mystery, danger, murder, drugs, guns, and crime; living a life of fantasy, which turned into a reality. Her life was filled with destruction and dysfunctional events. Her life styles lead her into incarceration. After her release, she vowed to assist others like herself and started a Half Way House for mental health returnees (D-47 parolees). She returned back to school receiving her limited license through the State of Michigan as a social worker. She is working as a substance abuse counselor assisting adolescent and adults. Encountering a long struggle of prejudice, slamming of doors and biased individuals because of her past, she is determined to conquer society and regain the life of freedom, while she continues to fearlessly and morally search herself daily.

This book is a memorial of her struggle. The grammar and sentencing structure is not completely in order; the author wanted to leave it in her natural street dialect. This was her street lingo in the sixties, seventies and part of the eighties. It allows the audience to feel her personality and ignorance to life and the situation of events as she encountered them.

Some characters in this book have passed on through death while others are still alive. She is not trying to hurt anyone or expose anyone. She is just speaking on her life experiences and events of trials and struggles she came across throughout her life. This book was not written to get money for the crimes committed but to shed a light for others to change their life and record for posterity the mixed up street life of Detroit in the late twentieth century. She is not proud of her past and very embarrassed by some of the items in this book.

She felt naïve not understanding the complete concept of consequences of her wrong doings. The ripple effect it had on all the lives around her. She lives for recovery now and has dedicated her life to it. She believes in recovery and the penal system. Without it, she has no idea where she might have been with her life choices. She owes her Higher Power for all her success and frame of mind. Her main prayer is for all those she has hurt in her life time, will find forgiveness, as she has learned to do the same.

She does not claim to be a writer and this book seems more like a diary than novel but many who have read it, stated it was interesting and kept their curiosity. It is segments of her life that has turned into a nightmare. She wanted it to help others with their self-esteem and choices in life. **"Never give up, giving up on giving up."**

# Characters of the Book

**Mother**—Marge

**Father**—Michael

**Step Father**—Tom

**First Older Sister**—Julie

**Second Oldest Sister**—Paula

**Third Oldest Sister**—Lilly

**Main Character**—Billy Joe—main person this book is written about

**Last Sister**—Nivea

**First Older Brother**—Ben

**Second Oldest**—Rip

**Third Brother**—Rick

**Billy Joe's First Husband**—Bernard

**Second Husband**—Dee

**Third Husband**—Vicenza Giuliano

*Billy Joe*

**Fourth Husband**—Zakeith

**Main Characters Daughter**—Sabrina

**Street Characters**—Cherry, Lena, Denver, Alan, Lori, Eddie, Doodle and Carney, Ju-Ju Bean, Acacius (Cassius), Aaron

**Characters in Prison**—Militia, Nina, Alicia, Peco, Denville, Donna, Bonnie, Western, Warden Little, Adeline, Deputy Warden Robert, Officer Shawn, Officer Oz, Officer Sales, Silvia, Wig, Lina, Jill, Deputy Faults, Tina, Sadie, Deputy Premont, Mrs. Purple, Celeste F

**Characters of different Employments**—T.J. Norton and his wife

THIS BOOK IS DEDICATED TO
MY DAUGHTER
MY GRANDCHILDREN
MY FATHER (MAY HE REST IN PEACE)

AND

MY BROTHER . . . . WITH ALL MY LOVE

# Suburban Slums
# "The Secret Life of
# one Woman"

The year was around the1979, and I am sitting in the courtroom listening as the judge is hitting his gavel upon the desk. My ears are muffled as if I was under water. Everyone is in an uproar. The witness just told the courtroom he could identify the defendant if he ever saw her again. The prosecutor asked the witness to stand up and point the defendant out. I just knew he was going to point his finger at me, as he stood up, looking around the room. I am the only one sitting here next to my attorney. As the witness stood, a dark cloud rose over the room, as if a storm was about to hit. My knees became weak and I anticipated the man pointing me out. However, to my surprise, he pointed to one of the jurors and the crowded courtroom literally went nuts. I leaned back in my chair; it was as if I could hear nothing around me, as if my ears were underwater. I could only hear the dampened sounds and my own heartbeat. I cannot believe this is happening to me. It is not as if I had been a good citizen or a perfect person. I always did illegal activities but I never got this involved until my

life was rooted with Vicenza Giuliano. My brother tried to warn
me but I am so bull-headed that I would not listen. I always
think I know everything. Now here I sit, twelve people to decide
my destiny. I am too much in a state of shock to be scared. I
guess you could say I am in denial. My whole life is flashing
before my eyes. What happened? What is going to become of
my daughter? What could I have been thinking of? Well, as I sit
back and realize that I destroyed my life, my daughter's life, that
man's life and his family. I came to see the good, the bad and the
totally insane.

# CHAPTER ONE

## ADOLESCENT YEARS

I was born in the 1950s at St. John's Hospital in Detroit, Michigan. My mother's name was Marge; my father's name was Michael Key. I have seven siblings. My sisters are oldest to youngest: Julie, Paula, Lilly, myself-Billy Joe and Nivea. My brothers from oldest to youngest are: Ben, Rip and Rick.

My mother said when I was born I had dark black hair and dark complexion. She thought I belonged to another family. A few weeks later, my hair started turning light blond, almost cotton white. My mother stated that she knew I was going to be a trouble child because I started walking before I crawled. I would walk around my crib like a monster. They had to place braces on me from my hips to my ankles. Mom stated she would try to put me down in the crib but I would force my way back up. Once she said, I climbed out of the bed. My legs and feet were crooked and I ended up being pigeon toed. My mother and father divorced when I was one year old. My dad said I was crazy about him and would run from the living room window to the kitchen window to see him when he came to visit.

There were stories that were told growing up just like any normal family. Our family stories seem a bit unusual to say the least. I heard the story a dozen times that I was raised by dogs because we had a Great Dane that thought I was her puppy. The family would watch and laugh as she snatched me up by my diaper and carrying me to the closet laying me down for rest. That dog would

1

not allow anyone to touch me. Growing up I was consistently getting into trouble. My mom would try to spank me using a switch off the tree outside. The dog would get angry with her. Once she was trying to punish me and the dog attacked her. So my mom took me in the bathroom to whoop me and the dog tried to knock the door down. Mom got rid of the dog because of it. I cried and felt like I lost my best friend.

I grew up on the west side of Detroit area. I had one friend named Lori, who lived in a house at the end of the block. Her grandma lived two houses down from ours and when Lori and her sister would visit their grandma's house we would play together.

My godmother and godfather lived across the street from us. Every year they would purchase an Easter hat and basket for me. I do remember once I went across the street because they called me over there. My mom beat my butt and legs for going. I did not understand why. I was very hurt by it because my godparents called me over. They were not married, but brother and sister. My mother named me after my Godmother Billy Joe.

Our street was long and had several blocks to it. My school was at the end of one of the blocks. I attended an elementary school called, "Academy Elementary." I was so smart that I attended kindergarten and my first words I spelt were "dictionary" and "encyclopedia" so they promoted me to second grade. I never went to first grade.

I loved playing with my friend Lori, when she came down to her grandma's house. I remember, once, Lori, her sister, my sister Lilly and I would dress up and play thanksgiving. We would take paper and make Indian feathers, and pilgrim hats, and feathers for the turkey. We would put on little plays and do dress up. I remember we had so much fun. When Lori did not stay at her grandma's house it was boring for me. She was my one and only friend.

I don't know why but I seemed to get into trouble a lot. I can't remember all the things I did but I do remember the spankings. My brother Rip who was older than me, was always experimenting with his chemistry kit and once he was working on an operation and it backfired on him. Rip and his friend was building a bomb or something and it blew up catching our garage on fire. The fire department had to come and put it out. Rip threw his friend out the window and jumped out there to roll him on the ground putting out the fire. My mom was not happy. We did get the garage fixed but mom worried about Rip playing with chemistry sets after that but for us, it was just normal kid stuff.

Rip was always using me as his Guinea pig. We were both standing behind the garage and he was smoking a cigarette. My mother came back there and Rip did not want to get busted so he handed me the cigarette. (Thanks Rip) Mom made me smoke a whole cigar to teach me a lesson. That cigar turned me blue in the face. I got so sick to my stomach and it was not even me who was smoking but I got punished. I also got a beating with a switch. I did not think I would ever smoke as an adult because of that.

We were a very dysfunctional family. I remember many times I was left alone until my other siblings came home from school. My mother would be at work. My sister Paula was attending beautician school. She would walk down the street to get there. I saw a mouse one day and was scared to death to stay in the house. I ran down the street to catch Paula and when I finally did I told her I was scared. Paula told me she had to go to school and did not have time to deal with this. She was already late. Paula was always more concern with her own issues than ours. She told me that the mouse was more scared of me than I was of it. I went back home and stood on a chair until Rip or Lilly came home.

My memories of my younger days are slim but as I grew older I kept having thoughts of one of my older sisters taking me downstairs in the basement. She would take me into a room that was on the right side of the steps in the basement. She would touch me in my private area, and have me touch her. I did not understand back then why she did that to me. I never asked her why when I grew up either. I was always too embarrassed to bring the subject up.

Later on, another one of my older sister stated my mother's boyfriend was touching my sister's private areas and she probably was acting out with me, what was being done to her.

Julie, my oldest sister, and my mother argued a lot. One day, I saw everyone crying. Afterwards, I found out Julie died in a car accident. I am not sure if it was a week or a day later when she and mom argued. Mom was never the same after that.

Dad said that Julie was on her way to his place. My sister said Julie had her own place. There were rumors that Julie had a boy friend named Mot, and my mother was with his best friend John. John and mom were hypothetically married in Ohio.

John was the one molesting my sisters. My other older sister got away from him, he chased her too. I don't know if that is why Julie and mom were arguing or if it had to do with something else.

I know when John broke off his relationship with mom, he took all of our furniture out of the house and left us on the floor. My father was so angry when he found out.

My father's best friend Ron had to talk my dad out of getting a shotgun and going to our house. He was so angry with my mother; he wanted to shoot her and that man John. My father told me this story several times. He told me he bought each one of us kids a bed to sleep on and told my mother do not get in any of those beds, that they were for his children. My father blamed my mother for having John in the house to take everything we

4

own and left us high and dry without anything. It is said that my mother's boyfriend John was an ex-con and mom had him in the house with us kids.

Julie was a dark haired lady with olive colored skin. She died when she was young. I can't remember exactly but she was either eighteen or nineteen when she passed. She lived in Tennessee with grandma until mom married my father. Then my parents brought her and my brother Ben up to Detroit to live with us. I believe Julie was around five or six years old when my father started raising her. Ben would go back and forth to Tennessee with his real father because he never lived with us like Julie did.

My mother had Julie buried in Farmington, outside of Detroit. She must have had the idea to move out there when she buried Julie. We did not move after Julie passed for several years. Julie had a full-blooded brother named Ben, but he did not care for any of us. They both had the same father. Both were blacked hair and had olive skin color.

Mom said she was married to Julie's and Ben's father and he was a bigamist. I figured my mother was just saying she was married. I don't know, did they even allow a person to marry that was married? I guess that question will never be answered.

They did not have their father's last name either. Julie had my father's last name my father adopted her. My father loved her as if she was his own. Ben did not want my father's name. He was also in love with my older sister Paula. He ended up marrying a girl that looked just like Paula.

Paula, Lilly, Rip and I were conceived by my father. My mother was married to my father for close to seventeen years before they divorced. They divorced when I turned one year old. There was four years difference between me and Lilly. Rip and Paula look like my mother. Lilly looks like Julie and Ben. I look actually like my father.

My father's family owned land out in Mexico. It had oil reserve contract on it and dad received a check when they rented it out to an oil company. He and his sister shared it. Rumor was that dad gave mom so much money to keep it out of the divorce.

I was also told many times that my sister Paula supposedly signed my mother's name on a couple checks that came in because my father did not want my mother to get her hands on it after the divorce.

I really believed that my father really did not care about land, and he allowed his sister to take the majority of the funds. My mother tried several times to get us kids to take my father to court for that land. Mom still brought up Dad's land several times throughout our lives trying to make a claim on it.

So that is a run-down of the family and who my siblings are. Growing up was a challenge to say the least.

My first memory of getting into trouble was when I was five.

Once I was on my way to Kindergarten. I took my mother's diamond ring that my father bought her when they married. I was going to show it at "show-n-tell" that day. I did not understand about us being divorced so I was going to show the ring and express they were no longer married. As I was walking in the snow, I tripped, fell, and lost the ring. Every day, when I came home, my mother would spank each one of us until we would tell who had it. Of course, I was not going to snitch on myself. So every day all of us kids came home from school, we would get a whooping with the switch from outside, off the tree. My sister Lilly kept trying to get me to tell on myself, but I would not do it. It came down to her and me getting spanked.

My sister Paula's boyfriend, or brother-in-law to be, "George", took me to every place that I could have walked that day to see if he could find it on the ground. We never found it.

Of Polish descent, George was tall with blond hair. He had ambition. He put himself through college and was going places. He was with my sister since she was fourteen or fifteen years of age.

So George has been in our family ever since I was a little girl. He did not get along with my brother Rip because George tried to be the man in our family. Rip felt like it was not his place to be the man of the family because we had a dad and Rip felt like he was to take over when our father was not there.

We never found the ring and mom stopped whooping us. Everyone in the family knew I took it. For some odd reason, things started when I was young. That was my first big jewelry heist.

I would attend school and loved it. I was really smart. I was cute and I had hair that went down to my butt. Mom would start up at the top of my head and make a braid all the way down. It was thick and full and, as I said before, it hung down to my butt.

I was in school and this black boy loved to touch my hair. We had a fire drill and I was standing in the hallway waiting for us to leave out single file. That kid touched my hair and I turned and snapped on him about it.

I went home later that day and told my mother about it. She took my hair and grabbed it at the top of the braid and cut it off with the scissors. I had a picky hair style. I was so hurt, I cried all night. I loved my long hair. She told me; "Now you don't have anything to complain about, this is a lesson to watch what you complain about or I will give you something to cry about." I ran to my room and hated I had no hair. My mom was so mean.

Meanwhile we would go to Belle Isle Park in Detroit; it was the most popular park. I was playing baseball with my brother and sister Lilly. She got angry with me for some odd reason. Lilly took the baseball bat and hit me with it.

My eye appeared animated, as if someone took charcoal and rubbed it all over my eye. I climbed up this tree and stayed there refusing to come down. A family photo was taken of this event. I was six years old in this photo. In the photo you can see the black eye, also the picky hair cut my mother gave me. Our new dog was on the side of the tree and our car was out in front of the tree.

My mom did nothing to Lilly for doing that. If it wasn't for my brother she would have killed me. Lilly was quiet but had a mean streak in her about me.

My father lived on the east side of Detroit, on the corner of some apartment building. He worked at the Chrysler plant for 43 years. He was fifty-one years old when he and mom conceived me; my mother was thirty-three.

My father had always been old to me but he was a great dad. All my siblings said daddy was mean with no emotions but when I was around him, he always showed a lot of emotion and love. I didn't really know the father they talked about. My older sister and brother stated how dad was to them.

When I was six years old after my black eye went away, dad asked mom to allow me to accompany him to Aunt Lilly's house. My Aunt Lilly was rich and owned most of Williamstown, Kentucky. Everyone knew them, and they helped to put Williamstown together so to speak.

Aunt Lilly was my father's only sister and was living in Kentucky. My Aunt Lilly and Uncle Rip, her husband, had adopted a daughter named Donna who is my cousin. They did not adopt her until she was almost in her twenties, to leave her their wealth. She also grew up around them and they were attaching to her.

My sister Paula, throughout our family life, seemed to be the only one in the family that kept a relationship up with Aunt Lilly and Donna our cousin. Aunt Lilly really despised my mother.

So I went to my father's place in Detroit and we spent the day with each other.

We would go to the zoo and eat at the hamburger joint which is one of my favorite things to do with dad. At the hamburger joint, we would sit on the bar stools and eat lunch . . . . I loved it. The atmosphere was warm and comfortable like I was a big girl hanging out with my dad. It was just like T.V.

Later that night, dad had me wash up and get ready for bed. I looked out the window and remembered one time, my brother Rip showing me how you could stick your head out the window, then wipe your face and see the dirt on your face from the factories. So I did that but it was funnier when Rip was with me doing it.

Dad and I went to sleep and as we were lying down, dad kept feeling me get hot and sweaty. He was very concerned and just watched my bios.

The next morning when dad and I got up, dad wanted me to go to the doctor for a check-up before we started on our travel to my aunt's house in Kentucky. I did not want to go but I did not want to be defiant to my father.

I came down with a fever every night, but I did not hold a fever during the day.

This concerned my father and he started to take me to different doctors. Many of them stated that there was nothing wrong with me. My father knew different. He continued to take me until my legs gave out on me. Then he carried me from bus to bus. He finally broke down in a hospital asking someone to help him.

A nice young distinguished looking African man approached my father and asked him what was wrong. Dad explained with tears of fear. The doctor called us into his office. He looked me over and wanted to admit me for tests. He believed he knew what was wrong but did not want to state it until the results came in.

The doctor sat behind his big oak wood desk, writing on some papers. It felt like twenty minutes went by before he looked up. He got up and slowly walked over to me, taking my vitals. After a few minutes, he looked at my father who had not had any sleep in a few days worrying about me. "I am not sure but I believe that your daughter has Rheumatic Fever. Of course, I would have to admit her; run a series of tests before I am able to accurately submit a full diagnosis of her illness. Just try to trust me and in the Almighty."

This made my father feel very comfortable because this doctor believed in a higher power. My father was so relieved that someone was willing to take a moment out to physically check me out that he just broke down and literally cried real tears and mumbled, "Please register her in; you have my consent."

I was placed in Children's Hospital in Detroit. They placed a net over my bed to keep me from climbing out. I hated it, and became very hostile and refused to comply with anything they wanted to do with me. I had been left at home for an hour or so alone but never anywhere in a big hospital or facility.

The girl next to me was dark skinned with nappy hair and enjoyed making others miserable. She would tell me that my mother would not be able to visit after visiting hours. I corrected her and informed her that my mother received permission from the main office because she works. She continued to dispute this with me until I refused to discuss it any further.

Later that evening, my mother walked in. I must admit, I was relieved because I started believing what the girl told me. With much pride, I looked over to her and stuck my nose up as to say; "I told you she would be here."

I laughed and smirked a little with victory. She closed her curtain and gave me my win. The visit with my mother was enjoyable, we never really got along but at that lonely moment, it was great to have her there.

A little cute dark skin boy walked into my room, and mom invited him over to my bed area. He told her that he would keep an eye on me for a small fee. He was a little hustler to his seven-year-old heart. His lips were big and full. They covered completely the lower level of his face. They were at least, an inch and half wide, and as a pair, it measured out to three inches all together. Yeah, his lips were that big and wide. Realistically, may be as a young kid, everything looks bigger than it really is. However, to me, his lips were the first thing you focused on when you met him. His hair was coarse, hard and coal black. In the early sixties Afros were very popular and he wore one well. Not very groomed or even, but all over, like it had no real shape. He was tall for seven years old and very street smart.

My mother agreed to give him the job. I was totally outdone with her as if I needed a babysitter especially one that was almost the same age as me. I did not agree with this and protested my mother's will on it. Of course, she ignored me and made the arrangements.

11

I could not stand him coming in my room every day asking me to kiss him. He would lean over my bars and throw those big thick lips my way. You could see the saliva bubbles on the dark pink area of his mouth. I would turn my head and push him away.

When I was in the hospital they would give me a thick yellow medicine in a white paper cup. It was nasty tasting and I hated drinking it. When I got a chance and no one was looking, I would get rid of it. One day when cleaning my area, the girl pulled my bed away from the wall and saw a bunch of yellow substance on the wall. She reported it and the nurse came in asking me if I was throwing my medicine on the wall behind my bed. I did not admit it to it and so they decided to start giving me shots in my arms. When my arms got too small, they started to use my thighs. After a while, my thighs got too small so they started giving me the shots in my butt area. I hated that shot; it was worse than drinking the medicine. I did not realize it back then but that medicine was making me well and helping me to live.

Every time my mother came to visit, I would complain about this situation to her. She would just laugh as if it was a joke and not something to taken seriously. I believed she liked me being uncomfortable with this state of affairs. The more I complained the more she laughed. These visits with mom were not going well.

Then, my mother told me that my father placed me in this hospital, because I was a bad kid and I had better straighten out. I cried and told her that was not true. My father placed me here to get well because I was sick. She kept trying to convince me otherwise. She ended up leaving and later on, I would lay in bed all night thinking she was telling me the truth. I started to cry and I felt so lonely. Would my daddy do that to me, trick me into admitting me into this hospital because I was bad? I rolled over and tried to go to sleep. I just wanted to go home.

The next day, my father came in to visit with me and I told the nurse that he was **not** my father because I was so angry with him. Then a tall black man walked in wearing brown leather, and I lifted up stating that was my father.

My dad was so hurt he just turned around and went home. He felt, if I wasn't interested in visiting with him, then he would leave. He was not going to push himself on me. My father was not one to stay where he felt unwanted. My dad was a proud man, having been to World War II and worked a stint on the railroad. Later he became employed with Chrysler Corporation, and worked with for them forty-three years. That is a long time at one company. My father was a very loyal man.

His father died when he was around six years old. He went to live with his Uncle Sam who owned a big tobacco farm in Mexico. Later down the line, dad went and lived and grew up in Mexico on an Indian reservation.

When my father was younger he was driving around with his friends. There was a man my father called Pegleg. They were being crazy like young kids and dad went off a bridge and Pegleg died. My father was accused of his death as the designated driver and was sent to the Masons instead of sending him to jail. Dad did not mean to cause that accident. They took my father in and he stayed with them for several years. That is how my father became a Mason. I believe his father belonged to them too. That's why they took an interest in my dad. My brother has his ring to this day.

Dad was very open to people and their ethnic backgrounds. Dad accepted everyone for who they were inside and out. My father used to tell me that you can't have expectations of people because it would be yours. You can only have them for yourself.

I really saw the hurt on his face when I told the nurse that he was not my father. I never realized at that moment how that statement would follow me for years to come.

As time flew by, it was a year later and I was becoming stronger and ready to go home from the hospital. My mom made a bed for me in the living room so I could watch the kids outside the window. I would roll the window open, and play with them. I was bed bound and my mother hired a lady to watch me while she worked. I was not supposed to get out of bed. I was on a strict diet of lamb meat only, no salt. I had to take penicillin shots every month until I was twenty-one years old. I made everyone's life miserable. (Smile) I had a pair of crutches to go with my attitude and a wheelchair.

The lady that Mom hired was a woman named O'Finna who lived with us and took care of my needs. It was cool. O'Finna had black curly hair and she was crippled with polio. She was about 4' 5" and very funny. She was a woman with a soft spirit. She was happy to be hired because many people were biased against her due to her physical condition. She was prefect for the job. She was given her own room and she just had to watch me and make sure I ate what was prescribed.

She had the habit of falling asleep and I would sneak out, get into the kitchen cabinets, and steal food. Of course, food I was not supposed to have. The strict diet was because of my heart.

The penicillin shots were administered to me in the hip. I was too skinny any place else. The situation was dire; I was told that I would never be athletic and participate in sports like a normal child. The doctors told my parents I might not live to 21. I hate to tell you this but I was out to prove the world wrong. I did everything I was told would never occur and did more than I should have. As I was growing up I often snuck out and played

14

sports anyway. I was a big tom-boy growing up and I did not let my illness hold me back.

My father really loved my mother but my mom married dad for security. My dad always said that mom told him she was pregnant after one date. So he did the right thing and married her. My father would laugh and say, "It took that baby eleven months to arrive." Dad would also say he was happy he had all of us children. I was a daddy's little girl and either hung on my dad or my brother Rip. Both of them taught me how to fight and take care of myself.

I came from a semi-large family. All of us were dramatic with a bit of sarcastic personalities. Ben left home when I returned from the hospital. My mother stated he left because I was ill and he could not use the car. She stated it was my fault that he did not stay. I believed that for a long time but I don't anymore because I believe the reason he split was mom.

Julie died in a car accident. Paula married young, and made a wonderful, wealthy life for herself.

Rip became rich with experience and knowledge. He also stood by me 100% through some of my rough times; he worked as a contract carpenter. He was like a father and mother to me; he was my idol. I love Rip with all my heart. I always wished I could have found a man, half the man he was. Rip comforted me like a real father. Matter of fact, Rip, my father and I were the most alike in the whole family. You can hold my picture up to my fathers' photo and see I got my looks from my dad. I did not look like the rest of the family. I looked just like my dad but as a girl.

Everyone else in the family including Rip looked like mom. They had her eyes and nose. I was so glad I did not get her nose. It is long and crooked with a hook on the end, like a witch's nose. I got my father's nose.

My sister Lilly does not look like anyone . . . my dad or mama. She looked a lot like Julie. Lilly's nose, eyes and olive skin remind me of Julie and Ben. I always wondered if their father came around mom and she had Lilly; because her and my father had been separated for four years before I came around.

Dad stated he lived in our basement and paid all the bills and allowed mom to do as she pleased. Then after about four years went by, he wined and dined mom and they went to bed and I popped up. Mom divorced him when I turned one year old.

Rip took me under his wing. I don't know if that was a good thing or not (smile). He would make me eat worms and bugs to hang around with him when I was little. He was so mean. He was always training me to be a fighter, and would give me money to beat up other little kids. Rip and his friends would laugh when I ate the bugs but at least he allowed me to hang out. A small price I had to pay. (Smile)

In our neighborhood there was this boy that was two years older than me, that lived about four houses down from us. One day I was sneaking around and went down there to play. This little boy beat me up and pulled my pants down in front of everyone. I was so embarrassed I ran home crying. I climbed up a tree which was my favorite thing to do when I was upset.

My brother saw me and asked what was wrong. I told him and he looked at me and asked if he went with me did I think I could beat that kid up. I said yeah and my brother walked down the street with me and I grabbed the boy in front of everyone and beat the crap out of him. I was seven and a half and he was nine. After that, I was king of the neighborhood. He would walk on the other side of the street when he saw me coming. I was so proud of myself. I felt like I had power.

My brother would teach me how to fight. If mom knew I was out there fighting and playing hard like that she would have beat my butt.

I used to carry a note to school stating I was not able to participate in sports or gym. I would take the note and tear it up and play anyway. When my mom would find out she would beat me. What was the difference, her whooping me or me playing sports?

My sister Paula wasn't like us, she had a completely different style than Dad, Rip and me. Where we were aggressive in our mannerisms she was passive but would get people back in a different way without using her strength, but her brains. She got pregnant and mom made them get married. She had her first child and her and George lived with us for a while. She really wasn't part of my life until later on. I really did not know her growing up. I heard she got treated like me growing up so she wanted to get out of the family. I think she was only sixteen when she got pregnant. I am not really sure but I know she was young.

As the years gone by, I got healthier and my mother felt it was better to move all of her children out of Detroit into the suburban area. My brother Rip was getting into trouble in Detroit and my mother wanted him growing up in the suburbia. Mom also stated that we had to move because of me. I was not allowed to have city water. I don't think that was true. We left Detroit and moved to Farmington, where Julie was buried.

It was nice but it was nothing like Detroit. What I mean by that is the style of clothing, events, and people in Detroit were far different than what was going on in Farmington. It was sort of a cultural shock. Everything was laid back and behind the times; stores left things out in the open or placing everything they had on the sidewalks for sale. In Detroit, people would have taken that stuff. Farmington was a nice town, and people left their doors open at night. That would have never occurred in Detroit either. Sometimes, people would sleep out on their porches too in the summer time. You were not going to find that in Detroit.

It was a bit of change in many ways, the people were different too. Some were a bit snottier, stuck up and felt they were better. I went to school with kids that did not have much living in Detroit.

When we moved to Farmington, I attended school with kids, who had family members as judges, attorneys, court justices of the peace, mayors and the list goes on. Now I am attending a school where kids were spoiled.

I was put back a grade and had to repeat the second grade for the second time. I was embarrassed and totally upset, because it made me look dumb. I really did not want to attend school just because of this situation. I was not happy about this. I attended a school called Cloverdale Elementary. I was not accepted and did not make friends. Kids laughed at my clothes and how skinny I was. Trust me, I got into a lot of fights.

My brother Rip had no problem fitting in. My sister Lilly went off into her own little world. She did not have many friends, and stayed a lot to herself. She was quiet and did not socialize at all; she really isolated herself. Matter of fact, she only had two boyfriends her whole life and married the second one. It was not because she was not attractive, because she was. She had beautiful legs and body, as if she was a Hawaiian girl from some tropical island. Lilly had long dark hair and golden skin. She was very beautiful but for some odd reason, she did not think so.

Then there was my sister Paula and her husband George. They lived in the suburbs with us for a couple years. After their daughter was born they moved into their own home and started a foundation of their own. Financially and intellectually they were above us and we were an embarrassment to them. So my sister Paula did not really deal with us besides a phone call or babysitting issues.

Mom did not like for us to go out of the yard and play with other kids on the block so she got us a swimming pool with a deck all around it. It was square with a ladder going up to the pool. She thought this would keep us in the back yard.

One day, Lilly and I were in the swimming pool together. We had been swimming and having fun until Lilly became angry with me. I would call her Lilly-mill-puke. She would become so angry when I would tease her. She grabbed me while I was in the pool. She held me down in the pool with a great deal of force. I could not get a way. Lilly was just being despicable when I came up. I cried out and yelled for help and she pushed me back under and my brother heard me. I felt like I was losing my air, like I was dying. To this day, I can't not stand going under water.

My brother came running to the pool saw what was going on. He grabbed Lilly out of the pool by her hair and threw her on the deck. I crawled out of the water and my brother helped me out. I was tired and unable to go another inch. After climbing out of the pool, I just lay on the deck crying and out of breath, gasping for air. He turned to Lilly and asked her if she was crazy and what the F—was wrong with her. He told Lilly, "You could've drowned her." Lilly just stood there looking at Rip without saying a word. I just loved my brother; he was always there protecting me.

My brother protected me against my mother too. One time after that pool scene, he went to Pontiac Juvenile Home for it. My mother caught me doing something; I can't even remember what it was that I did so wrong. I might have gotten caught with a cigarette or food in my room. My mom had me pick a branch off the tree in the back yard; she beat me with the switch.

19

My back was bleeding and I had about four or five large cuts on my back, all of them full of blood. My brother came home later that night and I was in the bathroom trying to pull my white t-shirt off the cuts, and it kept on sticking.

My brother walked in the bathroom, saw all the blood and cuts on my back, asking me "how" did that happen; who did this to you?" I told him to leave it alone. He would not let the issue go. Then I told him mom did it. He went out in the living room and I tried to stop him, but he was so angry. Mom was standing by the dining room wall. We lived in a brick ranch type house. My brother pushed her in the wall and told her, "Do not ever lay your hands on her again like that or I will do something about it."

My mom was in shock that he pushed her like that. Mom treated the boys like gold. They did no wrong.

The next day, she called the Pontiac Juvenile Home for boys and made up a big story and had my brother put in Juvenile.

I will never forget when we went up there to see him for Easter; mom told me I had to sit in the car, because I was not allowed up there. Then she told me that she wanted me to sit there in silence and realize that it was my fault he was there; that I was the cause of him being away from home on Easter; that I was an evil child with a dark cloud that followed me and everybody I come near; that people suffered because of me. I don't know how many times I heard her say, ***"the devil sits in your face girl"*** throughout my life.

Living with mom was a true experience. She never had anything to do with her family; mom had thirteen siblings. I remember two tall uncles coming to see us before at an early age. They had been in jail and were alcoholics. I also remember her one sister visiting us a few times. She was with a black man. (Who later became

20

my uncle?) They had nine children from that marriage which were my cousins. They could not be legally married because back then, blacks and whites could not intermarry. They could not legally marry until 1968.

Mom stated that this particular sister killed her first husband by pulling the plug and that is why she did not want her over our house. She had no connection to her family and did not want them around.

She did go get grandma from Tennessee in the mountains because she was alone. Mom went overboard trying to please her mother but grandma did not care for mom; you could tell by their relationship. She came to live with us and refused to live in the house. We designed the garage as a house for grandma to live in it. I hated it because once a week each one of us kids had to stay a week out there with her to make sure everything was okay. I hated it when it was my turn. There was no TV.

Grandma did teach me a lot growing up, like how to knit, make soap, butter, and make quilts. She even made rugs out of nylons. She was very talented. She would sit and read the Bible all the time. She really did not get along with my mom either but she stayed with us. She was around 300 lbs. or more. She had long hair and it was mother-of-pearl white. It hung down to her butt and grandma would comb it with a small comb. Then she used that to keep her hair up. She would twist and roll it into a bun stationing the comb to hold it. Grandma never really wanted much, just the material needs to make the things she liked. She did not care about conforming to this world.

We placed a stove and refrigerator in the garage for her. She did not believe in TV and felt it was the devils tool to destroy the world.

She did love chocolate candy bars. Milky Ways were her favorite. Mom would buy her bags of it. Mom would bend over backwards but grandma did not like mom's ways. Grandma took care of mom's children that she had out of wedlock. Julie and Ben lived down there with grandma in Tennessee while mom worked here in Detroit. Mom would send money back to take care of them. Now grandma lived with us in our garage. She never attended the family functions that we had whenever we had them. It was nice to have grandma in my life when God allowed it.

Well, like every kid, I loved to play games and sports. I wasn't supposed to do it, but I just had an ambition inside of me. I always seemed to be doing things I had no business doing. I loved baseball, and because of my illness and the doctors stating I should not participate with sports, I would have to sneak out to play it. I ran track, climbed robes, and did everything any other kid did. I was good at sports. I had incredible strength like my brother and father.

When my mother would find out that I was playing sports, she would get mad. However, my father would come to my rescue. He would tell my mother, "If the child dies playing sports, it is better for her to have lived a full enjoyable life, than to live a miserable life staying in the bed doing nothing. Let that child live, and be a normal child even if it means that God takes her. At least, she would have lived life to its fullest."

I was playing basketball in the back yard while mom was at work. I ran in the garage and grandma was rocking in her chair and I hit her old trunk.

It cut my thigh on my right leg open on a metal piece sticking out of the trunk. It was so bad it did not bleed and you could see the meat. I showed my grandma and she told me to put a Band-Aid on it.

Mrs. Parker next door saw what happen through the fence and came over to help. She saw my grandma was not doing anything. Mrs. Parker took me to the hospital. It is funny because my mother was pissed at me for Mrs. Parker taking me to the hospital. I got in trouble for it. Mom also told me that the doctor had a heart attack when she had to sew me up.

My mother was nutty but back then I never realized it as a kid, but she believed her lies. I was embarrassed of my mother and plus the fact my grandma lived in our garage.

When my mother moved my grandma to Detroit from Tennessee, it was nice to have some of her family around but it was totally embarrassing that we were playing the part of the Beverly Hillbillies.

It wasn't long after that incident that my grandma fell over dead with a heart attack. My brother and his friend John had a hard time picking my grandma up. My brother kept trying to cover grandma up, her skirt kept rising. She would wear nylons rolled up above her knee because they could not go all the way up with her legs being so fat.

They got grandma to the hospital but soon she passed away. At least she did not have to be alone in Tennessee way up in the Smokey Mountains by herself. No one would have known for many months that she was dead.

I do remember us going there as a little kid. I hated it because there was no one around for miles. It was way up on the mountain. It did not have running water or a bathroom. We had to use outhouse and a pump to get water. The cabin was small with no decorations. It smelted and had snakes. There were so many holes in the yard that had been covered up because the outhouse was there at one time. Flies were everywhere in the outhouse and the main house. You could not eat without being attacked. I hated it. Those were memories I had of grandma living in her habitat. May she rest in peace!

Well, after grandma died, life went on. I cannot pinpoint where it started, or how my life was turned around but it did. I can't really blame anyone but myself, many other kids had it worse than me and they did not turn out like me. Something was not clicking right in my head I guess. My mother made me stay in the back yard. I was never allowed to have friends over or go down the street. I was not allowed to talk to anyone. Mom always felt I would screw a boy too early and get pregnant, so she kept me under tight surveillance.

I really believed that because she had Julie and Ben out of wedlock; my sister Paula got pregnant before she was married and because of this family tradition, mom felt so worried that it would happen to me. Mom would state that men used blond haired women. She also stated that men thought all blonds are whores.

There were twelve boys that lived next door to us. They were referred to as the Parker boys. My mother would go crazy if I communicated with any of them. I would sneak to talk with them and hang out when she was at work.

My mother was just funny about things and life. She had a different way of looking at life and what was right or wrong. She turned me into a loner growing up. I am still that way today.

I wasn't really allowed many toys, she really did not believe in them. Mom did allow me to have a doll. Barbie dolls were popular. Everyone had one, but because their boobs were big, mom would not allow me to have one so she would purchase the Tammy doll for me. I got mad and cut Tammie's head off and stuck a pen or pencil in her tits. I took her head and made a puppet out of it, out of anger.

One Christmas, my dad purchased me an Easy-Bake Oven. I was so excited I could hardly wait to use it.

My mom took it, threw it in the garage. She refused to allow me to use it. I would sneak out and use it anyway. I took it out of the trash. When she found out, she gave it to a girl who lived at the end of my street. Someone I did not even associate with. Her father was an officer of the law, which did not mean anything to me at that time, but it just made me mad, every time I saw her. I hated the fact she was enjoying *my* Easy Bake Oven that *my* father purchased for me on Christmas.

Mom felt since we had a pool and a skating rink in the winter time, a bike, (that I was only allowed to ride up and down the drive way), was enough. That was my mother's idea of having fun and us having toys. We were allowed to watch T.V. until 8:00 pm. Every Friday night, we were given one bag of chips and two Country Town pops on weekends. We were giving one pop for Friday and one for Saturday that was our treat. Mom did not buy cakes, candy or sweet cereals items like that. She did bake a lot. She made sure she baked homemade pies and cakes from scratch every other week. She had us girls learning how to bake by the age of twelve.

I will never forget mom showing me how to bake a pie from scratch. We had two cherry trees and one apple tree in our backyard. Mom would have all of us kids out there on ladders picking cherries. Of course, we ate more than we picked.

After the cherries were picked, we would take them in the house and clean them off. Take the stems out, and then open them up to take out the pit. I'm reminded of that book title when I remember this time in my life: **"Life is nothing but a bowl of cherries, but all I ever get are the pits."** (Smile)

After removing the stems and pits, we would wash them again. We would get a big pot out and pour all the cherries that could fit in there. Grab a few cups of sugar and cook them down. Once they were cooked down, we would make our pie dough. Mom would take Crisco grease, added some flour, baking soda, baking powder, instant potato flakes, salt, water, baking soda and a pinch of sugar. She would kneed that dough until it was just right the old fashion way. Once we stuck the pie dough in the oven and baked it. We would pour some of the cherries over it and then cut strips of dough for the top part of the pie.

Well, it was my turn to show how I would be a good wife when I grew up. It was my turn to make a pie. When I made my pies most of the time, I would cook them downstairs in the basement because it was cooler down there, and more room.

I was coming up the stairs with the pie and tripped at the top of the stairs falling over on the vestibule area by the back door. The pie flew everywhere. I hurried and picked it up and ran back down stairs and grab more strips to put on the pie.

There were hairs in the pie and dirt from the floor. I did not want my mother to see it. She would have made me do everything over from scratch plus beat my butt. She would also be angry about the waste. So I covered it up. That evening when we were going to sit down for dinner, I told my brother not to eat the pie.

I explained to him why. He and I both did not eat the pie that night. So mom did teach me things, she always told me, I need to know how to cook, clean and iron clothes to be a good wife. As the old saying went, "The way to a man's heart is through his stomach". I heard that enough.

Of course Lilly could not cook no matter how many times my mother showed her how. Mom used to cook the meal for her fiancé and tell him that Lilly made it. Lilly was like Elly-May on the Beverly Hillbillies, where her biscuits had to be buried out in the back yard.

She was not good at housekeeping either. I use to hate when Lilly had to do dishes, because as soon as she did, mom would come get me out of bed and have me redo Lilly's dishes because mom said Lilly left food on them.

She would never correct Lilly about it just have me redo them. That was pretty much what she did with most of the chores Lilly did. If they were not done right, mom would come get me and have me redo them. I hated that, and could not understand why she did not just show Lilly how to do it the right way.

Mom was a trip, and she babied Lilly a lot. She always called her Julie. After Julie passed, mom gave Lilly all of her clothes to wear. I really think she was trying to recreate Julie through Lilly.

Time went on, and everyday living occurred. I mainly played in my back yard, because as I said before, I was not allowed out of my yard.

I was playing in the garage one day and one of Rip's friends was renting our upstairs in our garage after grandma died. Our garage had a nice upstairs to it with a furnished bedroom up there. It would get really hot in the summer time but stayed alright in the winter.

Anyways, Rip's friend was a bit weird; he had this statue made of every piece of gum he ever chewed. When he was done with the gum, he would take the gum and wrap it around this statue. It was weird looking at first glance but it looked like art. When you got close up on it and realized it was gum, it kind of made you want to throw up.

One day while playing in the garage, Rip's friend cornered me in the garage and wanted me to pull my pants down so he could see my private area. I did not want to do it but he kept telling me that Rip wanted me to do it. I felt funny but I did it and Rip came in and caught the man doing this to me. Rip was so angry that he kicked his butt from the garage to the street. Rip beat that man up for messing with me. He was always my hero.

Of course he did not live with us anymore after that, and we did not tell mom. She would have felt I did something to cause it. Rip and I kept it all to ourselves on what happened. Rip moved in the garage after that.

Rip and I kept many secrets that were not shared with others in the family.

Once I was on the deck of the pool swimming by myself, because mom would not allow us to have friends in our pool. As I was standing up drying off, I heard an alarm going off and looking over a couple houses where the sound was coming from. I could see the Farmington bowling alley and Deane Inn Restaurant. Those buildings were three houses down from our home. One could see into their parking lot. The Deane Inn Restaurant was a fancy place and the children of the man that owned it, went to school with me and were my friends.

Anyways, I looked over there in the parking lot and heard the alarms going off. Suddenly I saw about four men dressed in dark clothes running out of the building. I did not really see what they looked like, I just saw them running.

Later on, many years later, I found out that was my brother and his friends. They did that! Rip was lucky that he did not end up in trouble. Later on, he was shocked that I remembered that and saw them. I am glad he changed his life since then.

I don't know if I had bad luck or if I just had issues happen to me in my life time. Was I creating these incidents or what? I had another family member which was a brother-in-law who wanted to touch me sexually. He asked me to pull down my pants so he could see if I had any pubic hairs. It was at Christmas time.

I cried because I did not want to do it either, and he told me that everyone does it for people they love. Then he started to plead with me to show him, if I cared about him. I look back now and think about all the sick people that were in the world even back then. I never told anyone about this until I was in my forties.

Then my brother's girlfriend Gloria pulls my pants down to humiliate me all the time. I could never understand what she got out of that. She lived down the street from us, and my brother hung out with her brother John. John was my brother's best friend besides the Spear's Boys.

One time when she first did it, we were playing baseball with some other kids, while my mom was at work. Gloria got mad at me and pulled my pants down in front of everyone that was out there. I pulled up my pants and cried telling my brother what she did. My brother really did not like her; he just wanted to screw her. He did get mad at her for doing that. Gloria was just a mean girl and a loud month.

My mom worked two jobs and most of the time, I only saw her on her back laying on the coach sleeping from one job to the other. She was a hard worker. So Rip was the one that was really raising me. Dad lived downtown on Eastside of Detroit.

I spent a lot of time in my own surroundings with not many options. When I was able to sneak out of my back yard, I did. Sometimes I would sneak over the fence, or just wait until mom went off to work.

One time mom went to work and I snuck out to play with Debby who lived two doors down from me and Tina who lived across the street. Some of the kids and I went sledding across the street behind this one house. If you crossed the street and went behind the neighbor's yards, there was a big hill and the neighbors never complained about us going back there.

The hill might have been really small, but back then, it seemed to be huge. The hill went down to the wood and a creek. They said it was the Rouge River. We would take cardboard boxes and make them into sleds. Of course some of the kids got real sleds for Christmas and would use them.

We would also go out on the river in winter ice skating. I fell in a few times but nothing dangerous. Except one time, I snuck to go skating and Debby had to go home but I wanted to stay. So I did.

I had a blue fur coat on with a red belt to it my dad purchased it for me. I will never forget this. I was skating and the ice caved in. I was scared to death. The current was pulling me in. It was part of the Rouge River. I was by myself. I did not know God for real at that time but I look back now and know he was there with me and saved me.

The current was pulling me under the ice and I could not touch the bottom of the river. I could not even yell out; no one would have heard me anyways. I slid under and floated to a branch, and grabbed it.

I held on to it tightly until I was able to pull myself out. I was nervous and scared to death. I got out and was freezing cold. I had to walk home like that. I had ice skates on and my coat was soaked and wet. I hurried home and placed my coat in the dryer for a minute. I did not want it to shrink. I then hung it up and did not say anything to anyone. Mom would have beaten me until I could not standup if she knew I was out of our yard.

Winter has past and it was summer time. The flowers were blooming and the grass was green. I always loved to see the summer months appear. As a kid I did get into a lot of stuff. Once I was playing down the street, there was a hole in the ground and I saw a wild rabbit come out of that hole. So I stuck my hand down in there to get the bunny.

My brother told me I was lucky that the mother was not there or she would have bitten me. I pulled a baby rabbit out and took him home. I called him Chipper. I hid him in the garage during the winter time. When summer came, I placed him in a shoe box and put him up in the apple tree so no one would hurt him.

One day, I came home from school and could not wait to play with Chipper. When I went to the tree, the shoe box fell down and Chipper was gone.

Then later on I was in the house and saw Chipper through the window. He was just having a ball going from one place to another eating. Chipper would not leave our yard area, he would just go from one part of the yard to the other. It was cute watching him in his habitat.

Denny lived down the street next to the parking lot of the Deane Inn and I came home from school one day and he had my rabbit. He was telling everyone he caught a wild rabbit. But I told him, that it was my rabbit and he did not catch a wild rabbit. We got into an argument about it. But I ended up taking Chipper home with me. I took him away from Denny. I put Chipper back in my yard.

A few weeks later my mom finally realized that I had a pet rabbit in the backyard and questioned me about it. She told me that wild rabbits did not have any business being a pet.

A couple days later, Rip came to me and said, "Billy Joe, come on, my treat, I will take you to Burger King." I loved Burger King! That was my favorite hamburger in the whole world because they used a tomato. What I did not realize was my brother was taking me there because he knew my mother had killed my rabbit and cooked it for dinner. Rip did not want me to find out. So he took me to Burger King. But when we got back home, I saw the chicken on the table.

I looked at it and said it looked funny. Everybody at the table was looking at me strange. I could feel something was not right. Then, I realized it was not chicken at all, it was Chipper. I ran outside and called Chipper several times and looked for him. I never saw him anywhere again. My mother had killed my rabbit and made dinner out of him. I really hated her for that.

I grew up hiding things from her and the rest of the world. All I ever wanted was her to love me; show me that she loved me. She never hugged me, or told me she loved me. I don't remember hearing those words out of her lips ever. Growing up was very difficult for me. I started smoking cigarettes by the time I was eight years old. I stole them from other parents, because neither one of my parents smoked or drank. The other kids around the neighborhood would usually steal the smokes for me from their parents. Anything to escape from the prison I was living in with my mother.

Mom started dating a lot of men and some of them became my babysitter. I can't recall all of them but I remember at least seven of them. One was married and was my mom's supervisor or boss at work in the factory; his name was Mel.

He had a wife and children at home and he would come and babysit me. I once asked him *why* he was babysitting me when he had seven children to babysit. Of course that question got me slapped so hard by my mom; it slapped me into next week.

Another time; my mother went out with this older man with gray hair named Harvey. I will never forget him because he gave me a stuffed rabbit as big as me. I put it on my bed. I never got a stuffed animal before and mom did not really allow things like that. So that meant a lot to me. When mom broke up with him, he came into my room and took the rabbit back. I cried and mom got mad and gave me something to cry about, a spanking for complaining.

Finally mom met a man named Tom; he was tall and had tattoos all over his body. He was nice and polite. Rip did not get along with him at first because Rip was used to being the man in the family. Tom came with some rules and corrections and Rip bumped heads with him. Soon mom married him stating she needed someone to make Rip stay in line. Mom just did not want to be by herself. She was a manizier. (Like womanizer)

Tom was nice and would take me fishing, teaching me how to use wading boots while fishing. He would get upset because I would always make too much noise with the water and scare the fish (smile).

He would teach me how to use a 30-06 rifle for deer hunting. We would go out shooting and Tom would drink on these outings so mom would not bother him about it.

At first she did not bother Tom about anything he did. He had drinking parties over at the house. Mom would make sandwiches and buy the drinks. Tom's friends would come over and play cards downstairs. Every Friday there was a card drinking party that went on in our basement on payday.

Our basement was all furnished with a bathroom with a shower, large bedroom, living room and kitchen with a bar that separated the living room from the kitchen. Of course there was a laundry room down there too.

Mom allowed this, because before that, Tom was going out drinking. Mom did not like that. She wanted him home where she could keep an eye on him. So this went on for a while and little by little mom manipulated him to push it out of his life.

Mom and he would fight when he drank. I used to lay in bed scared and wondering if we were in danger. This went on many weekends and it was stressful. I had a pretend imaginary friend called Mary. She was an angel that would appear when I needed her. She would protect me and allow me to tell her all my hurt and pain I felt inside. I kept Mary until I was 12 years old. Then I got on drugs.

Sometimes Tom would get mad and take off in his tan Dodge Dart car and mom would wake me out of my sleep and have me run down the middle of the street screaming at the top of my lungs, begging for him to come back. Mom said he would not be able to turn me down because he loved children. She was right because he would always see me in his rear view mirror and stop the car before he got to the end of the street. I always hated running down that street late at night or early morning because the next day in school I would be tired. At that time I was mom's bait to keep Tom with us.

Tom had a lot of family and it was nice because we never had family come around. My mom had thirteen brother and sisters and we never saw them. I saw my aunt a couple of times. I never understood why mom did not deal with her or any of her family but I had a bunch of mixed cousins out here and don't know where to find them.

Tom had family come over every weekend we had steaks and hamburgers on the grill. It was the best time I can remember growing up besides being with my dad.

Then mom started pushing his relatives away one by one. She manipulated every situation and would dream up incidents that would really make you wonder if they were true or not. I was so used of her fabricate stories that I knew what she was doing. She was a drama queen and did not stop until she was able to control the situation. Soon Tom started backing away from friends and then relatives. They saw mom for who she really was. She knew how to get them out of the picture so they did not take Tom from her.

Tom had a wife before mom and they were not able to have children so they adopted a child and raised it as their own. One day his wife was driving with their adopted child in the car and had an accident. They were both killed. After that, Tom drank himself stupid. With mom being nuts and Tom on alcohol, I had to find an escape.

Once I reached sixth grade, well, actually the summer of seventh grade. I started experimenting with narcotics, weed and alcohol. I was eleven years old going on Twelve. It was as if I found a negative avenue to escape the pain and loneliness I felt growing up. I always had to stay in my backyard and was never allowed to go anywhere along with no phone privileges. I was not allowed to talk to boys and mom would have a fit if I did.

I was getting older and encountered more issues in my life. Tom was cooler than mom about stuff so I could go to him with things, where I could not talk to my mom about things.

Then mom found out she was pregnant by Tom; everyone wondered HOW? Tom still drank because he was grieving from his first marriage. Tom's family stated it could not be his. This was mom's opportunity to push them out of Tom's life.

My real father was still strongly in my life; he did not agree with a lot of things that my mother did but he tried to allow my mother to raise us and he provided for us. He liked Tom. I was going to start Farmington Jr. High after summer.

Mom was pregnant and Tom stopped his drinking. Mom, having his baby meant everything in the world to him. He always wanted children. When he could not have children with is first wife, he thought it was him. That is what the doctors told him. It was not him; it was his first wife that was not able to conceive. You can tell Nivea was his.

My father was seeing me every weekend. I would go to Detroit or he would take me somewhere. It was great to get away from Mom and Tom. With mom being pregnant, I was starting to feel more unwanted than usual.

Back when I was in fourth grade; I wanted to play a musical instrument so my father made sure I was able to participate in music class. They started us out with the flute. When I got into fifth grade I played the violin. My father paid for private lessons for me for many months. I believed back then, he paid 100 dollars a lesson for one hour. He purchased my own violin. That cost him about 400 dollars. Back in the 60's, 400.00 dollars was a lot of money. I played during elementary school and now I joined the junior high school orchestra after the summer.

Through the summer I meet this person named Alan. He had long beautiful hair that came down to the middle of his back. He also had a long blond streak in there just in one part of his hair. He was very popular in my eyes, and all the girls wanted him. Why he chose me I will never know.

I did not have a figure. I was straight up and down with no curves. Girls his age had boobs, and looked like women. I looked like a girl. He was two years older than me. I always looked younger than what I really was. My mother did not like him and would not allow me to hang around with him.

Denver and Alan meet me one night while my brother Rip was on the phone. They had a number you could call that was a party line. All the kids were doing it and getting dates. I was yelling on it and this guy yelled out his phone number and I called it. Rip let me. It was Alan and Denver. They met me at the bowling alley one day. I fell in love with Alan. He was so handsome to me. He was a hippy type guy that your mother would love to hate. He looked like a bad boy. Back then Cheech and Chong were big. Denver was his best friend and they were always together.

So I would sneak off and meet Alan. Once my mother followed me and Alan did not want to be bothered with my mother. It was not long before Alan became tired of sneaking around with me. I could never go out for a hamburger, or coke, I could never go to the mall or a show. Sneaking became an issue.

Alan would always be with Denver. They were close friends. So Denver would always want me to hook him up with a girl. I did not have any real girlfriends, I was not allowed to hang out at the mall or go out of my yard. So the newness ran out. Alan and Denver started looking for other possibilities.

I saw Alan drive by with another girl in his car. I was angry and when I met him at the bowling alley we fought about it and he blew up his car revving the engine hard. I cried and ran home.

I snuck Alan in the house one time after that and we lay on the couch kissing and Tom my step-dad came into the room. He told both me and Alan that it was time to leave.

I would sneak and see him as much as I could. That got old quick and he soon found a girl that had bigger boobs and left me for her. After that, I had self-esteem issues.

He did care about me even when we were older, we always ran into each other and we would try to reconnect. It was my fault though, I had changed so much using drugs, and I was unable to give Alan what he wanted and needed. I still hold a special place in my heart for him, and always will. Alan was my first boyfriend and the first one I kissed. Later on, Denver and I became great friends.

Now junior high school started and everyone is stuck up and has little cliques that they hang around with. I did not fit in with any of the cliques. I was a loner and got into a lot of trouble and did a lot of time in study hall. I hated going to school like all the other kids and coming home. I did not know back then I was dyslexic but I did know I used to love school until I came down ill with Rheumatic Fever which affects the heart, the joints and the brain. I went from being the smartest to the dumbest. The doctors stated it could have been the fever.

Debby my friend, who lived down the street from me and with whom I snuck to play with all the time, was finding new people to hang around with. She was not hanging with me like we used too. Then Debby's family moved to a nicer part of town in Farmington. Over by the mall area closer to the Jr. high school. So, I lost her as a friend.

Many of the parents down our street did not care for my mother, she was a divorcee and strange. Then with her marrying Tom and being pregnant at fifty years old did not help things either. They looked at my mother as a loose woman. She did not socialize either and did not really allow us to.

Lilly did not have any friends but she did have Keno her soon to be husband. Lilly was a good girl, she wanted to have sex when she got married.

I did not have anyone. So to entertain myself, I started using harder drugs. I wanted to try them. Most of the kids that did drugs did not care what people thought of them; they built their own world. The first thing I ever used was LSD. Boy did I go on a trip. After that experience, you would have thought I would not have done it again. However, it was just the beginning.

I took some LSD one day coming home from school. There was a long stairway behind our school that led to a park. That is where Farmington Junior High School would have their football and baseball games. Many of the kids who messed with drugs hung out on this stairway. So one day, I was going home and though I was not supposed to go home that way, down to the stairs, I did anyway.

I met a guy with long hair and he had some LSD for sale. He was selling them for a dollar. I went up to him and asked him if I could buy some or did he have to know me first? He stated no and asked if I had a dollar, because that was the cost. I got a dollar and bought my first pill. Of course, I stole the dollar from my mom's purse.

I went home and took it. I immediately began tripping on that LSD. I was pretty high and scared. My heart was beating fast and my palms were sweating. I went to my bedroom and stayed there because I was scared at the things I was seeing. I was looking around my bedroom and my hands felt funny, sweaty and I felt like I was dirty, like I needed a bath. As I looked up, I started to see strange things and got scared and hid in my closet. Sitting on the floor, I looked over at my blue jeans on the floor and I thought my blues jeans were talking to me.

I got up from the floor and ran out to the bedroom and onto my bed. I was laying there looking up on the wall; the window looked like a door. I could not seem to sit or lay still. I had energy inside that was unreal. Everything was weird and I felt like my skin was tight.

I looked up on the opposite wall and saw a photograph that hung on my wall. It was a photo of an African woman with a large whickered bowl with some kind of fruit substances on her head. Her body was abstracted and colorful. I could hear the African music in the back ground coming toward me. Somehow she came toward me and I got scared and flew from my bed back to the closet. I was tripping and needed to get away. I would go with the feeling for a moment then get scared and get up running.

When I sat in the closet again, my pants started asking me why I never hang them up. I was really going with the flow of things and it was causing me to get higher. I realized what was happening to me and I could feel my heart rate going up. I felt as if it was coming out of my chest. Every time I moved my hand or arm I could see trails.

I ran out to tell my mom. I did not care about getting into trouble. I wanted help. I told my mother I needed help. I expressed that someone must of put something in my candy bar, or drink at the football game after school.

I told her it was my first time I attended a football game. I asked her to forgive me for sneaking and reassured mom it was the last event. I knew I was not supposed to be at the football games. My routine meant, coming home directly after school. I was not to stop or attend events, or hang out with friends. However, at this time, that was not the issue at hand.

My mother and Tom rushed me to the hospital and they told her that since it was a little too late, she would just have to wait it out and let the chemical take its course because it was too far into my system. They stuck tubes down my nose and through my stomach to pump it but did not get anything out of there. I remember promising God and myself if I made it through this, I would never do it again.

It was not more than a couple weeks later; I was doing the same thing again but this time with more experience. As time progressed, I got deeper and deeper into the street life. I started to advance by taking chances. I would go into Farmer Jack's grocery store and stealing Apple Farm Booze. I would return to Farmington Jr. High School, lie out in the bathroom downstairs and drink the whole bottle, anything to sedate myself.

One day in science class, a teacher spelled out the word, Lysergic acid diethylamide for LSD on the black board. He called on me in the classroom, asking me to tell the class what that word meant. My face turned all red because I never paid any attention in school. After my illness, I was sent back two grade levels. So I ended up in classes were I was a year older than everyone else. Not understanding or knowing I was dyslexic caused me to think I was dumb. All the teachers that taught me, never discovered this. This caused me to lose interest in school and made me feel as if I was a dummy plus I did not learn like others and I felt something was wrong with me after my illness.

Furthermore, I did not write or read like I used to. Then the teacher made it worse; he requested me to stand up and tell the class what that word meant. I stood before everyone as I heard them laughing and snickering because I did not know the word. Then the teacher stated, "Sit down Billy Joe, but for future reference, if you are going to experiment with a drug, know what you are taking. This word, in other terms is known as LSD. Now Ms. Billy Joe Key, I bet that rings a bell in your conscience doesn't it?"

Everyone had a good laugh on me that day, but I thought to myself, yeah, you all are laughing at me now, but the laugh will be on you. I am going places, and you will not be laughing at me when I get there.

I could not even believe a teacher stating something so negative like that to me. He made me look like the classroom idiot. He was not good at helping and reaching a kid on the edge, he should have pulled me closer than pushing me farther away. Just as my mother.

After that day, this girl in my class started trying to get close to me. Telling me that everyone in class was a bunch of stuck up rich kids. We started to hang out together. She kept telling me that her parents did not understand her. She told me everything she thought I wanted to hear. Misery loves company and I was miserable.

It was not long before she started to cut into me about hooking her up with some drugs. For some odd reason, I did not feel right about this whole deal. Therefore, I kept playing her off. Then she started coming on stronger, and I told my connections, the older kids who I purchased from. They suggested that I sell her some aspirins and see what she does with it. So I took their advice and took some pills my father had called alfalfa. I put a gel coating around it from another pill, they were long and gel coated. I poked them with a needle and stretched them around the alfalfa pill; I thought I hooked it up.

I gave it to her and then asked her the next day if she tripped. She went off into this big story how she had a wonderful experience. I knew then she was lying. When she asked for more, I decided to charge her and get a few dollars out of the deal. I hooked up a couple more and sold them to her.

To my surprise, her father was a cop and she was giving them to him. Over the intercom I was called into the principal's office. I walked down the hallway wondering what the hell I did now. I was sitting in the principal's office, no one would tell me why.

I looked out the window and knew I was in big trouble when I saw my father walking up the sidewalk. I knew seeing my dad at this school that I was knee deep in trouble for some odd reason. However, being naive I never even thought about that girl turning me in.

The principal waited for my father to enter the room and sit down, before charges were brought against me. My dad was so hurt by this; you could see it all in his eyes.

I did not feel good about myself when I knew I was hurting my dad. My father expressed that he would attend to this issue at home and that the school would not receive any more complaints concerning my illegal activities.

That girl had a lot of nerve; she tried to talk to me as if nothing even happen. I stayed away from her. Everyone already knew her father was a police officer and did not deal with her. Oh well, now I felt played by both, the girl, and then by others for not clueing me in about the situation and allowing me to be played that way.

When I spoke on it to my dope man, they just let me know that it was my last time coming to them. Therefore, I was played out of pocket all the way around a lesson learned. As time went on, I learned many lessons. That was just the icing on the cake.

I was picked out of my violin class to join and be bussed down to Cobo Hall, down in Detroit. I was first chair first row. Those who were picked; could gain a scholarship to college playing in the Detroit Symphony Orchestra.

When I got off into drugs, I destroyed that opportunity for my future but trust me, that was not the only opportunities I had in life that I let go of.

My father was more than willing to pay for me to attend college and become anything I wanted in life. I did not want to be a drug addict; I just got caught up and became one. I only did it once in a while for recreation at first.

I was going to be turning twelve in October; it was so funny I started my period that summer. I even went to my brother Rip and asked him what I should do. Of course, he answered very typically by saying; "Steal them from Lilly and just put them in between your legs". I asked Rip how you hold them up. Rip responded; "I don't know Billy Joe, just stick them in your butt area and hold them between your legs". "Guys", what they know about being a woman. But at that time, he was all I had to direct me.

I did that until my mother realized that Lilly's napkins had been coming up missing. I did try hard to avoid this situation. I guess she was bound to find out eventually. I tried to keep it from my mom. My mom would not allow me to go to school when she found out. The truancy officer had to come and get me.

My mother took me out of school and stated that the boys could smell it. Which mean I would get raped or fall pregnant. They let my mother know it was against the law for her to keep me out like that. That is how screwed up my mother's thinking was.

My stepfather Tom didn't take me fishing as much anymore. He spent most of his time handling things with mom and his new child, Nivea. We did still swimming together in the back yard and that was fun. We still had family picnics without Tom's relatives. Tom's work provided work related picnics that we attended every year. My sister's soon to be husband Keno worked with Tom. So Lilly and Keno would attend these picnics too, which made them fun. We would pack up the car and ride out as a family.

One time we went, I was riding the go-cart and I got into an accident and messed it up. Tom just shook his head. We did all kind of things on those picnics and I really enjoyed them. Tom was really embarrassed that I wrecked the go-cart. I seem to blow everything I did. I remember how pissed he used to get when my fishing line got caught in the tree or rock, anyways may be that is why he stop taking me. (Sad) That was the last year I went to company picnics and fishing with Tom.

After Nivea, my little sister appeared, my mother started renting our basement for extra income. When the last tenet moved out, my mother offered it to my real father because of me getting busted at school. My dad retired from Chrysler's after forty-three years. He jumped on the opportunity to be with me all the time. So he made arrangements to move out of Detroit and move to Farmington with me.

He purchased some Greyhound tickets and took me traveling all out west in the United States. We went to Utah, Colorado, Salt Lake City, Wyoming, Yellow Stone Park and many other places. He felt like it would keep me out of trouble. He arranged this travel after I got busted at school for selling that alfalfa.

I had a great time with my dad. I am blessed to have those memories. We went on boats, rode horse; stayed at fine hotels and hiked trails.

We went to Jackson Hole, Wyoming; it was a town designed as an old western town. They had a show where play-acting cowboys came out shooting each other; the whole town was like a stage play so to speak. I went to live shows and we went on a stage coach ride. Dad let me talk to boys, go to bonfires and enjoy myself. We did so much together it was awesome. As all good things come to an end and so did our travel.

Where my mother was strict and would not allow me any freedom. My father would give me too much. I do not know why my mother was like that. I never had to marry because I was pregnant. However, I sure made up for that, because I did a lot wrong in my short lifetime.

Well, once the second baby came, yes my mother was pregnant again, Mom had a completely different family. This time she had a boy and they named him Rick. I started to take meals with my father and stay down in the basement with him until it was my bedtime. Mom wanted just their family up stairs.

I know many people thought it was weird that my mom was married to another man, and that her first husband lived down stairs in the basement. I did not care, because I had my father right there with me. Plus it was no worse than my grandma living in the garage. I loved coming home and going straight downstairs dealing only with dad and not mom. Dad would allow friends over down stairs. Rip, also, lived downstairs with my dad. It was good for them to bond together. Dad was hard on Rip.

Mom was so caught up with her new family that she did not have time to focus on me so it was me and dad. Dad and I watched movies together; I was in love with Bogart and all the gangster pictures. Dad and I ate together, went places together and he helped me with my school work which mom could never help with because she only had a third grade education. She could not spell, write and only read enough to get by. To this day, I pronounce my words wrong. People are always telling me I have an ascent but I think my mother said her words wrong, and I picked up her dialect growing up. I am not sure because many people say I sound like I am from New Jersey. Some think I sound black. I don't know, I think it comes from her and the dialect she has, combined with Detroit accent. She was my first mentor and taught me how to say my first words.

Anyways, I felt like it was just me and dad living together. I was not using drugs. I was just happy to be with dad. This was the happiest time of my life with him. Watching T.V. dad would hold me and give me love in a respectful way. I hated when I had to go upstairs to bed. I wanted to be with him all the time.

Rip and Lilly all moved out on their way to their own life. I was the only child with mom, my step-father Tom and the new addition Nivea and Rick. So of course, the house was too busy with my father living downstairs Tom, Mom, Nivea and a Rick plus me. You could see mom making her plans and her wheels turning in her head. We just never knew what the outcome would be.

She succeeded in pushing Tom's family away. He did not have anything to do with them because they did not believe mom had these children with Tom. They were wondering if they were really Tom kids just because he and his first wife could not conceive. You could look at those kids and tell they belonged to Tom. It did not take a rocket scientist to figure that one out.

Rip moved out of the house with his girlfriend, Sissy (soon to be his wife). They traveled all over out west. Rip purchased a fast sports car that was not a GM product. It was made in another country. My father became so angry at Rip. My father felt we should purchase American products to support your own country first. My father would only purchase from Sears because they carried American products. He stopped talking to Rip but dad did think highly of Sissy.

When they returned home, they wanted to live together before they got married. So my mom told Rip to ask me if they could borrow my savings bonds my father purchased for me. I had about 4,000.00 dollars in savings bonds. I told Rip I did not care, but of course, back then, I really did not have the concept of money. So Rip and Sissy got a duplex. It was nice looking and had a living room, kitchen, two bedrooms, and a large bathroom. They lived there for a while until my sister Lilly moved down south with her husband Keno.

The house that Keno and Lilly lived in was in Farmington on East Monroe Street. Keno got a job back home in the coal mines and wanted Lilly to move down there with him. So Rip and Sissy took over their house and left the duplex. My father helped them to purchase that house as a wedding gift.

It was a gloomy day and I was wondering where my life was going or if I would even live. I was always thinking about death and felt I would never see sixteen. I hated the change in the household and did not care inside my heart for my new sister and brother. I felt not wanted. I never really felt wanted by my mother anyways. I always wonder if I reminded her of herself or what. Later I found out it was my father that I reminded her of. She could not stand the fact that I looked like him. She was going to leave him after Lilly. That is why there was four years between us. Then she got pregnant with me and I looked just like my dad, more than any other kid.

I loved my home in Farmington. When we first moved there I hated it but over time, it grew on me. I ended up loving it and felt it was all I knew. I had no direction and felt I would grow up and be a psychiatrist and marry a gangster like Humphrey Bogart. He was my favorite actor. I loved watching movies with him in it while in the basement with my father. I was going to miss my dad.

My whole world and existence was coming to an end as I knew it. My father was moving out and taking over my brother's duplex. I loved living with him. My brother and sister moved out and of our original family, I am here alone with Nivea and Rick. I have a new brother and sister. What could mom be thinking of, having children at the end of her life? Even though I knew it was not the fault of the children and I was some way excited that they were here, I knew life was going to be different.

I also knew mom had Tom where she wanted him. He was a great man besides his drinking. The nights I ran down the street chasing him to come back home was a nightmare. Maybe this was a good thing for Tom. Who knows, maybe this will stop him from drinking. I had to look on the positive side of things. I just could not look on the positive side of my role in all this. I already felt I was not wanted. I was the "Key" kid, living in the house with my mother's new husband Tom, and their two new children. I was feeling the victim's role.

I was sorry to see my dad leave but I am glad he is not going back down to St. Jean Street on the East Side of Detroit. It was difficult to visit with him there. They seemed to accept dad over there and my aunt Laure (my mother's sister) lived somewhere over there. They did not like it when Rip or I visited. It was during the 60's when the great riots were about to erupt. It was hard to even be in the neighborhood because you would have to fight going to the store. The blacks were getting sick of whites controlling everything. So at least dad would be in Farmington and not back in Detroit. That was a good thing to me. So life goes on and the outcome is for the future to see.

# CHAPTER TWO

## TEENAGE YEARS

Well my father ended up taking over my brother's duplex in Farmington Hills. He moved out of our basement. I did not want dad to move but too many people where in the house now.

I rode my bike over there to dad as much as I could. Mom and Tom were planning a summer vacation up north. They owned a cottage on the lake up there in Tustin and would go every given chance to get away from the city. My mom saved all her tips working in the restaurant to purchase that cabin. She was good with her money. I hated it up there, there was nothing to do. I started back on drugs. I asked if I could stay with my father at his duplex while they were on their vacation.

Mom had no problem with it, only because she wanted to be with her new family. I was just added baggage to her and a social security check that she received for me since my father retired. Even while he lived in the basement she collected that check.

I had a blast that summer but trust me, I paid dearly for it. I broke into my mother's house and gave a wild party. Remember, we had a swimming pool in our back yard with a deck on top. It was square and big enough for the whole family. Well, that night it became full of beer bottles and whatever else you could put in a pool without a conscience.

***What our pool looked like***

I got so high, I didn't even remember what my name was.

There was a guy that showed up at the party I did not even know. He crashed the party so-to-speak. His name was Leon.

I was lying in my sister Lilly's old bedroom. I was trying to keep the room from spinning around. I was so sick that I end up laying in my own regurgitation. This guy Leon was making his rounds at the party. He was going in and out every room. He saw me laying there in my own regurgitation and must have got on top of me. I guess, he just saw a girl lying passed out and thought this was an opportunity for him. He got on top of me. I can't even remember how everything occurred. I know one thing, he screwed someone who did not or could not do anything back.

He was sixteen years old and I was only thirteen soon to be fourteen that fall. I did not even know him nor deal with him. He was a pig and I hated what he did to me. He took that part of my life from me. I thought I was saving it for Alan. I thought we would get married one day.

That pig raped me without my consent. I did not even know what he was doing. I remember him on top, and pulling on my clothes but it was as if my body was not mobile. As if my arms and legs were lifeless. I remember trying to move but would get sick to my stomach even more. Then I heard him laugh and get off me, I could see a blurry version of someone and tried to lift up only to throw up again and lay my head back down.

Well, it was not long before the neighbors called the police. They shut down my mother's house. The neighbor next door called them. Parker's father came over looking for his boys and got his son out of the house. I was in big trouble now. I could not even clean up the house or pool area before my mom saw it. It was a freak—n mess~! And so was I.

It was also the beginning of me not caring any more. I became another person from that day on. Something happen to me that night, I became addicted to the street life and drugs.

I have always felt violated in my life by my mother and many men who I came encounter with growing up. I snapped in side and felt, why should I care when the rest of the world doesn't.

With mom having the other family, my dad moving to another location, Rip and Lilly moving out, I felt like I lost my identity. I did not belong anywhere. Who was I? My head was going crazy with thoughts. I hated living with my mom and felt like I did not belong to this family. Many things were going through my head.

I just wanted to grow up and marry a mobster man or a gangster like Bogart. All the anger from the whippings that I received growing up with all those switches, living a sheltered life, being violated by Leon raping me, by others pulling down my pants and taking advantage of me, swelled up in me.

My mother who never loved me, caused my trust issues and I sedated my emotions with substance abuse and acted out with violence instead of communicating my hurt and pain. I even stole money from my step dad who had a collection of buffalo coins; I took all of them. I was going into addictive behavior and not caring about anyone or anything.

When my father lived downstairs, I never wanted to get high. Now, I was hurt and hated my life. I wanted to die. I never had loyalty with anyone but my brother and dad.

It was about me; I did not even love myself. My mother's rejection and the beatings she gave me for every little thing I did, caused me to shut down too. Mom was raised in the south and they did not spare the rod. My mother felt like the only reason she put it harder to me than anyone else was because I was the worse child she had she said, plus I reminded her of my father.

She used to tell me that Lilly had prettier hair because it was black and that blond hair girls were used as sluts by men. I heard that so many times over and over. She never hugged or kissed me growing up. She never made me feel loved or wanted. She blamed me for getting sick and for my brother going to juvenile. She blamed me for her life, for Lilly's solitary life style, for Ben leaving home.

Whatever she could blame on me, she did. She only wanted to use me for a sympathy card to get Tom or her other boyfriends before him.

Only when I was needed but other than that, I did not exist. I was a child support check to her, or someone to keep her house spotless, cleaning up after everyone including her precious Lilly.

After that night, I did not hold loyalty to anyone. I would rip my own friends off and lie about the littlest things. Don't get me wrong, I did tell big whooper lies before this. I was always lying about stuff and stealing whatever I could get my little fingers on. But something snapped that night. I changed for the worst.

My mom and step dad sold the house in Farmington on Dixon. During the party, someone stole my mother's black lazy-boy chair. My mother was pissed and felt I had disgraced her life in that neighborhood, and she never wanted to live there anymore. She just did not know, everyone in the neighborhood did not even like her and thought she was a disgrace anyways.

I believe she wanted to move up north, what I did, just give her the excuse to go. She would always use me for the excuses when she wanted to do something. She stated we had to move to Farmington because I was ill. Yeah right. (Sigh)

They told her to move me to a town and place that had better water. She always found a way to reflect the reasons on me.

She hated for Tom to being in the Detroit area, she wanted him away from his family and friends. He was a real likeable man and everyone felt Tom was the life of the party. Mom wanted him to give up everything, his job, brothers and sister, and his friends. Mom wanted him only around her and no one else.

I had to move up north with my stepfather, mother, Nivea and Rick. I did not want to go up there. Mom would not allow me to stay with dad because of the party. So I ended up moving up north.

Oh my gosh, it was so boring, I was always in trouble up north. I did not like the people up there and fell back in isolation again. I registered for high school and went the first day. It was awful, the kids smelled like they just stepped off of the farm. Some of them smelt like poop.

I ended up in one class where a teacher in Tustin had thought I was a freak. The kids hated me because I was from the Detroit area. They did not take kindly to strangers and did not like people from the Motor City. I did not make it any better. I did anything I could to act out and let people know I was from the Motor City.

I would look for grass that looked like marijuana. I would smoke anything I could get my hands on. I would go to the store which was a pretty far twenty miles away, and steal some booze to get drunk. I even abused prescription drugs in hopes of getting high. I did anything and everything to escape from being up there. I wanted to be home in the Detroit area.

The landscape up there was beautiful. Our house was on the lake. We could walk out the door about 30 feet and the lakefront was there. Cabins were all around the lake. Listening to the sound of motorboats and people laughing as they swam, boating, and waterskiing was a great sound. Campfires at night. It was breath taking, but when summer was over, so was the fun.

There was a farm right above my mother's cabin on the lake. They had a grandson who would come over and milk the cows. When we went to the cabin in the summertime, I used to talk with him. Now that we moved there, he was more aggressive.

That boy tried to get me into the woods, stating that city girls were fast and tried to screw me. When I would not, he went around and told everyone I did. We got into a big fight and it turned physical. We stopped communicating with each other. When we used to vacation up north for the summer he was the only one I would talk to. Now that I lived there he treated me disrespectfully.

When I went to school the next day I met this girl kind of like me, an outcast. Her name was Leeann. She had freckles all over her face but they were very appealing and long blond hair that was natural. She had such a full figure for a young girl her age. I believe she might have been around thirteen. She was kind of a full-blown figure southern girl that all the boys wanted to score with.

She and I became friends; no one could pull us apart. I hung at her house and she hung on the dirt roads with me.

I never took friends home. Mom was crazy and had many issues. She did not like friends or people over our house anyways, not when we lived in Detroit, Farmington or up north. I was very embarrassed of my mother.

Leeann and I started hanging so tough with each other that our teachers became concerned about it. They felt I was a bad influence on Leeann.

I told her many stories of Detroit of course; many were blown out of proportion and made to seem better than they really were. Leeann would bug me all the time to take her to Detroit one day.

I had to find a job to work because mom does not believe giving allowance. So I went into Cadillac which was the big major city outside of Tustin. I received my first job working as a server at Big Boy's right off of Highway 355. It was a little pocket money. Mom didn't give out funds even though I did do all the chores around the house, even when Lilly was home. I was my mother's housekeeper.

Every Saturday I was to rise at 6 a.m. and clean the bathroom with a tooth brush and bleach. This was a chore even when we lived in Farmington. Without me the house would have never been clean.

I will give her and my father this much, because of their work ethic, I was always taught to work at a young age. I was never allowed to use the telephone at the house. My mom did not believe in allowing me ever to use the phone to talk to friends. She would make a sour face and sigh sideways about friends coming over or calling. So Leeann was never allowed to call. She would meet me in Cadillac during my work schedule.

I liked my job because it was away from home and the customers liked me. There was a person that would come in all the time and one day this customer drew a picture of me on the back of a menu. It was cool and looked just like me. He gave it to me but over the years I misplaced it.

My mom would never take me to work so I would have to hitchhike to Cadillac every day. Sometimes it would be dark at night when I left and I would catch a ride home.

It was Saturday and Leeann asked me to go to a dance club in Cadillac. It was supposed to be a swinging club with no alcohol allowed. It was made for the kids in the neighborhood to have a place to hang out. I arranged for the day off from work. I told my mom I was working so I could get out of the house. She would have never allowed me to go to anything like that.

She would have said it was for whores. Mom was really negative about everything and saw the worse in everything. We met some people at a dance club. We hung out with them all night, and then went to a bonfire out in the woods. I had such a good time for a hick town.

One evening Leeann and I were a little toasted. We picked up a couple guys that evening. We all decided to commit a robbery. I came up with the idea. Of course, I had to play the big role of a Detroit gangster.

So we saw this restaurant in Cadillac where the window was left cracked open. That restaurant was right down the street from Big Boy's. I convinced everyone that we could get in there and get lots of money. They helped me up to the window and in I flew head first. I fell on the counter and landed in the sink. I hurt myself falling in but I played it cool and acted as if I was a pro. I walked into the back part of the kitchen and opened up the back door for the other kids.

We walked around in there for a good half-an-hour. They were busy stealing candy bars from the front counter area where the cash register was left open to demonstrate there was no money in it.

I went to the back and found a small safe that stood about two feet high and about two feet wide. I tried to get them to help me to carry it out of the back door. None of us was able to lift it.

They were so busy stealing large plastic mustard and mayonnaise jars of food as if they had never eaten before. They were not even thinking about that safe. I heard a noise and flagged everyone down to leave out the back door. Later that night, we found some acid and got high.

Then, Leeann and I stole someone's horses and rode home on them; we had such a great time. I turned and looked at Leeann and said, "Just think Leeann, back in the olden days, people were hung for stealing horses." We laughed and rode the horses down the dirt road.

When I got to my house, I let the horse go and he trailed back to his home as fast as his legs would carry him. Leeann kept riding her horse because she lived farther away than I did. When

Leeann released her horse, he did the same thing. Horses are smart animals. They know right where they live and they did not half step going back home to their surroundings. We both checked on the horses the next day to make sure they made it home.

The following day it was back to school. I worked and went to school.

I had a teacher at school who took an interest in me, or I thought he did. He was just trying to get information from me to see if I was bringing drugs in from Detroit. Some kid in school told him I would brag I did that.

Of course, I was not, but I tried to play the role of a street hood. That teacher gave me a book called, "*Go Ask Alice.*" I read some of it and then realized why he gave it to me.

He was on a mission to bust me doing something or bring something into the school. The problem was it was all talk, no facts to what I was bragging about. I rolled up some tea in some zigzag papers and pawned it off as weed. I did not care as long as I was getting attention.

What I did not see was the negative affect this action was really causing me. When the teacher stayed around me as if he could not let me out of his sight, I knew something was not correct. Then I was told to go home.

When I got there, my mother greeted me at the door. On the kitchen table was the tea that I rolled up in zigzag papers that was pawned off as weed. It was ripped up into pieces lying on the table.

I knew now, I was in big trouble. I tried to play it off as a joke or that a friend gave it to me as a joke, but my mother was not going for that crap. She told me to go to my room, take off my pants and wait for her. I knew what that meant "The switch."

I went into the room and waited but this day I refused to allow my mother to spank me anymore. I was thirteen and a half years old and she was not going to put that switch on me. I was sick of her and her beating me throughout my life.

I would say that is when I snapped. When she entered the room, I protested right away. I let her know from the beginning that I was not going to let her touch me. She went to raise the switch toward my face. I took it out of her hand and pushed my mother down. From that moment on, I realized she was nothing to fear. I was not afraid.

Another personality took over me. She was so devastated that I touched her. I was even shocked that I had the nerve to take that switch away and push her. I was feeling like King Kong at that moment. I was no longer afraid of her. She lay on the floor scared and called Tom's name for help.

The other side of this coin was dealing with my stepfather. He was not very pleased with my actions. Tom came rushing into the room to find his wife on the floor with fear in her face. He looked at me standing over her and stated,

"Leave this home. You have disrespected my wife and your mother." He was not having it in his house. I picked up my stuff and started to leave when my stepfather told me not to take anything with me. "Just leave, with no possessions," Tom stated with disgusted in his face. His eyebrows were turned up toward his forehead.

I was to leave with what I had on my back. Tom and mom did not care how I got to my dad's house. They just wanted me to leave now.

I was glad because ever since my mother re-married, I was always referred to as the **"Key"** kid. I no longer felt like a part of this family.

I know this sound like a cop-out but I never felt that my mother wanted me or loved by her. I felt she had wished I had never been born. I did not want to live there with them but the rejection of them kicking me out at thirteen was hurtful. I could not cry but felt unwanted again.

I went out to Highway 355 and hitch-hiked a ride, all the way from Cadillac to Detroit. When I got to my father's place I could not bring myself to knock on the door. I paced outside his house for hours. I had no knowledge that my father was aware of my presence out there.

Finally, it was dark and he came to the door stating to me, "If you are going to come in, come on, but make up your mind because I am tired and need to go to sleep for work tomorrow." I walked into his place and felt odd and uncomfortable.

My father looked at me and said, "Honey, I am not going to get off into what happened between you and your mother but I will say this, you have no right putting your hands on your mother regardless of the situation. She is your mother and you need to respect that. Now, get something to eat and try to get some sleep. We will go to Sears tomorrow and get you some clothes."

He then kissed my forehead saying good night to me. I felt so loved and wanted at that moment. Dad did not live a traditional life style like other normal families but I loved being with him.

I was a little scared my mother told me before I left up north that my father was a sex maniac and to watch myself because he kept a box of rubbers in the house all the time. I asked my father about this and why my mother would state that. My dad told me that my mother could not help it. I should not hold anything against her. My father told me to forgive my mom because she had a hard life. (Later on in life I realized it was my mother that was a maniac with sex.)

I was okay with everything my father and I talked about; it was off to living a new life with dad again. Dad allowed me to have so much freedom, I did not know what to do with it. I abused that privilege because I could not handle it.

With my mother, I was not allowed to go out of my backyard, permitted phone calls, blocked from having friends over, and denied to sleep over at other kids houses. I was not allowed to go anywhere after school or on the weekends and granted a limited amount of toys.

On the other hand, with my father, everything went. There was a lot of trust. I was allowed to have phone calls, stay out until twelve o'clock at night, friends over, or anything I wanted to buy. It was a completely new life style for me. A life style I did not handle very well.

I got heavy into the drug world. I carried the scares of my mother after that situation up north; my heart felt evil. I never spoke on my mother to anyone after that day.

My father gave me a bankbook with 1,054.00 dollars in it for my fourteenth birthday. I did not waste that money. I turned it over to more money. I got a connection and started selling drugs.

You could buy a pound of weed back then for 95.00 dollars, a gram of THC or PCP for 35.00 dollars, one hundred hits of pills like THC or acid, and mescaline, for 35.00 dollars. Joints went for .50 cents. Downers went for .50 cents a pill too but you were able to make sixty-five dollars off of them.

I would buy hundred hits of pills for thirty-five dollars sell them for a dollar each. It gave me a profit of sixty-five dollars. I started selling pills and weed. I became one of the dealers in school but mainly outside of school. I went to Farmington Jr. High and the parks.

I was a total outcast in school. I had only a few friends that really liked and cared about me. One of them was named Jenny and her brother Timmy; she lived in the apartment complex next to me.

She had an older brother who lived in California. He would come and visit sometimes. Their mother drank, but she was a good mother to those kids and all their friends. She provided the best she could for them. It was almost as if she lived her whole life for those kids. Too bad my father was so much older than she was, they would have been perfect for each other. She was living for her kids and so was my father. I rather felt sad for both of them.

Alan found out I was with my dad and where we were living. He told me he was going into the service, the Navy. Alan and a friend named Dan got busted and was given a choice back in the 70's. Prison or the service and Alan and Dan picked the service.

He told me he wanted to be with me and asked if I would wait for him. I told him yes and my dad invited him into the house. I was surprised that my father liked him so much.

My dad thought he was a nice guy; it was so different than how my mother would act. We saw each other a few times then Alan left and I went on with my life. He was going to be gone for three years. In three years, I would be seventeen years old. I held a soft spot in my heart for him. I never wanted him to know I wasn't pure anymore, that I had lost my virginity from that party. I never said anything to him.

Jenny and I started hanging out together getting high. Matter of fact, all three of us did, Jenny, her brother Timmy and me.

We did some energetic crazy crap together and never got busted. We stole bikes, shoplifted from the Mall, ripped off people and hung out with a motorcycle group called The Pokers. I did not think about it back then but they all could have gone to jail getting high with us and screwing sexually with us.

We were at the Livonia Mall one day stealing bikes, ten speeds. I went over to the bike rack and started cutting the lock off one bike that I liked. As I was cutting it, a man came out of the store yelling, "Hey, that's my bike!"

I waited until he got close enough to me and started swinging the bolt cutter at him. I hit him several times until he pushed away from me stating, "Take the bike girl, take it!"

I did just that . . . . I took the bike. I had anger inside of me that was unbelievable.

We all went back to the duplex and laughed about it. Everyone thought I was so tough and had a lot of balls for a girl. We got high and enjoyed each other's company until school the next day.

The weird thing about it is I never had to steal anything. My father would give me whatever my heart desired. I did it just to be doing it.

I remember a few days later, Jenny and I hitchhiked out to Walled Lake to visit one of Jenny's friends. We both did so much THC that night I am surprised we survived that evening. We must have taken at least twelve hits each of THC. I had a whole bag and we just kept grabbing hits out of the bag all night long eating them up like they were candy. I was so high that I could not feel the floor under my feet. I felt as if I was walking on air and my legs and body felt like rubber. I wish I could say that is the highest I have ever been but as time grew so did my habits of getting higher.

Jenny was so blown (high) that she freaked out and lost sight of what was going on. She started to freak out at the house that we were at. Realizing that we were out of our minds, the people we were with tried to play on us and catch us up into some weird sexual activities. I was blown, but not that high where I did not comprehend what was going on.

One dude freaked out and started to trip. He was lying on the floor taking a table and lamp lifting it up and down as weights then he cut his arm. Blood was running everywhere and he was tripping on the blood. He was yelling and tripping off the PCP he took. I grabbed Jenny and told her we had to get out of there.

We could not trust anyone to take us home so we snuck out and hitchhiked home. We did not even know how we made it. God was with us that night because we were fools running crazy with no direction.

It was not long that Jenny became pregnant and her mom sent her to New York to have an abortion. It was hard for Jenny she was only thirteen years old. I was fourteen now, my birthday was in the fall. She experienced many emotional and psychological effects from it. However, it was the best thing because Jenny was not able to care for a child at 13.

A friend of ours in school Liz found out about Jenny's abortion and blabbed it all over school. They started to make fun of Jenny and that pissed me off. I am very protective of my friends and loved ones. I do not like bullies. I am still like this today. Some things never change.

Jenny came crying to me during class. I became angry so I went to the girl's class and asked her why she was gossiping and spreading rumors about Jenny. The smart-ass girl talked to me as if I was a joke. I told her to bring her punk ass outside and talk to me like that.

When classes broke, she ran and got her older sister and came out side to confront me. Both of them were going to gang up on me. I had a different plan. As the little sister came walking up on me, I let her get close enough to get a good swing on her. Without warning, I swung and hit her as hard as I could with my fist across her nose. I knocked her glasses off her face; she went flying to the left and her glasses went flying to the right. It was very humorous but very serious. I busted her nose. It started bleeding and her nose was leaning to the left of her face. It was truly broke. Her older sister simultaneously came running up on me as if she was going to jump in to save her younger sister. I turned with swiftness hitting her as hard as I could.

She was knocked down then here comes the other little sister who jumped up and attacked me from the behind. I threw my body weight as I pulled her to the ground and straddled her like a horse choking her as I banged her head repeatedly several times on the ground.

Finally, Jenny pulled me off her and brought my thoughts back to reality. I lost myself. All I wanted was that girl to know I was not the one to mess with. When I let go of the girl's throat, she had marks on her neck like a ring of hickies. I severally choked her. It was a good thing that Jenny pulled me off her or I might have gone to juvenile. That is how my brother taught me to fight, hit them in the nose; they will be shocked with the blood and then you can finish them off.

We walked home that night proud as if we gained a victory. We laughed about it and got high. It was truly a day we both would remember for a long time to come.

I did Jenny wrong later on in our relationship. I do not know why I would cross people out that were my friends. It was as if I had no loyalty to anyone but myself. (I prayed she will find it in her heart one day to forgive me for it. Maybe she will read this book and know it's her and forgive me.)

Later Jenny and I started hanging out with some older people who lived in the same apartment complex as Jenny. The one guy's name was Jerry. They would allow us to come over and smoke their weed. Then, they thought they would get us high and eventually fuck us.

They had a nice duplex with lots of guns and a motorcycle. They would buy weed by the pounds. At the time, I did not think about ripping them off but one of the guys there started to like me and it started from there.

There were two dudes that lived there but there were many that hung out there; it was the party house. They had jobs and worked; many of them were at least in their 20's. I started staying over their place a lot without Jenny. I would go over and hang out every day after school. It was a place for me to get high for free and buy drugs.

The next day in school, I was in study hour class, as sitting in the back part of the class room I noticed this girl watching me. I was tripping off some acid and talking out loud. I was holding a conversation with myself designing a plan of escape. I was pointing my finger at the pipes in the room and explaining how I was going to shrink myself and go through the pipes and out the radiators, then, through the window. Lena the girl that kept watching me was sitting in class listening. She looked dead in my face and stated, "You're crazy; I think you are a little special."

I just laughed and the bell rang. I left and saw her later in gym class. She approached me and told me, she wanted to be my friend. I questioned her as to why? She just stated there was something about me. I asked her what nationality she?

She had olive complexion, and curly dark hair. Lena had real small framed and slanted eyes. She told me she was Jewish. I ignorantly asked her, "Did you guys kill Jesus Christ?"

Lena looked up at me so innocently stating, "I didn't kill him, I wasn't even there!"

We both laughed. I just looked at her and told her she could tag along with me. Who would have ever known that Lena would become my one and only friend throughout my whole life?

I went home from school and started hanging out at the duplex with the guys. The one dude that acted like he wanted me was acting like a little bitch. When I would not agree to fuck him, he would treat me like crap and tell me to go home. If I lay up with him, kissing and rubbing his dick, he would get me high and hang out with me. He was disgusting; he was around 22 years old.

I started feeling used by him too. I was beginning to believe that guys only used girls. He would talk to me really sharp and make comments to put me down. So I would leave. I did not like to be over there when he was there by himself. He would really treat me like an asshole if I did not screw him every time I came over. Nor would he offer to get me high unless I was doing something back for him.

He was older than me too I was jail bait but back then, I did not know that. He never took me out or was seen with me, only at his duplex. I didn't like being used but it seems I only found men that did.

While I was over at the house, this dude came over. He was really cool and we talked all night. I really liked him. He wasn't trying to hit on me and treated me only as a friend. His name was Dave. He was tall and a dark complexion with black hair and beard. He looked Arabic.

I was chilling one day over at their house and Dave came by. He was going to re-up on some drugs for them. I realized he was their connection. He told them he would go pick them up some stuff. I was really surprised. He asked if I wanted to ride with him to Detroit. We drove for a while and finally came to the house where he coped. ('Coped' is street slang for 'buying dope'.)

It was pretty cool and I had a great time. He went upstairs to cop the dope and left me downstairs with a bunch of guys. They were all hanging out at this house and they called it the Marlow House. There were about 7 to 8 guys that were regulars there. This was a place to get out of the cold and heat get high without any cops bothering you.

There was this one guy there named Nick. I was very attracted to him. We talked as I waited for my friend. He was dark complexioned with long hair. He was full blooded Indian. He asked me if he could have my phone number. He told me he was not like the rest of the guys there and he had a job. My friend came back down stairs and we left going back to Farmington.

Nick called me a few days later. At first I was worried he would not call me. Then finally we talked on the phone. He asked to take me to dinner. He had his own car and got directions to our place. He came over to meet my dad. My father liked him. We went out and things went well with us. I really liked Nick and thought he was the one. He was tall, dark and handsome.

We went out about three or four times. Then, he backed away from me which I did not understand why. Later on, many of the other guys at the Marlow House told me he thought I had crabs and I did not even know what crabs were. He would never ask me out any more, that really hurt my feelings.

That night I was so hurt by that I just got as high as I could. I always seem to get rejected by people. Shit, if my own mother did not want me why would I think anyone else was different.

I hung out in Detroit on a street called Marlow house that night. They were dipping a coffee cup in the bag of dope and pouring it on a record cover. We would pass it around with a rolled up dollar bill to snort with. I was so high that I was walking through the dining area and must have passed out. I could feel myself going down but did not feel the floor when I hit it. I don't even know what I was snorting. I never asked.

The guys in the house threw me out in the alley but one of the dudes living in the house went back there and got me. He breathed down my throat, giving me mouth to mouth; it must have worked because I remember feeling a puff of air coming out of my mouth. I was really cold and he wrapped me up with his shirt or coat picking me up, carrying me outside to the porch.

There was a porch swing out there he just sat with me in his arms, rocking me back and forth. I can't even remember his name. He had long hair down to the middle of his back. It was brownish blond and very full with dreadlocks. He was a hippy, very quiet and the first white person I saw with dreads. He told me later that I was talking about a lot of crazy stuff that did not make any sense. I believe that man saved my life that night. I believed I O.D. and he brought me back.

71

I was intrigued and interested in things dealing with the street. The street life kept calling me. I would hang out in Detroit and I started spending more time at the Marlow house in Detroit. Part of the reason was to see Nick one more time, the other reason was to be associated with someone from the hood. I felt more wanted in the hood.

It was around the Schoolcraft and Evergreen area. I would hitchhike down there ever night. Those guys introduced me to heroin. The only thing is when I purchased it, they all sat in the car with me and did most of the dope. I knew I could not go through them and had to watch who they got the dope from. At the Marlow House, I met a few guys that I got high and hung out with.

Their names were Eddy, Step (who ended up dying in a motorcycle accident), Nick (the one I went out with), Gene, Karen, Carlos and a few others. I hung at this house every day getting blown to the point I did not know which way was up or down. I started hanging out with some of the guys outside of the hang out.

I would hold many conservations with Gene and I loved the way he could pull out a knife from his pocket with the blade out. I kept trying it myself until I mastered it.

Eddy and I started dating but it did not last long. He was another one that did not care about me; he only wanted to have sex.

I had been hanging out all night and I did not want my dad worrying about me. On my way home, I started hitchhiking from the Marlow house back to Farmington. I jumped in a car with a white dude. As we started driving down the street, I realized out of the side of my eye he started masturbating while we were driving. Wow, I was blown away and felt really funny being in that car. I was so embarrassed that I would not look over at him. I was even scared to say something.

I searched for the door knob to grab without him knowing. My heart started beating fast and I was so nervous I could feel my hand and arm shaking. I jumped out of the car as it was going 40-45 miles hours and my leather jacket was the only thing that saved my life. I rolled and got up and started running in the middle of the street as **he chased me!!!!**

It was like 3:00 a.m. and not many cars were out. He got out of his car and was standing there masturbating looking at me.

I was screaming for help. Not one person stopped or heard me. My heart was pounding like crazy. I felt like I was going to die that night and thrown in a ditch somewhere.

He finally ejaculated in the street. I ran home as fast as possible walking down the middle of the road all the way home. I can't believe people drove by and moved out of his way going down the street they did nothing????

**Are you serious?** Not many cars went by me, maybe two, **but seriously?**

What a nightmare that was. It felt so good when I arrived home safe. I must have walked 10 miles home that evening. I was so scared every time a car would pass me, thinking it was that weirdo.

I was so happy to be home, eat and went straight to bed. Dad was in bed but turned on the light in his room to check the time. I just lay in my bed thanking my lucky stars for being home. I swore up and down that night I would never hitchhike again.

The next day in school I saw this dude named Len. He had been talking with me for weeks here and there but would act mysterious when speaking with me. It was almost as if he was embarrassed to let anyone know we were talking. I started talking to him when Nick dumped me. We did this several times and many times I would go to his house or he would come over to my dad's place.

We never seem to go out in public with each other. I spoke on it several times with him. Many times, Len would just ignore me. As soon as we would make love he would get dressed and the date was over. He would leave early and not hang-out with me throughout the night.

Oh, of course he would get more pills and weed from me. I was selling and he would convince me he would sell them for us. So I would not get into trouble.

When it came time for him to bring me the money, he was always short. Or he would not bring anything back saying he was saving it for us. He would give me other stories like he had to get this or that. Some lame excuse of why all the cash wasn't there. Like a dummy, I would just say okay because I did not want him to dislike me.

He was one of the most popular guys in school. I really thought he liked me. I was proud that I was his girlfriend. He would never bring any of the money to me but always act as if it was us together. He would tell me he was saving the funds for us to go places.

He also played or managed a band and had to go to a concert this weekend coming up. I was really upset because he did not want me to attend. I kept bugging Len until he agreed for me to come. I went down to the Grande Ball Room on Grand River on the Northwest side in Detroit where the concert Len was playing in.

He turned out to be a jerk like all the rest. He was just using me because I had dope and was selling in school. He wanted to be a part of that.

I thought this was a party that we attended together as we were an item but the truth came out at the Grande Ball Room that night. I was there with him and his family. He asked his mom and grandma to keep me occupied so he could be with his real girlfriend.

I went into the bathroom with his mother and grandmother; we were getting high. There was a girl in there that was talking about Len. She was talking to this other girl about him getting rid of me after he got my bag of dope. I heard all of this while in the bathroom stall. I waited for them to leave and went to confront Len. His mom and grandma tried to stop me.

I went through the crowd with my heart beating, my nerves shot and a clump in my throat. I saw him talking to his friends. I asked him to come toward me. He refused and stated; "If you have something to say, say it in front of my friends."

I told him what I had heard and the next moment felt like an hour.

He laughed at me asking me, did I really think a guy like him could be interested in a girl like me.

I was really hurt by that wondering what he meant; "what was wrong with a girl like me?" I ran out of the place from embarrassment; everyone standing around started laughing too. When I looked over and saw his real girlfriend laughing I died inside. I felt like the biggest loser.

I started to hitchhike back home. I felt like crying but could not make the tears come out. So much hurt in my life kept the tears from coming down.

A car pulled up with seven black dudes asking if I needed a ride. At first I was scared but got into the car anyways it turned out to be great.

They got high with me and were really nice. They saw I was upset I explained to them what my so-called boyfriend just did to me. They felt bad for me and took me all the way back to Farmington.

Once they got to Farmington, I had a friend escort them back so the police would not bother them. In the Farmington area at 3:00 in the morning was not a good deal for a black person. I never saw them again but they were a bunch of great guys.

I did not return back to school so I started hanging back at Jerry's duplex getting high. I went over there every day and that guy who liked me, started with his crap again trying to screw me.

I got pissed off and called Gene at the Marlow House. I told him that I knew this dude in Farmington that had some items. I told him that Jerry and his roommate had guns, stereos, weed and much more in his place. I was mad at all the men. This guy treated me like shit too. So to get back at all the guys who treated me like crap? I would get them first. So Gene and I decided to hook up and hit them while they were at work and we did just that!

I broke into the apartment, by breaking out the side window. When Gene came by, we loaded up his white van with weed, guns, stereos, TV's and anything else we could grab. We were making a fast buck.

As we were leaving, I saw the keys to the motorcycle and grabbed the helmet. I just could not pass it up. I grabbed them going out the door as Gene and Jesse (a guy that Gene brought with him to help) called out for me to get into the van.

A neighbor from across the way heard and saw Jesse. She became scared, (Jesse was African American) and called the police. You did not see black men in Farmington Hills in the late 60's and early 70's.

I yelled out for them to go without me. I hopped on the motorcycle and turned my head to Gene asking how to place it in gear. Gene came over showed me and asked if I wanted him to ride it. Being greedy I knew he had wished he had grabbed it. I told him no I could handle it. I took off on the bike having never ridden a bike in my life but I was riding that day! It was a Kawasaki 900.

As I was cruising down the street, I was afraid to stop at the light. The bike was heavy. I did not have enough weight to hold it. I cut through the gas station. I drove over to my school, Clarenceville High School.

Wow, what a rush I was excited and proud of my actions. I got my best friend Lena and showed off the bike. I took her for a ride. Then everyone wanted to ride it. I was receiving a short amount of fame at that moment. I was popular for a short time. I was eating up the glory of it.

I wanted to be the big shot. I let everyone take a ride on it including this person Tim that I knew who was friends with Derrick, Gee, Terry, Len and Don, Terry's brother. These guys were all the popular guys in school. They hung with that jerk Len. I had met all of them at a park selling drugs before I started going to school there. They only liked me because of the drugs and things I had. Derrick came over and told me he could hide the bike for me on his property. So, I rode over there with him to hide the bike.

Later that evening, I went over Jerry's house like nothing ever happen. I walked in the door and to my surprise, they invited me in. I was as strong as acid coming back after I robbed them. I sat down on the couch. They told me that someone robbed them. I expressed how sorry I was for their misfortune.

Then, one of Jerry's roommates placed his hand under a pillow and pulled out a pistol. He clicked the hammer back and told me we can play Russian roulette or you can tell me where my bike is. I played it off as if I did not know what he was talking about. He clicked the gun back and pulled the trigger. The gun did not go off. I kept telling him I did not know what he was talking about. He clicked the gun again. It did not go off.

I was sweating and worried about the next click. He then turned the gun around to show me that there was one bullet in the gun just in case I felt he was playing mind games with me. When I saw that bullet, it gave me a reality check. I told him, I would tell him where the bike was.

We drove over to Derrick's house. Everyone over at that house was on probation. We got the bike back and there was three hundred dollars' worth of damage done to the gas tank that Derrick did.

Well guess, who got blamed for the damage? I went to juvenile for it. They did not keep me, my father agreed to pay the damages on the bike. He paid the whole three hundred dollars. I was released in my father's custody. That was the first time I was placed in juvenile, but not the last time. I could have gotten Jerry and his roommate into trouble for pointing a gun in my face and clicking it. But I did not want to call wolf after the fact.

After that I went back to Jerry's apartment and broke in. I took a bunch of pills and tried to kill myself. I was so embarrassed and did not want to go back to school again. I was considered a snitch and did not get any money from the stuff Gene took or sold either.

I was a big dummy all the way around. I was taken to the doctors at National Surgical Hospitals to get my stomach pumped they placed tubes down my nose to my stomach they pulled everything out. My dad was there with me and my brother came down to pick us up.

I walked out of the ER and my brother walked up to me and hit me hard in my chest and knocked the air out of me. I flew back into a chair against the wall. My father jumped up stating softly; "Not here you guys!!" When I got pushed back in the hospital chair I looked up at Rip.

Dad kept asking us not to do this here in the hospital.

Rip stated, "If she is going to do something stupid like that; then she needs to do it right and don't put us through another scare like this. You want to die, then kill yourself . . . . Don't take us through this shit again."

My brother and I started to pull apart from each other at this time. He did not approve of the drug scene, or me taking myself through this, or me being weak, trying to be accepted.

My father insured me I would return to school and face everything. My dad always told me, if you fear something, it rules you, it keeps you in prison. If you face your fears head on, it usually isn't as bad as it plays out in your mind. We went home and dad and I had a long talk. He encouraged me to take advantage of life's offerings while I am young.

He told me, "Billy Joe, you are not going to be a teenager long. These years will fly by and one day you will look up and realize life has passed you by."

We hugged and I went to bed. I love my dad. That statement ended up to come true later in life.

The next day, I went over to the Marlow House, I did not see Gene there. There was a guy named Carlos at the crib. Once in a while when I would go over there him and I would smoke weed together and maybe hit some THC together.

Our school was giving a 50's dance "The Bo Diddley's" and I did not have anyone to take me. So I wanted to go and I asked Carlos to accompany me. He agreed. I was happy to have someone go with me. I went back home and the next day at school I had purchased two tickets.

A couple days went by and it was Friday night, party night and school dance. I was so excited. I had a date and dad gave me money to purchase a nice outfit. I went all the way out to Detroit to get him, and we came all the way back to Farmington for the concert. Carlos did not feel funny about being in an all-white school because I was there. We went on the dance floor and started dancing.

Some white guy who thought he was, a big hot shot came up to me and Carlos tapping us on my shoulder. He told me we don't dance with *"N"* on this side of town. I stopped and looked at him stating; "the only *"N"* I see is **"you."**

What the heck did I go and say that for, he busted me right in my nose while others jumped on Carlos.

They all ganged up on him, beating him down. I went to the bathroom to see how bad my face was. My nose was on the other side of my face. I pulled on it to straighten it out. It cracked real loud and moved back in place. Who needs doctors? I realized I left Carlos so I ran back.

They had taken the fight outside in the parking lot. I found a chain on the parking lot and started hitting people off Carlos and we got the hell out of there. We hitched a ride to Detroit rode the bus the rest of the way. Carlos would never really talk to me after that.

I don't know what ever happen to him, as time went on, but I heard he moved and then some people blew up his house. I did not mean to bring him into a situation to get hurt. I really liked him as a person. Pray he has forgiven me.

I went home that evening and placed a steak on my eye. My father would work at Drano Inn on West Adam Street as a cook. He could not retire. If dad stopped working, he felt like he would die.

He came home flicking the light on. He saw me lying on the coach and asked me why I was sitting in the dark? I jumped up to show him my two black eyes and broken nose. My father stated, "Wow, what does the other guy look like?"

I said, how did you know it was a guy?

Dad said; "I didn't, I was only kidding; you mean a guy did this to you?" I told my father yes, and you have to go to school with me because they kicked me out.

We went to school that Monday. The Principal kept telling my father we can't have this kind of behavior in our schools. I had told my father what the fight was about. My father cannot stand racism.

My father knew what the Principal was trying to say, but my father wanted him to come straight out with it. The Principal wanted me to quit because I brought a black to the school. He stated it in so many words, but would not come out and say it. My father kept beating around the bush, trying to make the man state why he felt I should drop out. Finally after toying back and forth with the issue, he finally said it.

"Because your daughter is involved with drugs and brings blacks to our school system; parents pay good taxes to have their children go to school in the suburban area. They do not want other children to bring the city here."

My father told that principal, "I don't care if she drops out, because I do not want her to learn to be a bidet."

Now, I don't think my father was totally on my side, because he told me a few things after we left. Dad was not biased at all, but he did not believe in placing people in situations that were not healthy. My father felt I did just that. He was wondering what kind of reputation was I creating for myself and why? He offered to send me to self-esteem classes.

After that he signed me up to take karate with my brother's school and business. (My brother and another man ran a Karate Martial Art & Fitness School on East Monroe Street.) Dad felt this would allow me to learn discipline for offense and defense. He felt it would give me more confidence with myself. We went home and dad just shook his head asking me what I was going to do with my life if I was not in school?

Dad felt school was everything and you could not get by without it. He was not going to agree with me about dropping out. We went to bed and did not discuss it. I did not quit school; I continued to attend.

Many of the guys in school never wanted to be with me or asked me out. I was not popular in that department. I never did fit in. I was only used. So I hung with Lena and sometimes Jenny and her brother.

A couple days later Lena came over to the house. Lena and I did a lot of things together, she was my best friend. We both hung with others but the majority of the time we were together. We would even celebrate the holidays together.

Christmas was around the corner and we had celebrated a few of them. I told Lena I felt cheated; she asked me HOW?

When we celebrate Christmas, you give me one gift. When we celebrate Hanukah, I give you a present for seven days of the holiday. Lena and I laughed as she expressed, "I can't help it if your holiday is a one day affair and ours is seven days."

"You don't have to give great gifts or go purchase them, they can be gifts from the heart." Lena is so funny and I loved being around her.

Lena's parents gave her a hard time about me. They felt I was not the type of girl they wanted her to hang around with. It even got to the point where they would not allow me to come over anymore. I would have to stand outside on the sidewalk and yell Lena's name out so she could hear me.

I will never forget, one day, I was in Lena's neighborhood stealing this mini bike and riding it through the complex. I had to keep the bike running because the throttle had to be tied with a wire, to keep the choke open. I hung the wire around the handle bars. The bike would not stop. I could not unloose the wire fast enough as I rode by Lena's house and was going to pull up in the drive way, and could not get the wire untied.

I could not stop the bike.

I drove into Lena's family's house. I hit the brick of their house under the main picture window in the front part of the home. Her dad was sitting on the chair reading the newspaper when I hit the house. He jumped up stating: "What the heck was that?"

"It was me, hitting the house." (Smile) He was truly mad and did not want me over there for nothing in the world.

Lena felt at times like she was having a hard time growing up at home. She would complain to me all the time. Lena wanted me to go everywhere with her. I was like a protector.

Lena came to my house out of breathe stating; "I can't take it any longer Billy Joe. I have to go see my brother." I was trying to get Lena to calm down and see what was going on. She stated with great passion that she wanted to go to Arizona.

Lena stated I am hitch-hiking down there. She did not like the way things were happening at home for her so I left with her. She was my friend and I could not let her go by herself. I had it good at home. My father and I were just getting over all the bad things that had been going on and worked things out. I really did not want to go but Lena was my friend so I had to go with her.

Dad just signed me up for the Karate classes. My brother was talking to me again. I was not doing as many drugs and things were starting to change for me. But as well, I could not set my loyalty to the side. My best friend and sister needed me. So we were on our way to Arizona. We were hitchhiking down 94 Freeway and the cops rolled by.

I was trying to grab all our contraband and hide it. They pulled up next to us asking how old we were.

Lena tried to tell them we were older than we looked. I was fifteen but I looked like I was twelve. They told us to get into the cop car. I was getting the LSD acid out of the ballpoint pen I had. I gave one to Lena and took one myself in the back of the cop car. Then I handed her the weed to swallow. I swallowed some myself. They could not take us to the police station, because back then it was against the law. They rode us to the Juvenile Home for girls in Paw-Paw Kalamazoo.

They took us in giving us a shower and stripping us down. I was caught with a switchblade in my shoe. It was over three inches long you could pressing a button and the blade came out. They gave me 30-hour lock down for it. Lena would come to see me but, I was angry at the whole world. I felt like I always was blamed for everything, always caught, no matter what the surrounding situation was. I was feeling sorry for myself and took the victim's route.

Lena was so small she had to jump up and down to look into my small window.

The room was small with a steal door. There was a window about the size of three feet by three. It was double plated glass, surrounded by steal. The bed was bolted to the ground and a small plastic mattress on top. No sheet was given for safety reasons because of the threat of suicide. There was a toilet and a sink connected to one another in one corner of the room. It smelt like a toilet was in the room too. That was my quarters for thirty hours.

By the time I was released, Lena's parents had already come to pick her up. Lena wore my 42-inch bell-bottom blue jean's home. I told her she could, but I was mad, because her pants looked like floods on me. I stood around 5'6 and she was 4'5. So you can image what I looked like.

I stood staring out the window wondering why I did the things that I did. Here I am locked up like an animal again. I did not know it at that time but my future would hold that same scene and I would ask that same question in my adulthood.

I saw a Greyhound bus pull up and a few people got off. To my surprise, my father was one of those people. I knew I was in big trouble. My dad rode the bus all the way from Farmington Hills to Paw-Paw Kalamazoo to get me released. My father for some odd reason believed in me. I look back now and wish I hadn't sent him through so much hell. He never did get to see me get my life together.

(Author's excursus: "There are so many things that we do in our lives that cannot be overturned or corrected. That is why, it is so important to think things out and make a healthy decision before you react. You had better be able to pay the consequences. Stand up to the music as they say. There is a flip side of that coin. I always stood up but regretted every one of my decisions.")

After I was released from the juvenile in the custody of my father, we went back home and for the first time, my father laid down some rules. He was getting tired and could not deal with the hurt and disappointment any longer. I stood by my father rules. Lena's parents placed her into a drug rehab clinic downtown in Detroit, someplace called Lafayette. For some odd reason, she and I grew a part for a while after that incident. However, we got back together.

Her parents hated me and refused her to see me again. It would hurt me that they thought I was the cause of everything. I usually went along with what Lena wanted to do because I always protected Lena. I felt like she needed me to keep people from saying anything to her or from getting in trouble. I did not want her to be like me. I had dark and deep secrets. I just hated that her parents thought it was me. I always seem to get the bad rap.

Lena was my best friend but even she would tell you, I was not anyone to play with. I was strong and quick to fight. I had many dark secret pockets of anger inside and would not share them with anyone. Not even my best friend. I kept a lot of pain inside. It's funny now, I talk about everything. However, back then, I was very secretive and I was not an easy person to get know. You could be my best friend and still feel like you did not know me.

Lena never knew I had a mother or any of my other friends. I never spoke on her to anyone; they thought it was just me and my dad. A lot of my friends and associates thought my mother died but would never ask me. People thought my dad was poor because of the way he dressed and did not care what people thought. It was the opposite, dad had money.

While I was in juvenile my brother Rip came over to the house asking dad if he could borrow my stereo. Dad always purchased everything from Sears because they carried American made products. It was modern and very nice. When I came home, I went into my room and saw it was missing. I was really upset and asked dad where it was. He explained to me that Rip borrowed it and that he would give it back. A couple weeks went by and Rip still did not return it.

I went over Lilly's old house where Rip and his wife were now living on East Monroe Street. I knocked at the door and Rip let me in. I asked him about my stereo and he told me, "You left Billy Joe, so I am keeping it; you have it swell at home, you keep doing this dumb stuff, for what? You have some issue and you need to address them. You have it better than any of us kids now."

I told Rip that he did not live with my scars from mom. At that point, Rip became outraged stating, "Get over it, Billy Joe. We all have scars but I am not out killing myself or going in and out of juvenile. You used to be my favorite sister but I don't know who

87

you are now. I am not giving it back. Suffer, because you have it good and you don't appreciate it."

Then Rip asked me to leave. I was so pissed I could not believe him. I felt like Rip should have embraced me with love, not toss me to the side and not help me. I had issues, but he never wanted to help me emotionally, he only wanted to get mad at me and not speak to me out of anger.

I ran home and told dad, he was calm and cool telling me he would get it: "It is your stereo Billy Joe, and I will get it tomorrow. Your brother is just hurt by your actions. We all are puzzled by your actions. They just don't understand your mother hurt you deeply emotionally."

Dad then stated he should have taken custody of us kids. He could have but did not want to hurt our mother like that. We watched TV together and retired for the evening.

Dad went and got the stereo; I saw it in my room after school. I was so excited but when I looked on the side of it, I knew it was not mine. I had carved my name on the side of the wood. I walked back into the living room and told dad and he sat me down.

"Billy Joe, you need to learn which battles to fight to win the war."

It's funny that was my problem all my life. I never knew which battles to fight. I guess that is why I never won the war. Dad did not get the one back from my brother and we left the issue alone.

I was hanging around the neighborhood. I met this guy Fred through another friend. I started hanging around him but he was a much older man than me. He lived in this big green house on Middle belt Road. Fred was about twenty-five years old. I was only fifteen. I met him at a party in the apartment complex through Jenny my friend. He really liked me a lot and once we met he did everything to see me all the time. He would invite me to his house. We saw each other for a few months then Fred stated how he would like me to be his woman.

What a laugh, I was only fifteen!!! He purchased me a gold ring with diamonds and Safire stone in it. It was very pretty and you could tell he spent some money on it.

I went back to school as dad requested and it was not long before I was in more trouble. I ended up in juvenile again.

Officer Tina, a cop, and her partner came to school to check my locker, searching for drugs. Of course, someone told on me that's why the police were searching school lockers. She did search my locker but the Principal really called about me not attending school.

Officer Tina was a hard-ass. She had a heavy attitude. We bumped heads at first until she got to know me and my situation. They wanted to keep me in juvenile until I was eighteen years of age for truancy. Are you kidding me? For-real??

They were unable to find the drugs. My mother was supposed to come to a hearing to help my father get me out because she had legal custody. Officer Tina did not like my mom from the jump-start and got very frustrated with her attitude toward me.

They stuck me in juvenile hall. I had a scheduled hearing, and the committee was deliberating about my history and situation. I was waiting in the hallway for the decision which the evidence did not sound good. I was supposed to wait for the outcome of the hearing but I did not stay long. When I heard my mother wanted me to stay in juvenile until I was eighteen years of age. I escaped as soon as an opportunity presented itself.

My father was trying to tell the Judge, "That I had been in trouble but that is all behind Billy Joe. She is working on it and I am helping her." The judge was concerned with the fact my mother had the legal custody not my father.

Officer Tina, her partner and I waited in the hallway for the outcome.

The Judge was talking on the conference phone with my mother. My father along with the Judge who had her on the phone, also talked to her.

I was in the hallway with the officers and asked for a cigarette and the officers told me they could not give me that. I expressed, "Hey, I am going away until I am eighteen, please." They felt sorry for me and gave me one. The officers got a call on the radio and walked around the corner.

I went down the hallway and rolled open a small skinny window in Detroit Juvenile Hearing division. I was looking down realizing I was up a couple floors. I looked at how small the window was and kept telling myself to go for it. I looked behind me, Officer Tina and her partner had left. I placed my head through the window, it was hard but I got through it.

Then I worked my body through and had trouble getting my butt out. I was only a size 0 so I was really skinny but so was the window that narrow. I worked my butt out and went out the window awkwardly. As I fell to the ground I scraped my arm and leg on the side of the building going down. I landed in a bush with pickers. I got up and hopped through the parking lot. I knew it was over now. I need to go as fast as possible.

I started hitchhiking and the first person that rode by shook her fist at me. I had a black tee shirt on that stated Pontiac Juvenile Home. I turned it inside out on the main street.

The second person picked me up. They were in a pickup truck and had me get in the back. I lay down so no one would see me. I got a ride home and went to Fred's house to hide. I did not want to go to my father's for fear that the police would come there to get me.

I do not know why I trusted Officer Tina but I called her to let her know why I ran. Then I called my father. I hid out at Fred's place and chilled there until they were able to arrange something for me. It was cool at first; I was living in a house with seven other hippies.

Everyone paid separately for a room. Of course, my father paid my portion. We did not have a refrigerator and stove, so my father went to Sears, his favorite store and purchased one, so I could keep food in it. There was a party every night and I was always high on drugs. Sleeping with Freddy and not realizing he was a child molester.

Officer Tina and my father felt it was good to leave me there until they could work out the details with my mother and Juvenile Hall. They had no idea the drugs or what was really happening over at this house.

Officer Tina did not like what my mother had to say about me. My mother told them to keep me until I was eighteen. She stated that I had been a thorn in her side from the day I was born. My father asked her for custody and my mother refused. She did not have anything nice to say about me and Officer Tina became very angry. Not understanding how a mother could not care about her child or wanting a solution to my issues.

Later on, my mother agreed to sign for me as long as my father agreed to allow my mother to keep my social security check. I received a social security check ever since my father retired from Chrysler when I was twelve.

Mom got child support checks from my dad until he retired. Dad would send double payments for all us kids. Each one of us kids got social security checks. I believe Lilly and I were the only children that got one. She also received them all the time I lived with my father while they were living up north. She never stopped receiving them. My father allowed it and never said anything until now. He let Marge (my mother) know if he could not get me out of juvenile then he would make sure she did not receive another check.

I was a check to her. She never cared about me, just the check she received for me. While Officer Tina and my father were working out the situation, I was still living in Fred's house.

Everyone kept eating my food and did not respect the fact my father purchased that merchandise. It was always some chaos in that house, romantic drama every day. Fred became obsessed with me and wanted to get married when I became of age. I was not in love with him. I really felt obligated to screw him living in that house even though my father was paying my rent.

If my father knew he was screwing me, he would have had a shit-fit. I felt if I did not do it, he would not accept my father's rent money for me and I would go back to juvenile.

Lena would sneak over to the Green house (what I called Freddy's house) to see me once in a while. We hung out like old times. She came over one day and I was tripping. I ended up ripping off a shotgun from one of the people in that house. I was taking the shotgun down the street to the corner gas station under an army jacket. I planned to pull it out on a person who worked there named Pete. I knew Pete from school. He would talk to me here and there in the hall ways. A few times, very few, we would meet up and talk. I went out on one date with him. He was not really my type, as my father would say . . . . because he had a job and did not get high.

Lena tried to stop me as she stood in front of me trying to keep me from walking out the door. Lena pleaded with me not to go out. I finally tricked Lena and locked her in the bathroom and left.

Lena was so smart: she climbed out the bathroom window and chased me down the street to stop me.

I walked down Middle belt Road. It was a busy road and strange that no one saw a young fifteen year old girl walking down a busy street with a shotgun under an army jacket.

This guy Pete told everyone that he screwed me and that was not true. I became so angry that I planned on shooting him. I saw Pete and called him over to me. As he approached me, I lifted up the army jacket over my head and pushed the coat off as I brought the gun back down facing him. The gun became jammed and another man came up behind me who worked with Pete taking the shotgun out of my hands.

Lena came running up out of breathe yelling, "Billy Joe stop! Please stop!"

The man held me down on the ground while Pete and I discussed it. They unloaded the shotgun while we talked.

Pete expressed that the guys just assumed that by the way he described our date. I calmed down and they let me up. It was true; I did sleep with a lot of guys. I really just wanted a steady boyfriend but people took it the wrong way as I was a slut. I just wanted someone to like me.

Lena and I returned to the house and put the gun back. No one at the house knew we did that.

Something was not right with me mentally. I would get into rage like that then calm down later. I believed I had a personality disorder caused by events with my mother. I knew I was a sick girl with a lot of emotional issues. You can punish two children the same way, and one child will take it to heart and the other one will roll it off like it was nothing and keep going. I took it to heart.

No one knew anything in the house. I was getting sick and tired of the Green house. Every night parties at the house. I could not sleep from the noise. I could not watch TV because of the noise. There was no structure or love in the house, just a bunch of hippies having free love and getting high.

Lena started hanging with other people. I wanted to go home and could not wait to see what the results were between dad and Officer Tina. I really did not like being with Fred and felt trapped in this relationship.

I did not realize it back then, but Fred was a sick man. It did not even dawn on me, that he liked little girls. I was missing the family life style, sitting down at the table to eat dinner with dad, having rules and chores to do. I missed being close to my dad. I felt very alone with no direction. Even being young, parties every night became depressing. I just wanted to go home so bad I could taste it.

Yeah! A few weeks flew by and dad came over to the house. He sat me down to let me know I was finally able to come back home. Dad and Officer Tina got the agreement with mom. She signed the papers allowing me to come back home with dad. So I went home.

I could have danced out of excitement. I was happy to be there, but I was still using heroin here and there, especially after living in that Green house with Fred. He would purchase it for me to keep me sedated. Being home with dad my time was spent going back and forth to Detroit, copping dope, and bringing it back home and getting high.

My father and I talked about me doing something else with my life since I was not in school. Dad wanted me to get a job and go to night school or an alternative school for active children. So I decided to get a job. It was summer time and dad felt it would help create responsibility for me. I got a job at "D & T restaurant." This was my second job after I had worked at Big Boy's in Cadillac. I was able to use that on my reference.

I loved working there and I got along well with the manager. I would come to work in roller-skates and wait on customers. The manager and I would smoke weed together. Things were going well and I was making money. I received plenty of tips and a paycheck. Dad said if I saved half he would match whatever I saved up and get me a car. I was able to get my license at fifteen because dad was a non-driver. I saved my money.

My father was proud of me and how well I was doing. The guy that owned the restaurant was a little weird. He had an ex-wife that sometimes came over and bitched telling the boss man what to do. She was gay and had a women who was her significant other but the boss and her were still legally married. Weird set up.

He hired these two girls and they did not work very well. They would clown around and leave work early and we would get stuck doing all their work.

I caught them making dope deals with this guy who came in playing off like he was a customer. I told them, I was going to tell and they said **so what,** they took money out of the cash register and walked off. I told the manager and she did the paper work to let them go. They were a trip.

The manager trusted me a lot. She let me do a lot of the important things around the restaurant. I was still getting high but on many things not just heroin.

One day, the manager gave me the key and told me to lock some items up and then get a copy of the key made. They needed two copies for the restaurant. So I left and went down to the key shop and had the copies made but for some odd reason I had a three copies made. I did not say anything and held on to it. That day at work, we had a really good day. We sold a lot and made some good tips.

The manager asked me if I wanted to come over to her house and smoke some weed. I thought that was really cool and felt special. I went over there after work and we had a good time. We sat and got high with her husband and some of my friends. She fixed some platters of snacks. I stayed over there until twelve midnight. When I came home that evening, my father asked me, "I thought you were not going to do this anymore? I thought you had decided to change your life."

I told my father that I was over my boss's house, that's why I was late. Dad told me to go to bed and please at least call before I come home late. I told him I would. I went to work the next day, me and the owner got into it. He was messing around with this dude and I ran into it. They were doing sexual things. He became angry with me for seeing it. I told him I quit and jumped over the counter and walked off. That was some sick shit to me at that time.

The manager tried to talk me out of it in the parking lot. I told her that I did not want to work with him, he was sick. He had more issues than I thought, but I found out, he was bisexual and a heroin user. So was his weird ex-wife. The manager knew all of this; she told me to let it roll. I just couldn't do that. This was the first time I was faced with this issue.

He was mad at me because I came in while he was sucking someone's dick??? "To me, I should have been mad not him." I did not tell my dad I left. I hid it from him.

A couple of weeks went by and I called Denver a friend of mine and Alan's. I asked him, if he could give me a ride. I told him I had a joint picked out to rob.

He agreed to pick me up. I went over to D & T and used the key that I had made and went inside. There was no alarm. I walked to the back where he kept the deep freezer and opened it up.

Inside there was a few bank bags of money. I could have grabbed all the bags but I was only able to grab four or five of them. They were very heavy because some of them were full of coins. I grabbing the bags, walking out as I locked the door. I just knew that Denver was waiting for me down the street where we agreed to meet.

To my surprise, he was not there. I kept walking down the street. I was so mad, because I did not know how much longer I was going to be able to carry these bags without someone seeing me. I kept walking faster. Sweat was pouring down my arm pit, my heart started beating heavier. I saw cops riding by and I had to hide or act like I wasn't carrying money bags. I was terrified. The cops kept rolling by.

A car pulled up to me. I was very fearful of whom was pulling up next to me. I peeked inside and it was Denver. I breathed out as a sign of relief. A shadow of relief was on my face. I got into the car and asked him where the hell he had been. I told him I could have gotten busted.

We drove over to the manager's house counting and split up the money. I did not have to split it with her or her husband but I did. We each got a lot but I can't remember how much. I was able to give my dad my half of the money for my car. I also told dad that summer was almost up and I was going to think about school. I was lying and did not want dad to know I had quit.

Later on, I rode my ten speed bike to the D & T to get my last check. They owed me and I noticed that no one was there. It was odd because the bosses car was parked in the parking lot not behind the building.

I rode over there and saw dirt on the windows. I went up to the door, and he had put a gun to his head and shot himself. The dirt on the window was really his brains and blood. I got scared and left. I rode all the way home and was tripping about what I saw.

I went to the funeral and his ex-wife, who was a lesbian, kept telling me that I was the cause of his stress. I shot back, "It had nothing to do with me, bitch. He was secretly a heroin addict, a skin popper, (a person who injects their heroin under their skin and not in a vein) and he was in debt up to his ears. That robbery was just the icing on the cake, he was deeper in debt before that robbery." I cussed her out and laid low for a long time.

I was really scared after I saw that man's head blown off. That really messed with me, and caused dreams. I never told anyone that I rode up on him dead in that car in the parking lot. I was too scared. I was only fifteen years old. I was still messing with heroin here and there. I started pushing away from the street life.

That night I went to sleep. I had a dream about Julie lying in a casket. I went up to the casket and Julie sat up and told me to leave the heroin alone or I was going to die.

I woke up in a panic full of sweat and then told my father the next day. Dad started crying and told me he asked Julie before mom and he separated to make sure she watched over all the kids. Dad was convinced that was Julie's way of coming back in spirit to save me. After that I kicked and tried to dry myself out. For three to four days, I was clammy, sweating and regurgitating yellow bio, with cramps in my stomach and legs. Cigarette smoke and food made me sick to smell it. I just lay in my bed and told my dad I had the flu. He got me some Alka-Seltzer Plus Cold medicine and Sleepy Time Tea with rose-hips. I was finally through with the evil spirit of Ms. Heroin.

I was still doing break-ins, and petty stuff here and there. I don't know why, because my father would give me anything I wanted.

I met this black guy named Tyrone in Detroit when I was coming home from the Marlow House. We dated a few times. The guys in Marlow House kept making fun of me and told me that it is not good for a white woman to be with black men that I would become marked. I really did not care what people thought. We used to go down to the Grande-Ball Room drinking and smoking weed, listening to music but I left the heroin alone.

Once we went to see Sly and the Family Stones at the Palace in Detroit. I was so high that every time I went down a hallway to find my way around, I would end up in the same place. It was so weird. I was so wasted that I kept going around in circles. While I was sitting on the steps trying to figure out where Tyrone was, I witnessed a dude who was so high, jump through a window which cut him up pretty badly. They brought in the EMS and took him to the hospital. He must have been wiped out on PCP.

I really enjoyed going places with Tyrone. We hung out at parks together. We went down to Hines Drive Park and sold our weed and pills. One time we were there and a big raid went down at the park. My father just purchased a nice pair of Platform shoes for me. They cost 30.00 dollars; back then, that was a lot. Tyrone told me to take them off and throw them away so we could run.

Helicopters were all around on top of the park. Police cars were surrounding the area. We had drugs on us and we needed to get out of there. I refused to throw my shoes away; he told me I needed to do that **now!** So we could run through the woods. So I did and went back the next day to get them. We ran through the woods and got away. We were lucky; many people got busted that night. I had a good time with him. But he was not what I wanted.

I was sixteen and I was ready to settle down and make something of my life. I wanted to quit getting high and quit school. I was not accepted there and everyone acted like I was a total freak from another world. I told my friend Tyrone it was over and stopped seeing him. I started hanging out around my dad's place.

Dad was happy because he knew I was home at a reasonable hour and I was not hanging out with bad people. It's hard when you don't fit in and no one likes you. Growing up during the teenage years is crucial in life. I did not socialize well because growing up I spent the majority time of my life under my mother and in the back yard.

I had a sister that avoids everyone. I had a brother that was out-going and in his own world. Mom made him the king of the castle. We were to iron his clothes for him and wait on him whenever he requested it. Mom always treated the boys in the family like they were gold. They could do whatever they wanted. The girls, she treated like her slaves and under her foot.

I had a lot of head issues and did not fit in with the other kids at my school. I thought different and acted different. I started a new school at 14 and have gone to three different schools in two years. I wasn't diagnoses with dyslexic until later on in life. I had a reading problem and kids would make fun of me. I refused to read out loud in class. Teachers passed me just to get me out of their class because they did not want to deal with my oppositional defiant personality. I knew I would never get a job beyond working in a restaurant or factory like my mother.

My mom was never able to help me with my homework growing up because she only had a third grade education. My brother was too busy with his life and Lilly was in a bubble of her own world. Paula never really bothered with the family, only once in a while. I always felt she did not think we were good enough. Julie was dead, and Ben . . . . who knows where he is or if he is alive. So much for family.

I was not popular in school but considered a freak. I was ready to just let time pass until I could get a job and move out. My father did not know what else to do for me. He knew I had a lot of head issues. I did not want to go back to school. Dad wanted me to go to any school as long as I received my education.

I started to hang around home area and took babysitting jobs so I could keep money in my pocket so I did not have to keep asking my father. I hated babysitting because I was very fearful of being a child abuser like my mother. But it was money and I needed it to purchase my cigarettes and whatnots; I hated asking for money from dad. I was sixteen.

# CHAPTER THREE

# ON MY WAY TO THE CHAPEL, CHAPEL, AND CHAPEL

I finally ended up dropping out of school and hanging out at this girl's house in the apartment complex. Her name was Cherry. She was a single mom living with this guy who worked and was her keeper. She liked me a lot and wanted to be some kind of a mentor to me. We hung out daily as she smoked cigarettes and drank Pepsi one after another.

She had long black hair that she dyed like that. She was not attractive but with her confidence she was. She thought what was between her legs was the best in town. She felt entitlement. She would give me cigarettes and feed me. We hung together and it was a place to go, plus free cigarettes.

She wanted me to meet her brother. She felt he needed someone younger to be with. His last girlfriend was older, almost 30 years older than him. Well to say the least, I met my first husband there. He was older than I was and Cherry's brother.

We dated and went to places. He took me out for lobster dinners and bought me flowers. We ate at The Detroit Dine-Around. I really never had a man take me to a place like that. We would do everything together. I still hung with Cherry but not as much as I did her brother.

We did country drives together, buy cider and hot donuts. We went on hay rides and horseback riding. We would pick cherries and applies at farm locations.

I saw this bunny rabbit once when we went out for a country drive. When my birthday rolled by, he brought me the rabbit and gave it to me. I was so happy and in love. Then he asked me to marry him.

We moved in together and started keeping house. I was sixteen years old and he was twenty-two years old. My father was not pleased but wanted me to be happy. Dad was worried that I was pregnant. I was embarrassed by the question and assured my father I was not. He felt we should wait. He did like Bernard because he worked making good money.

We did everything together, hung out at Michigan Ave Park, in Detroit getting high and parting all the time. We were a free living couple having fun, but many things change when you start living together.

I found out that he had a fetish for XXX rated strip joints. He sat and watched XXX rated movies at these places. He would lie to me where he was going. He was addicted to porn. He had that spirit in him that was demonic. He was also getting his dick sucked by men at these places. He liked watching the sex on the show and had men take care of his needs. I could not keep him out of Go-Go places either.

He did nothing but drink and became violent. He would come home and beat me. I would fight him back, but most of the time, I would have to trick him. Bernard would always lie to me about everything he did. I was so miserable with him. He would leave me home all night and be out at those places. We moved over on the River in Ecorse, on Second Street.

I had gotten a job at the hamburger joint on the River. It was right on Jefferson and Southfield Road. Bernard hated for me to work, but I could not just stay home all the time. He made really good money, but he drank so much, plus the porn, that we never had anything. What we did have, he would break it when he got drunk.

He was a machinist and a setup man; he ran screw machines. His brother taught him the trade and he was great at it. He could tear a car down and put it back together too. Bernard had an IQ of 145. It was nothing to him to read a volume from an encyclopedia for pleasure. He was an atheist and believed in Darwin's theory of evolution.

One afternoon, he told me he was going over to his friend's house to have a few beers. He did not get home until 1:30 in the morning. I was very angry having to stay in that apartment all by myself for hours. I was a young girl and did not want to just sit in a room but he convinced me that it was on the up and up.

Later the next day, we went over to the store together, and stopped at his father's house. They lived in the slums down in Detroit over by Lafayette. We ran into these so-called friends the one he said he was at their house drinking some beers. The friend called out to Bernard and said; "Hey, we haven't seen you in a while, what's up?"

I could feel my face fill with blood as I got madder and madder that he lied to me. My stomach felt as if it was up in my neck. I could not wait until we left, to question him about where he really was last night.

We were driving down the street in Dale Ray area of Detroit. I just pulled my fist back toward the seat and hit Bernard as hard as I could as he was driving. Then I grabbed the wheel and tried to steer us into a tree.

Bernard kept yelling, wait honey, let me explain! I had felt like a fool as if he went out on me. I had held all that anger in until we left his father's house. Bernard then explained he had been with another man there and not a woman.

I became sick to my stomach wondering what I had gotten myself into. We pulled around and picked up his little brother. My husband told me not to talk about it when Berry was around. I agreed, but when we got home one word followed another after another and when I found out the whole truth, I just could not hold my temper.

I fought with him and I ended up stabbing him with a kitchen knife. Bernard was standing on top of the bed; he was waving his hands as I was standing below with a knife. I had gotten a knife because I was scared how Bernard was acting.

It was almost like I just went totally blank, saw red in front of my face and pulled back my hand and butcher knife as he was telling me to **"stab me"** so I stabbed him; I could actually hear the knife cutting into his skin it was an awful sound. The blood shot up like a faucet. I just stood there looking at it; it actually looked like a waterfall. The smell of the blood made me think of metal. Berry asks me why?

We took him to the hospital and he got 23 stitches in his hand on the inside, and 27 on the outside. His little brother Berry was terribly upset with me stabbing his brother. He was calling me names as I was driving Bernard to the hospital. We came up with a story to tell the hospital so the police would not get involved. After we sat and discussed the whole issue, I tried to be more understanding and see if I could **allow** Bernard to be himself.

Bernard had a lot of issues about his mother and dad. I had a lot of issues because of my mother. We were both messed and dysfunctional trying to balance each other out.

He told me his dad mistreated his mother all the time. That she was not happy with him but she had all of the kids. He then told me that he always went to the store with his mom, but that one time, she was on her way and Bernard wanted to go but she would not allow him. She just had a baby, which was Berry who was only a couple days old.

She got hit by a train while going over the railroad tracks in the country.

Bernard was really hurt and did not understand why she died. Bernard told me often, through the years, that he felt like she committed suicide because there was no way she could not see that train coming. Bernard broke down and cried like a baby in my arms.

I vowed that day to never pick up a weapon against him no matter how scared I was. I then tried to be an adult about this situation dealing with whatever was keeping Bernard from staying home, to bring it there for him.

As time went on, there was one incident where he brought home another man to have sex while I watch. I tried to watch but I could not go through with it because it made me sick. It was not exciting to me like it was for him.

I walked out of the bed room into the living room area. The man he was fucking asked Bernard if he could fuck me or would Bernard fuck me and allowing him to watch. Bernard stated **NO,** but I would not have done it anyway it was nasty to me and disrespectful. Bernard had some demonic spirits and it was really hard for me to participate with his desires.

Anyway, Bernard kicked him out of the house. The whole house smelt like two men's asses.

We fought about it later and then Bernard told me he made a mistake he did not enjoy it. I knew that was a lie, because I was there. I could see this was not the first time he had done this. He just did not want me to be a part of it because of how I felt. We ended up getting married anyways. I was crazy for marrying Bernard but for some odd reason I did not want to back out.

My girlfriend Lena was my bridesmaid. She was the only person at my wedding besides my father. The other kids in my family did not have much to do with me nor did I have much to do with them. Lena and I went and got my dress and fixed my hair. I always wore my hair straight and never wore a dress.

It did hurt me that my brother did not participate in my wedding. My brother and I did not talk back then because he hated that I was on drugs and thought if he stopped talking to me.

I thought I was straightening out my life. However, it just got worse as time went on. All was changing now; I was getting off drugs and getting married, I thought!!! It was a new beginning.

Lena and I were ready for my big moment **"Marriage."** It was the worse snowstorm of the year; it was 1974 and we had a big snowstorm. Lena and I spent hours, fixing my hair, curling it, fixing my long crème colored dress. Never wore high heels but there is a first time for everything.

Lena and I left my father's place as I slipped falling down the steps on dad's porch. I was so mad, the snow was coming down on my hair, and my dress got all dirty from the snow and the dirt under the snow it was a nasty day.

We went to the church. I got married at St. Paul's Lutheran Church on Middle Belt Road in Farmington Hills. The pastor came out of retirement to marry us because he married everyone in my family including my mom and Tom.

We walked to the door, with the snow coming down on us like crazy. I tried the door and no answer. We went to the next door, no answer. The snow was up to our knee caps. My legs, feet and dress were wet. My feet were freezing from the snow. My make-up was running down my face.

My hair was hit; it went from a curl to straight. I should have known then, that this was a bad warning sign. We ran to the back of the church, saw a man cleaning the church, and knocked on the window for him to let us in.

We finally got into the church and found my husband and father. My husband looked at me and stated, "Man, you look bad, are you okay?"

After everything we went through to get into that church. I was so mad at Bernard for even saying I looked bad.

The pastor had us repeat after him but for some odd reason, I was unable to say my vows. My girlfriend Lena said them for me. I used to tease her about it stating, she really married him not me. She had to say my vows for me, I was never able to say them. I was too nervous. My words were twisted, and Lena got tired of waiting for me to say them, so she did. I wonder, was that legal? (Smile)

Our marriage lasted about three years. My marriage was awful; some of the years were good and others not worth speaking about. It was made for the movies.

My husband brought home at least 500.00 a week as a machinist. He made good money for the 70's. That was not our problem. He just always missed work. He worked on the near West Side of Detroit, at a plant, called, Micro Machine Products. He worked the midnight shift.

There were three other men that worked this shift with him. I would fix a big plate of food for the guys, so they would not tell when I would sneak in the place. I would run my husband's machines for him, while he lay in the bathroom, sleeping off his drunk. I would work all night long, tired and full of oil from the machines. Then, about an hour before the other people would come in. I would get him up and go out to the car, and sleep. We did that for a long time without being caught. I was an enabler for him.

My husband was an alcoholic and very abusive. It was a living nightmare with him. I went from an abusive mother to an abusive husband. He broke things in the house and cost us money all the time getting him out of jail, replacing wrecked cars, and insurance companies canceling us; unpaid bills, and always having to move because our bills were not paid plus, the many beatings he gave me.

He drank up every bit of the money we could get our hands on. I accepted this behavior for a long time. Him beating on me and me hitting him back when I could get a punch in. It's hard to fight a drunk because they are not conscious, i.e. they have no 'presence of mind'—they have no control over themselves in their madness; Bernard didn't care and would fight to hurt.

Bernard came home destroying all our stuff in the living room. I was so tired of begging my father to purchase us stuff. I knew this was another night of hell. I let him do as he wished. I played yes sir so he would not hit me. He took me by my hair and swung me around knocking me into the wall and tables. He bashed my head against the wall. I cried and begged him to please stop. He screamed out what a piece of crap I was.

I was under his torture for hours. I was pleading for my life, running out side to keep him from hurting me. When I ran outside, I saw neighbors putting on their porch light on wondering what was going on. I stayed in our car waiting for him to fall asleep as I always did.

I was cold and uncomfortable not able to get any sleep. Finally I went to the house and looked in the windows to see if Bernard had fallen asleep. I opened the door because he did not lock it. He played music and drank himself to sleep.

I tied him up after a night of hell. I started hitting him with a bullwhip we had. He kept asking me if I was crazy and what was I doing. I hated that he would always tell me I was crazy. He knew my mother would tell me that.

I would catch him off guard and hit him back anytime I was able. I was miserable with him. It reminded me of my mother. There were many nights when Bernard had gotten so drunk that he busted our T.V. and knick knacks in the house.

I was trying to stop him when he blackened my eye by fighting with me. Things cooled down and I finally was able to go to sleep only to wake up in terror of hell. Bernard woke me up and dragged me out of bed. I did not have any clothes on. I was sleeping in the nude. Bernard fought with me and threw me out of the door. I stood outside without any clothes on and had to knock on the neighbor's door and ask them to help me.

I was so embarrassed and felt like a total fool. I did not want to be with Bernard any longer. I learned that day to always wear something to bed no matter what.

When Bernard was not drunk he would treat me like a queen. He would always make things better by taking me places because he acted like an asshole the night before, typical domestic violence syndrome. As they say, the honeymoon stage.

Bernard decided to take me on vacation and visit my sister. That turned out to be a mess. While we were down there my brother-in-law wanted me to go for a ride with him on his motorcycle which I did.

Then he tried to hit on me (throw a pass at me) behind my sister's back and behind my husband's back. He asked me to grab his dick as we were driving down the street. He tried to place my hand on it. He told me he had always wanted me since I was little. (I remember when I was little, he had me stand by the Christmas tree, asking me to pull down my pants so he could see if I had any pubic hair down there).

I told my husband about it and Bernard wanted to beat him up for it. I told him no because of my sister that I cared about her emotions. We left right after that and went back home. I never told my sister.

I will never forget that I called my mother and told her what had happened and she called me a liar and said that was not true. Mom stated, why he would want you when he has your sister. I hated talking to my mother and after that, I kind of kept her out of my business and life as much as I could.

After we returned home, Bernard started getting high on heroin again. At first, he started hiding it from me. Then I found out and we argued about it. It was not long before I started doing it again. We started hanging out at the parks on Hines Drive Park, going up to Beer Hill in Northville area. We started selling our drugs and getting high every night.

Bernard was uncontrollable. With his drinking and doing heroin, it was a mess.

Talk about the 12 Steps of being unmanageable, Bernard was the main character. I was slipping right back into my hippie days. I will never forget this one night that we went up on the hill to sell our stuff. This person was showing my husband a raccoon that he had sitting on his shoulders. My husband tried his hardest to get that person to sell it to him for me.

While Bernard was talking to him, a person came up to me asking if I had anything to sell. I told him I had some packs of heroin and some bags of weed. He wanted to see the bags. I showed him one. He wanted to know if I had a pound. I told him all I had left were a half of a pound. He wanted to see it. I held the 1/2 pound up and the person was looking at it and the next thing I knew, something hit me in the face.

I went down on the ground and felt my face out of pain. I had blood all over my hand. That dude had a sharp item in his hand which he put it between his fingers, balling his fist up. He hit me in my face with it. He took the 1/2 pound of weed, and started running down the hill. I yelled for Bernard, screaming that my face was bleeding. Bernard saw the person running down the hill. Many other people saw him running too and saw me standing on the hill bleeding.

They all went running down the hill after him. A couple people came over to see if my face was all right while my husband was trying to catch the person.

The bleeding would not stop. A person got some water from somewhere and tried to clean off my face to see just how deep it was. The cut was deep.

When Bernard came back, he said they were unable to get the person. The dude saw some people with a big tire tube. He jumped in it and rolled down the hill and got a way.

My eye was cut bad with a knife or sharp item he had in his hand. I was taken to the hospital. I kept telling Bernard I did not need to go but he would not listen to me. I am glad now, because I had to get seventeen stitches in my face right under my eye. I also received 21 stitches in the inside. I still have that scare to this day. We returned home and called it a night.

The next day I woke up thinking every weekend was the same old crap. Every week, he drank, and every week, I would have to defend myself from him hitting me. I was getting sick of it day after day. Every week I would try to fix different things for dinner for Bernard.

He called the house telling me he was bringing someone home for dinner. That was odd for him. Bernard never brought people home. He came home with a friend named Dee. He introduced me to him. Dee had long blondish brown hair and his mustache went down to this chest. It was an ugly sight to me.

Dee seemed to be a nice guy but Bernard did not like the way he was looking at me. I did catch him checking me out every time I turned around. I was not interested. We ate dinner and had an enjoyable night. This was a change. At least Bernard was drinking and not acting like an asshole.

It was getting late and I wanted to go to bed. So Bernard drove Dee home after we had dinner. When he got home, Bernard asked me if I thought he was good looking. I stated he was alright. We argued that night for nothing. I was not interested in that man. This was just Bernard's weird way of control.

A few weeks later Bernard was drunk and came home smashing everything. I tried to calm him down but it was not working. I always did this every night and waited for him to fall asleep so I could finally go to bed and sleep.

I kind of kept one eye opened as I slept. I never knew when Bernard would wake me out of my sleep. Bernard seemed to be in a deep sleep. I could rest now.

A few moments later, I heard a noise and I awakened to see Bernard opening the dresser drawer peeing in it. I just shook my head. I was tired of arguing with him. I figured I would get it in the morning when he was passed out.

The only thing that was great with our relationship is we would go places on a thought. If we wanted to go down south we did, if we wanted to travel up north we did. Bernard and I did go places with each other but he would still get drunk and wreck the fun or embarrass me.

After about three years of abuse. I announced I was getting a job. Bernard was unhappy. He did not like me to work. He did not want me to go to school. It was just another form of control. I went and got a job and was happy with a little independence.

Then one night my husband and I were driving down I-94 going home from a bar. I was driving because Lord knows, he could not drive. He was so drunk. As I was driving, I could see a car in my rear mirror coming up fast on me. I did not know whether to move. It kept getting closer and closer.

I just knew he was going to hit us and he did! The impact of the hit caused the steering wheel to get jammed in my stomach. I had to go to the hospital. My stomach was hurting as if someone was pulling my insides out. Bernard was mad and cussing the drunk out. I was thinking, "Yeah right, how many times have you done the same thing?"

When I got to Oakland hospital, we went through emergency and they pulled me in giving me X-Ray. At the time, I did not know it and the hospital did not check me or try to find out whether or not I was pregnant but I was. I was pregnant with our first child after three years of marriage. I was so naive back then when it came to sex and knowing your body as a woman. My husband taught everything to me.

He taught me about douching and how babies were born. I thought that they cut babies out of your stomach and that was what stretch marks were. For someone that was fast when it came to drugs and making money on the streets, I was dumb in other areas.

I never knew how babies were born until I was 17 years old and Bernard told me. I am not saying I did not do things when it came to sex. I just did not know about the details of how babies were born. No one ever told me and I never asked.

After the X-Rays, I kept having trouble. We went home but I did not feel well. Of course, Bernard felt like I was faking because the hospital could not find anything wrong with me. So I got no sympathy from him. My back was hurting and I had a headache. At times, I could not even walk across the kitchen floor. It got so bad that I wanted to die and thought I was. I went from one doctor to another, none of them could figure out what was up.

This one doctor took a pregnancy test, it came back positive. They gave me a physical exam but they did not think I was pregnant. When they felt inside of me nothing was in there.

So finally, I went to this Mediterranean doctor. He was so good-looking and dark complexion. I was embarrassed to have him check me because I found him so attractive at first glance. His name was Dr. Radisson, a gynecologist. He took my test and sent it out of town to Pennsylvania to a lab. He stated the results will return in two weeks.

While we were waiting for the results, I ended up in emergency again with bleeding and lower pain. While in the hospital, they called my doctor and he came right over. He had been at a dinner party by the clothes he had on. He had made a joke asking why I could not wait until Monday. So his nurse could make an appointment for me because my test came back positive, i.e. the rabbit had died.

Can you believe it back then that they waited for the rabbit to die? (This is how they checked to see if someone was pregnant by using a rabbit. If it died, the patient was pregnant.)

I was admitted to the hospital. There was not much anyone could do to ease the pain. Nature just had to take its course. It took ten hours for me to miscarry this child. It was funny, because no one could tell I was pregnant, but I aborted a son.

I cried and hated my husband for it. I felt it was his entire fault, because if we hadn't been at that bar, coming home, that car would have never have hit us.

After a couple months went by, I did not feel the same about my husband but I still hung in there with him. We moved from Vern Highway and Spring Pit to Woodmere in front of Patton Park. I was so happy and finally Bernard rented a house for us to live in that looked well. It was right across the street from a park. It was perfect for us to raise a family.

I ran into Denver my friend from my teenage years. The one that robbed that restaurant with me who had the owner that shot himself.

I invited him and his wife Karen for dinner. He told me that Alan was home from the Navy. I stated I was happy for him and pray he finds life and happiness. I was so embarrassed because they showed up but Bernard did not.

I told Bernard we had company coming over for dinner. He went out to the bar and drank. He did not want to be bothered with company after work. This is why we did not have people over. I made excuses for him but I knew he was out with a woman, man or just drinking.

After that night Denver told Alan when he saw him that I was living in Detroit. He told him my husband was a dick and did not even come home and I was in a bad marriage.

Alan was searching for me and found out I was living across the park with help from Denver. He found me and waited until he saw Bernard leave. He came up to the house. I was worried about my husband coming back or knowing I was talking to Alan. We decided to leave so we could talk.

We got a hotel so we would not be seen by people. We watched some TV and talked like we needed to catch up on life with each other. It was great seeing him. I just lay in his arms wishing life was different.

I hate to say but it was the first time Alan and I slept together. It was so nice lying in Alan's arms that night in the hotel. I was glad to see him home from the service.

I wanted to tell him what I was going through. I wanted to tell him about my mom. I wanted to express how miserable I was. I wanted to let him know that I was raped at that party. I could not bring myself to express anything besides I was glad to see him.

Alan wanted me to leave Bernard. He wants us to get back together. I wanted to also but part of me felt Bernard would die if I left.

We had an enjoyable night and I went back home stating I was at my fathers. I knew Barnard would never question my dad. But he did have an attitude for me being out all night. I never did things like that. We argued but this time it was worth it to me.

And then just like that, I disappeared from Alan's life. Both of us felt dirty inside cheating like that but our behavior still was defiant. Alan soon gave up on visiting me when I would not have time to see him.

Months later Bernard and I were still getting high every weekend hanging out at the Patton Park selling drugs. One night, my husband and I did some acid together. We ended up making love. I got sick afterwards. I felt I was pregnant again.

Bernard told me that was stupid. You do not know if you conceived right after making love. However, I just felt like I was. I was sick to my stomach and threw up right after making love. A few months passed by and I missed my period.

I got scared and thought the whole thing was going to happen again. I went back to the doctor and he told me everything was going to be all right this time around. I was having a baby.

I was worried because I knew I was high on acid when I got pregnant. I fixed a nice dinner for my husband and me. When he came home from work, I told him the good news. We were in love once again . . . or so I thought.

I stopped getting high completely. I wanted my baby to be healthy. Bernard did not like that. He felt like we were too young to stop partying. This caused more issues with Bernard and me.

His drinking got worse and so did our arguments as months passed by. Sometimes, it got so bad, that I would lock the bathroom door and sleep on the floor. I could protect myself and fight with him. But because I was pregnant I had a responsibility to protect the baby.

I was eight months and could not take the chance of my unborn child receiving any harm. I just slept on the floor in the bathroom, but I knew I would leave him after the child was born.

She would rise up in my stomach from our arguments and it would hurt and feel uncomfortable. I would take my hand and rub my stomach trying to calm her down. Once I saw the imprint of her butt.

He was just like my mother always beating on me and putting me down. He would tell me things like this, "Do you think anyone would want you?" You are uneducated, ignorant, and skinny. Who would want someone like you? You are lucky I stay with you or you would die as an old maid."

I kept my job at Teddy's Catering. I worked my whole nine months and the girls gave me a baby shower at work. It felt so good because I really did not have any friends. I went on leave a day before she was born.

I collected unemployment and was out of the hospital just in time to collect my first check of 93.00 for two weeks. I was proud.

Bernard and I were still arguing he would stay out in the bars and streets all night long. I would be home waiting for him. I was so lonely and felt life had much more than this to offer.

When it was time for me to have the baby, I woke Bernard up around 2:00 in the morning to tell him I was ready. He asked me if I had bloody show. I told him no.

He then asked, did my water break, I told him no.

He went back to sleep and told me I was not having the baby.

I woke Bernard up again and told him, yes I was having the baby, and if he did not get up and take me to the hospital, I would drive myself. Our car was a stick not an automatic. So Bernard got up to take me to the hospital and drove over ever bump in the road out of anger. He did not believe I was having the baby.

When we got to the hospital, the nurse told me I was dilated at 8. I asked her what did that mean. She told me that the baby's head was almost out. I asked her to please go tell my husband that because he was mad at me for coming in and felt like I was having false pains.

He was such an asshole he would not even help me walk to the hospital. He told me, I was going to feel stupid when they send me back home. He would not even carry my luggage in there. I had to carry it in myself. So the nurse went out there and told him. Bernard and I had the baby naturally. We went through the LA mom's classes but at the time she was being born I sure did not focus on them. Sabrina was beautiful to me.

I had broken out all over my body when I was eight months pregnant with red bumps filed with fluid. They thought I had scabies, and gave me crème to put all over. But it did not go away. Right after Sabrina was born the doctor told me to look at my leg. To my surprise, all of it went away. It was my nerves.

I could not believe that baby came out of me. I was really nervous about taking care of a little thing like that. I wanted to name her Sabrina Sunshine but Bernard would not let me. He said it sounded like an acid trip but she was the sunshine of my life.

After my daughter was brought home, I freaked out and left Bernard one day with the child after going to the store. I did not come home. I was so scared with our fights and unhappiness. How would I take care of this child?

I did not have any education and could not support her if something happens to our marriage. I was having flashes of the future I did not want to be stuck with him for years down the road. I wasn't sure what to do. Maybe Bernard's family could take care of her. May be my sister Lilly? Lilly wanted a girl badly. All kind of thoughts went through my head. I was terrified to raise a child with Bernard.

After a few days I went back home. I stayed in a hotel down the street using Bernard's credit card. I cried about my child and knew I needed to get back to her because Bernard was not the right person to leave her with. I came to my senses.

I went back and Bernard wanted to know if I was crazy. He asked, "Why did you leave me with this child?" I told him I was scared and thought I was going through baby blues plus I didn't feel that I would be a good mom to our child.

He was upset but not like I thought he would be. Bernard told me he was scared too but you can't just leave a child that needs to be breast fed. Bernard had trouble getting her to eat because she refused a bottle. He was really happy I came back. Bernard thought he was going to raise her by himself. He was scared too that I wasn't coming back.

I started to work part time against Bernard's permission. My neighbor next door watched Sabrina. She was really nice and had a daughter named Debby who had a daughter Sabrina's age named Moni.

It gave Sabrina someone to learn from. Moni was a lot bigger than Sabrina and smarter.

I started saving money, ten dollars here and twenty dollars there. I also skimmed some of Bernard's money when he wasn't watching or would know of. Bernard was still drinking like nothing had changed and just stuck me in the house with a child and more responsibilities. I could not go to a lot of places with him because it was not an environment for a child. So of course he would go without me. I felt trapped and my worst fears came true.

That evening I asked Bernard to stay home so I could have a night by myself and relax. He stated tomorrow after work, we will have dinner and watch T.V together. The next day I took Bernard to work so I could use the car and buy groceries. I went home and baked a dessert and made a nice tuna casserole which was Bernard's favorite. He told me he loved the vegetables I put into it and the crunchy topping.

So I took my time and made it special for him. I was so excited thinking wow it will be like a new beginning. I made Bernard's bath water and set his newspaper on the toilet seat like always. I laid out his clothes and made sure the house was clean.

My father bought us a living outfit, a kitchen set, washer and drier. My father also purchased a bedroom outfit for us and our T.V. If it was not for my father we would not have had anything because Bernard destroyed all of our stuff. Plus we were still paying on furniture he bought with his ex-girlfriend. He owed thousands of dollars and made payment on it every month.

Bernard came home that evening and I proudly meet him at the door. He took off his clothes at the door way (like always) and laid them there on the floor until I picked them up. He went into the bathroom to get into the tub. He read his paper and talked to me from the bathroom. I would go in and sit on the toilet seat and listen to his day. I did that every day to be a part of the world.

Bernard got out and dried off and went to sit down at the dining table. I took the lid off the casserole to show him it was tuna casserole. He stared at it for a long time until I asked him what was wrong. He started yelling at me, "You are asking me what is wrong, what the fuck do you think is wrong Billy Joe. You feed me tuna casserole every other week and every other week. I eat the shit but do you know I hate your tuna casserole!"

Then he picked up the casserole dish and swung it into the wall over the sink in the kitchen. I could not believe he did that.

I yelled out . . . "You are going to clean that up because I am not."

The baby started to cry.

Bernard became enraged and grabbed my head and shoved it in the wall and smeared my face in the wall and stated, "If you don't clean it up, then you will eat it bitch!"

I started crying and had tuna casserole all over my hair and face. My neck was hurting from his hands. My face hurt where he shoved it into the wall. How could this man love me and treat me like this. The baby started crying louder. Bernard went to the baby and started yelling at her to shut up. He picked her up to shake her. I ran in there and tried to push him away from her begging him to keep her out of this.

Bernard slams the door and left the house. He was looking for an excuse to leave. He had one now. He was gone until late that morning. I just rolled over and went to sleep and was pleased he did not bother me.

Time kept going by and the same stuff happened every night and weekend. I was getting sick and tired of it all and Sabrina was turning nine months.

One evening he came home drunk as always but this night he took a kitchen knife after the baby and me. He accused me of sleeping around on him and told me it was someone else's child. I had told his sister that I had an affair on him with Alan.

Bernard had many affairs on me. I caught him with plenty women, and guys. I caught him with this one girl at the bar on Vernor Hwy, Southwest Detroit and took a beer bottle and hit the girl and him over the head. The bar people kicked me and him both out. This does not excuse my behavior but he was no angel. This book would be 20 pages longer to explain all the things he put me through. I had gotten pregnant with Bernard's child months after Alan and I was together.

I made the mistake of telling his sister Cherry and she told Bernard. I also told her about him sleeping with other men, that he was bisexual. She told him that too. I just knew she told him about our conversation. She told him the child was not his. That was not true. The baby was his and I told him to take a blood test to convince himself. He became outrageous. I could not control him.

He took the butcher knife and raked it over my face as I was holding our child in my arms as he raked it over our child's stomach, he stated, "I could kill both of you so easily."

I tired talking to him about putting the knife down. He would not do it. He walked over to the big picture window and I put my daughter down on the coach and charged at him with all I had inside of me as I pushed him out the window. You would have thought I was a football player going out for a tackle.

He went out the window on the front yard. He was cut up and the police came. They took him to jail, for being drunk they thought Bernard fell out of the window. I lied and stated that he had the knife and fell through the window being drunk. They wanted me to press charges but I would not do it. They released him after he sobered up. A couple of days later I packed his clothes made him dinner and his bath water like always.

When he came home, he washed up for dinner and that is when he saw the suitcase. He asked where we were going. I told him, we weren't going anywhere that he was. I told him, I wanted a divorce.

Of course, he did not make it easy on me. He didn't give me any help with our daughter, with food, and left me with all the bills and penniless.

The stove, washer and dryer, furniture, bedroom set was all purchased by my father. The car was from my father too and in my name. Shoot, my father bought us seven cars in one year because of his accidents from drinking.

I drove Bernard to his father's house. I dropped him off with his suit case. I knew things would not be easy but it had to be better than this life. All the money that man made and we had nothing but what my father gave us out of love to help us make it.

I had asked my mom if we could come there for a couple months with her. She had a summer house behind her house. She told me, it was my issue and I had made my bed, now lie in it. I ended up selling everything but the bedroom outfit and washer and drier.

My daughter and I moved back in with my father. My dad was up in age, but strong as a horse. I did not want to bother dad because he was seeing a woman. It was the first time I had ever known my father being with anyone, after him and my mother's divorce. He and his friends would play cards every week. He was having the time of his life.

I felt like I failed. I was not able to keep my marriage going. Now I had a child to take care of. I really never wanted kids but when I was pregnant with Sabrina I wanted her more than anything in this world, more than my marriage.

I wanted to go back to school but was afraid because I was dumb and could not read well. I only had a fifth grade math level and fourth grade reading level. I was too embarrassed to go back even though I knew I had to do something to support Sabrina and me.

# Chapter Four

# Back to Drugs and Crime

Dad got rid of the woman and would not see her anymore when we moved in. I felt so bad because dad lived his whole life for his kids and I really did not want to impose on him.

After moving in with dad I saw my girlfriend Lena, she was working at the XXX Rated Theater. I was surprised and told her I needed to find employment. Lena stated she could get me a job there. I told her I might not be able to do that with what I have endured with Bernard. She told me don't worry about it and just look at the pay.

So dad agrees to watch Sabrina until I was able to find someone. Dad was great he would watch Sabrina until I got home every night from work. I had two jobs. One working as a cashier at an XXX rated store that my girlfriend Lena got me. She knew I needed to feed me and Sabrina. I also worked midnights as a security guard. I never seemed to have time for Sabrina. I was always working.

I knew I needed to give dad a break. He never complained but I know he loved going to the racetrack and with the baby, he would put his wants and desires on hold. Sometimes, Lena would watch her, but she really did not know what to do with a child. She was worse than I was. (Smile) Dad watched her most of the time.

I came home one day, and dad was outside with the baby playing. I got out of the car . . . "Dad, what are you doing?" Sabrina was hitting dad over the head with a stick, and he was on all fours, just allowing her to express herself.

I put an ad in the Farmington paper that read: "Looking for a full time babysitter." I cannot even remember what I paid an hour back then. I just know she got at least one hundred and fifty dollars or so back then for two shifts.

Later on Alan and I ran back into each other and we started talking again. He moved my bedroom set in his mother's garage because my dad's place did not have enough room for that or my washer and dryer. We spent some time together. He had his 1967 GTO that he purchased when he left the Navy. Alan loved his cars and was great building them. We never really went out on any dates. I kept looking at Alan as a man that did not do much for his woman.

We saw each other a few times and talked, made love but I wasn't into a relationship at that time. After going through all that domestic violence with Bernard and all the demonic spirits of evil, I was tired inside and too hurt. I never would tell people the abuse I went through with my mother both mentally and physically and Bernard just made it worse. I got with a man that was just like her and worse. I kept everything inside and did not talk about my hurt and pain. Alan never knew what my mother put me through.

I know Alan was not like that but I did not have a lot of trust with him because of our earlier history together when he left me for that girl with the bigger boobs in school. I just did not want to tell him. Plus, I never wanted Alan to know all the guys I had been with or that I lost my virginity thru rape. Moreover, I never wanted him to know I used heroin or other drugs. I never wanted Alan to know I had been with black men either.

He would not have really cared for he uses to fix all the Detroit Black Gentlemen's motorcycles on Schoolcraft and Grand River. I guess, what it all boiled down to was, I was so afraid of him finding out that I wasn't worth shit and wasn't worth the effort. The best thing I could do for Alan was walk away because soon after that, he married a younger girl with big boobs and had his son Shan. (Smile)

I stopped seeing Alan, and just worked a lot, saving my money for a place for Sabrina and me. Dad and I noticed that Sabrina was not eating for a couple of days. We thought, maybe she was just sick. Then dad noticed she would ball her little hands up in a tight knot and cry, every time we put food on her plate on the high chair. Dad, called me out of the bathroom one morning, and told me to see why the baby was doing that. We became concerned and took her over to Community Hospital off Main Street.

It was the same place where I took shots for my illness until I was twenty one years of age. The doctors had checked her out and came back asking my dad and me many questions about her and our conduct toward her. Dad wanted to know what was going on and why they were trying to point fingers at us.

The doctor explained that Sabrina was malnourished and dehydrated. We could not figure out why? I would send food every day in her diaper bag and every night it would be empty. While dad watched Sabrina, I went over the baby sister's house to find out what was up.

To my surprise, her boyfriend was there. We started talking nicely at first. Then the conversation started to get heated. Come to find out, her boyfriend knew me in high school and liked me. We never went out or dated. I do not even remember him to be honest.

Anyways, this sick bit—was jealous of him and me for no reason and she was taking it out on my child. She would put food up on her high chair and every time she went to grab something, she would take a ruler and hit her little bitty hands. Sabrina had not been getting anything to eat . . . . How, long was this sick behavior going on? Who knows? I knew one thing—I beat the living crap out of that bit—and told her about herself.

Her boyfriend left the property and would not even help her. Someone called the cops on me. I tried to explain to the police, but they did not want to hear it. They said I should have contacted the police and let them handle it. Then my dad tried to talk to them for me.

I just could not believe those cops wanted to take me in and not that sick bitch. After that incident, I was very cautious who watched my baby. They were not up on child abuse back then. Thankfully, I did not get charged for the assault.

Well, time went on and we finally moved out of dad's place. I felt so bad because dad liked the race track; I continued to work two jobs; Bernard would not pay child support. He was ordered to pay 46.00 a month, assist with clothes, and keep Sabrina on his insurance card. He only kept her on his insurance card. He would get drunk every week, get placed in jail, and call me up, cussing me out. I would go down to the jail and sign a paper stating that he paid his child support. I felt if he did not want her or take care of her, I would.

I took the baby to Patton Park where Bernard and I used to go when we lived on Woodmere and we played on the swings. There was a bunch of cars gathering around the park because it was the place to hang out. It was getting late and that is when everyone started to hang out, i.e., the dope fiends. I gathered Sabrina and her toys and started packing the car. As I was leaning over, I heard some dude say . . .

"Hey lady, watch out." I looked around to see who it was. I shook my head and said, "If it isn't Dee McGee."

He looked so surprised and asked me if we knew each other. I started laughing and said, "Yeah, it's me, Dee, Bernard's ex-wife." Then he remembered me.

"Oh yeah, I know you now!" "What's up? You and Bernard are not together anymore?"

I told him no and did not really go into it. I knew they were semi-friends. Then as I was getting ready to leave, Dee came to the car door and asked if he could have my phone number. I told him at this time, dating was not an option.

I explained that I had my daughter and could not spare extra money for a babysitter. In addition, I had bad experience with babysitters and that was a nightmare for me. He stated he would love to come over the house and just watch T. V. with us, nothing funny. I gave him my phone number.

When Dee would come over, it was so much fun. He would get on the floor and play with Sabrina for hours and hours. I could tell this person was nothing like I thought he was. He had a kind heart and he loved Sabrina or kids. We had a great night and become very close friends from that night on. Dee was always there for me. Dee also cut his hair and cut that ugly long mustache down low. He looked much better.

I was so tired of being broke. Even working two jobs was not enough money to pay for preschool and a babysitter at night. All my money was going to bills. I never was able to purchase clothes and had to buy cheap clothes for Sabrina. Most of the food I bought went to Sabrina.

She had to have fruit, vegetables, and lots of milk. I was so tired and ready to give up. I was not good with being a mother and making sure bills were paid and Sabrina had what she needed. My mother kept asking me to give Sabrina to her, but I did not want to do that knowing how emotionally screwed up I turned out. But I just could not seem to make ends meet.

Dee came over that night telling me about a few sweet deals making some money. I was all ears. I knew they were illegal but I did not care, I was tired of being broke. I could have asked my father for help but I wanted him to stop paying my way out in life.

Dee and I started to hang pretty tough. We both liked getting paid. We started getting high together to have the nerve to do the crimes. The only thing I hated about getting high with Dee was he would get so high he would O.D. every time.

I would have to beat him in his chest and slap the crap out of his face to bring him to. I would have to call EMS to take him to the hospital. I hated every time he would do that and it would wreck my high. Now, I was getting high again. I did not use any of the money I needed to pay my bills with. Dee usually paid for the drugs.

Dee and I saw how much money these guys spent on XXX Rated movies. Guys would buy movies to take home, blow up dolls, and other items. I told Dee, I wish we could knock this place off. Dee told me we could. He gave me the plan. I would have him come over to the place and hit me in the head and call the police as if I had been robbed. Well, the XXX Rated Theater could not pin it on me. They ended up just moving me to another location. We got a lot of money and it became an addiction once we did that.

I was also tipping the till, which means I would not count everyone coming in the door. I would count less than what really went in and kept that money. When guys came in with their girl, they had to pay ten dollars for themselves and five for the girl. I would count every other one coming in, taking the money and placing it in my pocket. They were losing lots of money because of us so they had me working at the other one they owned by Middle Belt Road.

Once it started happening there, they just let me go, but they did not fire me. They laid me off. I did not even know anything about W2 forms. I don't even remember filing for my taxes.

I went full time with the security guard job. I had to work midnights and I got a promotion to sergeant. I was scared because I took Sabrina to pre-school and now, I would not be able to do that.

Dee stated he would move in with us and watch Sabrina at nighttime. I was not sure if I wanted to do that. Dee convinced me it was strictly platonic. So I agreed, but as time went on, he did not want to go out on dates with other women and he wrapped himself around the baby and me. Then I started stealing items when I was a security guard.

Of course, Dee and I were rap partners (meaning we were street partners). We started to get deeper into crimes we were committing.

Things started getting rough and bills started growing. Sabrina kept coming down sick and it was hard to go to work, knowing she needed me. We went up north for the weekend to get away from everything. My mom asked us to come up so she could see the baby. So we stayed at my mom's house while we were up there. I complained about everything and stated I did not know what to do or how to handle motherhood.

My mom offered to help by keeping Sabrina for a while until I could get back on my feet. I couldn't believe she was willing to do that. She did not know Sabrina because ever since Sabrina was born, I never brought her up to visit my mother. I was not able to be around my mom more than a few hours before she got on my nerves.

They had cut my hours down and Dee lost his job. We were going to be kicked out of the apartment. I agreed to let my mom keep Sabrina . . . just until I was able to get back on my feet.

I was so desperate or I would never have done that. I really did not feel good about doing this; I just did not want Sabrina to live like this. I could take care of myself but I could not feed Sabrina and me. I could go without, but I could not let her go without or not have warm clothing or a roof over her head or when they turned off the lights, I could not bear having her live by candlelight. Sabrina cried bloody murder when I left her, I felt like such a bad parent and I guess, now that I look back on it, I was.

It felt strange not to have the kid, I missed her a lot, but it felt good to be free and not to worry about another human being, just myself.

Dee and I got a one room flat. It was cheap, only about $75.00 a month, no kitchen, no living room, just a bed in a room. He was having a hard time finding a job. So, now, he went and got some weed, by the pound. The man, who gave it to him, gave it on consignment. He hid it from me and tried to sell it without me knowing about it. We both stopped getting high because we could not afford it.

I knew Dee was selling something because I could tell by people always coming over. He went off privately to talk with them.

Then, there were phone calls at late hours. I knew what was up but I just did not know what he was selling.

I called him out on it and asked him if he was doing that. At first, he lied to me. I got mad and told him I was moving out. He begged me not to and we discussed it. Then I told him, I would help. I let Dee know everyone I knew that gets high. We started selling lids ('lids' are portions of dope by the Oz), and many other drugs.

Dee and I started to do armed robberies on top of selling drugs and moving up the financial ladder quickly. Dee and I were doing con jobs and selling drugs.

We placed all our money into a bank and lived only on the bare essentials. I wanted to save up enough money to bring Sabrina back home. I was hurting inside being without her and did not want her to get damaged by my mother's personality. I also wanted Sabrina to know I would never leave her. Now I look back on it, I was the one she needed to be protected from.

We knew a lot of paid clinics and thought about hitting them up. I know some people reading this book and wondering what paid clinics are. Well, let me try to explain. Paid clinics are facilities that are run by crooked doctors and nurses. They are only about the money and trying to score as much funds as possible. They have a clinic that's in a bad area of town. Inside are bulletproof windows where the receptionist asks you what you are looking for? They have certain customers that they deal with. Once she feels comfortable that you are not the police, she will send a nurse out to meet with you. Usually you have to tell them so-n-so sent you down, that way they know who sent you.

In the background is a mean looking person standing against the wall with a nine-millimeter gun strapped to his chest. He is the bouncer of this facility. He is going to make sure you are not going to try setting this clinic up on a robbery. The bouncer will make sure, if you are going through withdrawals, you don't get out of hand, that you pay your bill and go about your business.

So that is what Dee and I did, we hit about three or four of these paid clinics and got scripts for different pills. You pay fifty dollars for the script, then go get it filled and sell the items on the street at a more marked up cost per pill.

It would cost to fill the scripts $2.00 because I still had Bernard's insurance card on me from his employment. He never took me off his insurance (through the divorce, he was supposed to pay me 46.00 dollars a week, and keep us on his insurance, and provide $200.00 a month in clothes for Sabrina. Of course, Bernard paid nothing.)

Dee and I sold weed, valium, Percodan's, Tylenol 3's and 4's, dillies, dilaudids and barbiturates. Financially, were we doing well?

Dee landed another job and with our sells and the jobs, we did alright. We saved up some money and got a nice car for Dee. It was a GTO and it was fast and put together with big tires, a souped-up engine and a great paint job.

I saw a beautiful mother-of-pearl white Buick car with half-red vinyl top. I wanted it so bad. It cost a few thousand dollars more than what I had to spare. My father told me, if I came up with half of the money, he would pay for the other half. I did. I was riding in style. We were living the life.

Then Dee wanted to get serious. I was not ready for that. I liked being single and my own boss. After Bernard, I did not want another man telling me where I could go, watching my every move. I loved Dee but not like, he loved me. I liked him as my rap partner, my friend, but not as my lover. I still went out with other people and Dee just sat in the background and let me do as I pleased and would always be there for me. Dee and I were not having sex we just shared a place together.

I thought of him as a best friend, but he thought of me as the best woman he ever wanted. Boy was he blind.

I got a place in at Century Square Townhouses. They went by your income and, boy, were they nice. We had a living room, kitchen, dining room, and two upstairs bedrooms with a bathroom downstairs and one upstairs.

We had our own entrance and front porch. It was the suburban area and even though I loved Detroit, I always lived in the suburban areas of Detroit. Detroit was the place to go to make money and party, but the suburbs were the place to build your castle. Now, I needed furniture. I took one room at a time and started to fill it up with furniture.

My father helped me to purchase some of it. I will never forget taking my Dad to Joshua Lord's Furniture Store. There were rumors it was run by the mob. My dad went in there and we picked out what I wanted, my dad told the man, "I would not support your business because I do not believe in supporting the mob. But my daughter wants it from here, and my daughter gets what she wants."

I was so embarrassed, but I knew how my father was. He was about being totally legitimate.

My living room was first, then my kitchen. My bedroom set which was saved at Alan's house, I picked up, and then, I started on Sabrina's bedroom. I had a blast with her room. I got a white canapé bed, with matching dresser, cartoon bedspread and curtains. I filled it up with a Barbie dollhouse, cars, swimming pools, Ken doll, and friends. I even bought the camping equipment. Everything a little girl's heart would desire.

Everything I ever wanted and did not have. I got her all kinds of clothes to wear. I tried to get a different outfit for every day for two weeks of wearing. I purchased her shoes to match and little under garments.

My father was so impressed with my dedication to create a home that he took me out and bought me a bunch of clothes. It had cost my father a few thousand dollars. He did not care, as long as I was happy. Then I started to purchase pictures and nick-knacks for the home. I purchased dishes, pots, and pans. Everything a person would need to create the warm welcoming home. What my father did not know was that it was all drug money. He would be so hurt and angry with me if he knew. That would've killed him inside.

Then Dee and I went up north and got Sabrina. To my "surprise" my mother did not want to give my daughter back to me. She felt like I was not a good mother and that five months had passed by without even a call. True enough, I did not call. I had many reasons, one being that I did not really get along with my mother. When she talked to me, she would always react negatively and condescending to me.

I did not want to call until I was ready to take her back and give her the home she needed. I can't even believe my mom would think she was a better mother. I was so busy trying to get things together, that I did not want to call and give false promises. Shoot, my mother left her two children with her mother for five years before she married my father.

I wanted to come when I had it altogether, not before then. Of course, everything I did was wrong in her eyes, like she was the mother of the year award. We argued about it, she had my stepdad take Sabrina outside.

I told her firmly, I was not leaving there without my daughter she was my responsibility and I appreciated what you two did for me. I offered to pay her money and she took it. I gave my mother a few hundred dollars for every month she was there. I did not want her to feel that she did anything for me out of the kindness of her heart.

Tom did more than my mom because Tom is the one who potty trained her. Tom was the one who fed her and took care of her. I ran outside and grabbed Sabrina, and told Dee to get the car warmed up. All she had on is a little red hooded zipped up sweatshirt and a pair of under panties, no shoes. I grabbed her up and she started crying being scared. I put her in the car and she started kicking and screaming at the top of her lungs.

She was so scared by the way I grabbed her up plus not seeing me for five months. I told Dee to take off, that she would stop eventually. Boy was I wrong. That child cried all the way back to Near West Side which was a three-hour ride from up north.

My ears were tore up inside. Just as we got toward home she went to sleep. When we got her home, she started crying and would not stop. I just did not feel this was normal. So that evening, I took her to the doctors. They found out she had an ear infection and strep throat. I had a flash back when I was younger, when mom did nothing about me being sick and ended up with rheumatic fever.

That's how I got rheumatic fever—from an ear infection that went so long untreated that it turned into a strep throat infection. I would've never gotten rheumatic fever if mom would have took me to the doctor instead of going out with ever man in town to support her.

Sabrina received medical care and got better. The doctor caught it in time and I was happy. I was still having flash backs of my mom and what she did to me as a child. I knew I should have never taken her there. From that day on Sabrina seemed happy and we were a family again.

Time was passing and life was going on. Dee lost his job and wanted to move in with Sabrina and me at our townhouse in Near West Side Detroit. Of course, I let him. He had been good to us and I was not going to let him down when he needed me the most.

Things were still going well with us selling drugs. We were still making money but it seemed to go just as fast paying for material items and bills. I started working at a bar on the morning shifts at the LA Barron's Lounge on South Dix in Detroit. I was still doing the midnight shift as a security guard on Allen Road at Consolidated Gas Company. Dee would babysit during the night.

Then this person approached Dee telling him he knew how to get into Dee's old job that fired him. Dee was all ears. They came up with a plan to go into the office and steal the safe in the office. They ran across a box of work checks and the print machine that automatically printed out the boss's name and the amount of the check.

You would set the amount and slide it through like a credit card. The amount would print out and the boss's name would ink across the bottom of the check automatically. We screwed up a few checks trying it out until we had it down pat. We finally got it together.

Dee and that person tried to cash a few of them but many places would not cash them. I agreed to cash them. You could not take them to a bank and we had to get rid of them fast before they found out. I was a nice looking girl, young, long blond hair down to my waist. I stood about 5'6 120 lbs. and about a size 5. I was built with a little plumb butt, and long legs, with a breast size of 34 B; green eyes and a nice complexion.

I would go into bars and most of the owners would cash my check right away. I was busting them out for $340.00 to $430.00 dollars a check. The other guy assisting Dee with this con did not want to give me anything at first. He said my cut should come out of Dee's cut. Dee let him know very sternly that I was taking a chance and that we were not together only friends; the checks gets split three ways or nothing.

So I started busting them right and left. When the bars ran out, I started going to party stores. Some even had me do my thumbprint. I would burn wax on the bottom of my thumb or cut it up, whatever it took. I am sure it did not really cover up my prints but I thought I was doing something.

Sometimes, I would have to buy items in the store, or pay an amount for cashing it. Everything I got was a bonus. I got things for Sabrina, or me. Once the checks were gone, so was everyone's money. Not mine. I had saved up 3,000.00 dollars in the bank and did not tell anyone.

Then Dee got another fraud job set up for us. He would always let me in on every deal he came across. This person wanted to purchase some pills. The script was running out too because the police were hitting and closing down many of those paid clinics throughout Detroit.

We were unable to get the amount this person wanted. Dee got a bunch of pill bottles the same size. He took a weight machine that you weigh drugs with and with that, he counted out little tiny fishing weight sinkers and had them fill an empty pill bottle to equal the weight as a bottle of real pills he had.

Then he got a box that was unused, some glue, and a piece of cardboard to go down the middle. Dee then lined the bottom of the box with pill bottles filled with fishing line weights. Then he placed the cardboard on top of them and lined the rest of the top part of the box with pill bottles full of fishing line weights.

Then at the corner of the box and the middle; Dee got about twelve or more bottles of pills; placing them at each of the four corners and middle of the box filling the rest of the box with fake pill bottles of fishing sinkers.

He carefully glued the box tight; then placed it in the trunk of the car. Then we dressed up and put on our very best suits on. We drove down to a nice restaurant and sat until the person showed up. He looked like a businessman, I stayed in the car.

The man meeting Dee drove a nice car and looked like money. They sat down and started talking business. Then they excused themselves and went out to the car. I saw Dee open the trunk of the car. I could not see what he was doing.

Then a few minutes went by and the other people were taking the box and placing it in their car. He handed something to Dee, got into their car, and drove off. Dee motions for me to hurry up and get into the car.

As we were driving down the street, I kept asking Dee what happened and he wouldn't say anything. He waited until we were away from the area and then busted out laughing; Dee threw thousands of dollars up in the air. I could not believe my eyes. Dee was excited while he told me he opened the corners of the box and pulled out a pill bottle, they did not ask to see any more, they made the deal with me.

Dee expressed how nervous he was and scared that they would bust him. We went home and partied that night. Dee sold all that fishing weight for a couple thousand dollars. I just looked at Dee and thought that he was the best hustler I had ever seen.

A few months later, child services, CPS, came to my house and wanted to check my cupboards and see my home. Then, they wanted to pull Sabrina's clothes off her looking for any marks on her. I never laid my hand on Sabrina. I vowed I would never spank her after what I went through with my mom.

I was so embarrassed, all my neighbors were watching. I did not know which one called them, or why? They wanted to know about Dee living there. I told them I was not collecting any assistance and I did not know why I was being treated like this. The lady explained that my mom was concerned because I was not married; she was apprehensive about my daughter; my mother stated, I was never home to take care of my child.

After the woman left, Dee said, let me marry you then, they cannot say anything. I was crying; being naïve, I thought they were going to take my daughter away from me.

I was all woman, regardless of what anyone else thought, I had her, and I could take care of her. I did not need any man to do it for me. I was mad at Bernard and my mother. Then I thought about me putting Sabrina at risk with selling drugs.

Mom kept pressing the courts concerning Sabrina's wellbeing. She had a lot of nerve as messed up as I was growing up. I ended up marrying Dee and that was a big mistake. The first time we did it, I got pregnant. I did not want to be like my mother and have kids by different daddies. I kept telling Dee that we did not need this child now. He wanted it. He wanted a family with me so bad. I felt bad, because I just did not love him as if he loved me. I had respect for him and I would have done anything for him. I loved him as a brother. However, I did not want his child.

His father gave me the money for an abortion. I had the money but he gave it to me anyways. He felt like Dee was not mature enough to have a child and his mother was very possessive of Dee.

She did not want Dee to have a child because she wanted Dee to herself. She lost one of her sons through drugs. She did not want to lose Dee. I hated later in life for having that abortion it really screwed me up emotionally for doing that. Dee never saw or talked to his father again for giving me that money. He did not even attend his funeral. I felt responsible for that separation. Dee did not hold anything against me.

After the abortion, I had a hard time living with myself. I took the $3,000.00 dollars I had in the bank and went to California to stay with a girl I knew named Margaret that used to live next door to me when I was married to Bernard on Woodmere in front of Patton Park.

When Sabrina and I got on the plane I was so scared. Then a nun got on the flight, I felt that it was a sign of death. I started crying and the nun asked if I was okay? Sabrina turned around and told the nun I was scared. I quit crying right then and there and laughed at Sabrina; she was so smart.

We arrived in California and Margaret was living with this man and they allowed us to move in. She was a trip, bisexual and a freak. She liked it when men would beat her and cut her with glass and objects while having sex.

This was a big mistake for us to be out here. Everything was very open in California and sex was displayed out in the open. I placed her in pre-school while I looked for employment.

After three months, money was running out and I had to make a choice. I called Dee and he was still there at my apartment, taking care of it, waiting to hear from me. At least Sabrina and I had a nice vacation in California. He sent Sabrina and me the money to come home. After I got home, a few months went by and I let him know I wanted a divorce. We weren't even married a full year.

I told him that I cared deeply for him but I was not in love with him like a man and wife. We started fighting and he punched me in the face. I was so surprised because Dee had never done that before; he had never laid his hand on me. But he did this time.

I went down and saw stars as I was grabbing the counter for balance. I placed my hand on a knife. I came back up with swiftness stabbing Dee in his back. He ran upstairs in the bedroom and locked the door so I could not get in. After life with Barnard I would refuse for a man to hurt me anymore. As time went on, I became cold about someone putting their hands on me.

I kicked the door until it went through and stuck my hand up in there and opened the door. It was too late by the time I got in there. Dee had taken my purse and robbed me of all the money I had for the rent. He must have been very hurt and leaving like that out the window. I do not know where he went, but he stayed gone for about three months.

During that time, I got my job back at LA Barron's Lounge off South Dix in Detroit. I did not make a lot of money check wise but made up for it in tips. I brought home enough to pay for my apartment, buy clothes for Sabrina and me and pay all the other bills. My check was just extra funds.

Sabrina and I started to live life again. I stopped using drugs and selling them, we went to the zoo and parks every week. I was making enough for us to live on and have fun. I was feeling great being off drugs and enjoying my child.

145

While at the park enjoying the scenery I met a person named Mike with a yellow Corvette car. He made a lot of money and was crazy about me. We talked and hung together that day. I could tell he was digging me. He asked me for my phone number and I gave it to him. I dated him for eight months.

Then Dee showed back up one day, out of nowhere. We started arguing at first. We talked about him being hurt and aborting his child. He did not want to lose me as his wife but did not want me out of his life. He agreed to be friends.

He gave me an opal ring which is my birth stone with diamonds and rubies around it. I still have it to this day; Dee also gave me the money he took from me that day plus interest. I think he always believed we would get back together. He met Mike who drove the Corvette. Mike would take me and Sabrina out to nice restaurants and buy Sabrina lots of gifts, from clothes to toys. He always paid for my babysitter and bought me new outfits to go out with.

Once he had his mother watch Sabrina, while we went to Detroit. It was great, riding up there in his bright yellow Corvette T-Top with people looking at us and the wind in my hair. We stayed at a fine motel and ate at fine places. I had such a great time with him, but he wanted me to finally have sex with him. I had been dating him for five months and did not have sex with him.

I liked his money, his company, but I was not interested in him sexually. I did it with him anyways. After we went back home, I did not want to see him anymore. I kept making excuses about going out.

After a month, I called him up and told him I was pregnant. He wanted me to keep the baby. I told him no, that I wanted an abortion. He agreed to meet me and give me 350.00 dollars for the abortion.

I met with him and got the money. I never saw him again after that. I was not pregnant. I just wanted the money. I don't know why I did that to him. I always was mean to people that seem to be nice to me. I laid low for a while and just hung out with Sabrina.

Sabrina and I got some roller skates and got the neighbor next door to give us a ride us on her back bumper while we roller skated through the apartment complex. She was a beautiful black woman and Sabrina played with her daughter.

We were always over at each other's apartment. I was really glad Sabrina had a friend. Her mom and I would have coffee when we were not working but we did not really hang out. We were both busy and she went out on dates with her boyfriend. I did not have a boyfriend at that time. But she was company for me and Sabrina. Bernard was in and out of Sabrina's life, sometimes he would bring a gift over for her and sometimes we did not see him for months.

I never cared and did not press him. Dee was going out with a girl and getting high. I was trying to stay away and keep my head right and be there for Sabrina. Dee would always find his way over to us to hang out with me.

# CHAPTER FIVE

# O.G's / GANGSTERS; THE NIGHTMARES BEGIN

Then one night, a girl named Lori who lived a few townhouses over came by. Her brother sometimes baby-sat for me and she wanted to meet me. I did not work at the security guard job anymore only as a barmaid. I worked the morning shift was home around 3:00 every day made enough money to take care of Sabrina.

Lori lived there with her dad and 2 brothers. Their mother had died and they were trying to hold it together. Lori's dad collected some kind of check and Lori worked and hustled to bring enough money home to take care of all their needs.

The brother had kept telling her about me how they baby-sat for me at times for an hour or so, usually when I had to wash clothes. The boys were fourteen and fifteen years of age trying to make a couple dollars. She came over with her brothers to meet me. Lord, I did not know that my whole life was going to change by this meeting.

Her brothers felt we needed to know each other. She was just a few years older than I was. She went out with men for money, and worked in an office in the daytime. She was always schooling me on how to get over on people.

I was not interested in her methods or lack of morals. I thought of her as a streetwalker but it was nice just to have a girlfriend to hang around with. She was a heroin user too but I kept away from doing that with her.

We went out to a few bars and got drunk, picked up guys and having them pay for our drinks all night long. She did not care about letting a person know they had nothing coming if they did not put out the right amount of cash.

As we bar hopped, there was one bar we went to that had a wet t-shirt contest. She was going to enter it. She was a red head, about 5'2 with green eyes. No butt and maybe a 34c and a size 8. She really felt she had it going on.

You could not tell Lori that she was not drop dead gorgeous. She thought her stuff between her legs was a gold mine. She wanted me to try out for the t-shirt contest, but I was not interested. I knew Lori felt like she was going to win anyway because she was a cup size larger than mine. Then all these people were coming up telling me to enter it. Then one person said there was a prize of 100.00 dollars if we win. So I said why not I knew I would not win.

So I stood up there with ten other beautiful girls, some with big tits. I just knew I was not going to win. Here it came. They took the large beer pitchers and filled them up with water and had one person stand in front of each one of us and pour the water on our white t-shirts.

I was so surprised when they announced the winner . . . . I could not believe it . . . . they picked me! I was so happy and felt so sexy and beautiful that night. Wow! I did not see that one coming. I was so proud. I could tell that Lori was mad too. She tried not to show it, but it was all over her face. I was not the type of person to rub it in.

Days had gone by and I kept turning Lori down to go out. I told her, I had not been spending enough time at home with Sabrina. Then October came by. It was my birthday. Now that I look back, October turned out to be a bad time for me for a while.

Lori wanted to take me out for my birthday and for a little celebration, she set me up on a blind date and got her brothers to babysit. I agreed and went with her. We stopped at this dump in Detroit and picked up a person who had no manners.

She kept telling me he was a roller. Meaning, he was selling dope and making a lot of money. I had given up that life, and was trying to do everything legitimate.

We went to some dump down in the heart of Detroit on Third Street. Some bar called The Corner Pub, it was sometimes known as the Red Dog Bar. This place was a trip. There were bullet holes in the wall were the place had been shot up. It looked like a real dive.

We put a few tables together so we could all sit at the same table. There were six of us altogether, the person that was with me called himself Eddy. I knew this was going to be a night to remember. It turned out to be a real nightmare.

Have you ever did anything or went somewhere and knew your life was about to change? It was a like a whirlpool and you were not able to stop the motion but you knew things would never be the same. It was as if you stepped into Twilight Zone of no return. I felt something that night but did not stop it. I allowed myself to get into a whirlpool of the Twilight Zone. Your inner self is trying to guide you but you didn't listen.

We sat and drank while listening to the music. Eddy could not keep his hands to himself. Yuk!! It was getting on my nerves.

There was this person standing up at the bar with a dark haired girl that had tits that stuck out; she had to be a 44DDD. She was a bit on the heavy side with her Dolly Parton tits. She was big!!! He was a thin man, wearing a Dickman work uniform. He didn't have any hair on top of his head but he did down the sides. He did not look as if he had a lot of money. He kept staring at me.

I turned around to my blind date and told him, "That man keeps staring at me; he is making me nervous." Eddy turned around and looked at the bar and turned back around quickly.

"Do you know who that is? That is Vicenza Giuliano; he has a lot of connections and money."

I looked back over at the old man and said in a low voice, "He sure doesn't look like it to me."

As we were laughing and talking, listening to the jukebox, Vicenza Giuliano came over to the table with a drink for me. He placed it in front of me, told me his name, and asked me for mine.

I told him my name and told him to take the drink back. Everyone at the table knew who Vicenza Giuliano was, but me. They all looked very surprised and the room got quiet when I told him that.

He looked at me perplexed and asked why I didn't I want the drink?

I told him, "If you were any kind of gentleman then you would see I was with company and you would have had bought everyone a drink, not just me."

Well, Vicenza Giuliano liked that; he liked a woman who could handle herself. He went back to the bar and everyone asked me if I was crazy; do you know who you are talking to like that?

151

Vicenza Giuliano ordered drinks for the whole table and kept them going all night long. I was impressed. It was getting late and I asked them to take me home. I was not much of a drinker after being raped. I was always cautious about being alert when drinking. Eddy tried to screw me that night but I was not interested and he became angered and would not give me a ride home. What a freaking bum!!

I went home and checked in on Sabrina. Everything was quiet and relaxing at home. I took a shower and lay down for the night.

Two days later, I got a phone call. It was Vicenza Giuliano. I asked him how he got my number. My number was unlisted. He explained to me that car dealers get unlisted numbers and addresses on file. He got my number through that. He had a friend who owned a car dealership and found out my first and last name. We talked for a few minutes and I found him to be delightful with a sense of humor. I hung up and wondered what he was up to.

Then, a few days later Vicenza Giuliano walked into my work. I worked as a daytime barmaid for La Barron's Lounge on Dix Hwy in Detroit. I worked during the lunch hours and all the steel factories were around there. People would cash their checks, drink and give great tips. I would take a couple hundred home every day.

It was great and my boss was great too. His name was T.J. Norton. His wife and him treated me like family; they were the best bosses I ever had. They knew I had a child and would allow me leniency when Sabrina's pre-school was closed for the day.

Vicenza Giuliano came in, he looked very different than that night I met him. He was wearing a three-piece name brand suit, tie and a handkerchief to match. His shoes were sharp and matching his suit. He seemed to always be wearing a Dobbs hat. He looked like a mobster out of a television show.

He was full blooded Sicilian, very dark skin, tall but not too tall, his voice was deep and raspy. Every time he came in, he would leave me a hundred-dollar bill for a tip. Sometimes, he only had one drink, if even that.

One day, I told him that it made me uneasy leaving me money like that. His response was, "Don't you have a child? Don't you both need this money? Then don't question any man wanting to give you something unless, he steps out of line and tries to get something in return."

"Wow! This man is on the market." I thought.

I just looked at Vicenza Giuliano; I just could not figure him out. He would come in, get a drink, read the paper, look at me, talk a little to me, then leave a big tip and split. He did this for a while. Then one day, I asked him, "Why do you come in here?"

He looked at me with lust and said, "You are a smart lady, and I do not have to tell you why I come in here. You know the answer but if you want to just hear me say it, I will."

I looked at Vicenza Giuliano and said, "You want to take me out, don't you? But aren't you old enough to be my father?"

Vicenza Giuliano replied, "Age is just a number Mama."

That was the first time of many that he referred to me as mama. Vicenza Giuliano said, "Let me just take you out for dinner and if you like me, then we will go out again. If you feel uncomfortable, then I will not bother you anymore."

I agreed to go out with him. Boy, what a great time I had. He bought me the whole outfit to go out. It was very modern too. He purchased two outfits for me to choose from. He got the undergarments to match, outfit, shoes, purse, and hat. I really did not wear hats but being with Vicenza Giuliano I learned to wear one. He even bought Sabrina a complete outfit: socks, shoes, and undergarments and a toy.

He was attractive in a strange way. I was so impressed when we would go out. He would take me to the finest places, movies, or live plays afterwards, and everyone knew him. They would break their neck to serve him when he walked in the door. I loved being with him and loved the attention he gave me. Vicenza Giuliano treated me like a princess.

Then he took me to his apartment. I will never forget it. On the mailbox, it had his name and a person named J. D. Poach next to his. I figured he was rooming with someone else. Later on, I found out that this was just a hide out for J.D. Poach

While we were upstairs in his apartment, he gave me some lines of cocaine. I haven't got high in a long time. I never did cocaine before either. Heroin was always my choice of drug. I did the lines and we talked all night long. We did not do anything sexually we just lay there all night long talking.

Vicenza Giuliano gave me the coke to see if I was a cop having me talking about myself. I could not believe I did a lot of coke that night. I could not go to sleep. The next day he took me home and I got ready for work.

It was really early in the morning, running Sabrina over to the pre-school and off to work. We kept on dating; he would still come down to the bar every day to spend time with me. We would go out together every night. I introduced him to both

Dee and Bernard. Of course, both of them did not like Vicenza Giuliano.

I was pretty sure that Vicenza Giuliano did something illegal, but I was not quite sure what and how much. I remember Eddy telling me at that bar that he was a drug dealer. I knew when we went to restaurants to eat, they would treat him like a king. Everyone knew him and gave him lots of respect. I would just stare at him and be happy to be around him and get treated like a queen.

Then one night, Vicenza Giuliano brought me flowers and asked me to be his woman as he called it. He gave me a diamond ring in a wineglass at dinner. So I accepted and he moved in with Sabrina and me.

It was funny, I went every place with him when we were dating, but once he moved in, he wanted to always leave me at home and tell me my place was in the home. He did not even want me to work. He felt if I was going to be his wife, I did not need to work.

Vicenza Giuliano took me to Hudson department store and had them get me outfits for every day for the week and some. He sat down reading his paper telling the lady he wanted to pay for everything right here; he did not want to go from station to station. He pulled out a wad of money out and she jumped through hoops. He purchased all suits for me: skirt suits and pants suits; underwear to match and shoes plus hats.

He felt I represented him and wanted me to look professional. Then he took me to an old store on Woodward and purchased my first fur coat. I was amazed by the glamour of everything. Vicenza Giuliano really taught me how to dress.

Every night, he went out until the bars closed. Every night, I was by myself. When I would complain, he would tell me, "The streets are no place for a woman. You have a child here that needs you. I realize you are young. But soon you will be my wife."

A little later, I found out I was pregnant. I knew I was having Vicenza Giuliano's baby and I was a bit happy but I really did not want children by different dads. Vicenza Giuliano went out that night. I went upstairs to lie down because I was having back and stomach pain. I kept calling all the bars looking for Vicenza Giuliano. I started throwing up in the toilet upstairs, in the townhouse. Sabrina was sleeping in her bed.

I must have passed out and the next thing I knew, Bernard was standing over me, slapping my face asking me how many fingers he was holding up.

I answered him and asked how did he get in, what happen to me? Bernard told me the door downstairs was open. He was missing us and thought he would come by. Bernard had not been by in months, since I started living with Vicenza Giuliano. It was a miracle that he showed up that night.

I was lying there nude; I had gotten hot and tore off all my clothes and I was laying in my own vomit. I must have passed out and Bernard saved my life. He wrapped me up in a blanket and carried me out to his car.

It felt like knifes stabbing me all over. I was in so much pain I just knew I was going to die.

He got Sabrina dressed and took me to the hospital. They told him he got me there just in time. I had lost four units of blood in my stomach. I would have died if he did not show up. Bernard saved my life, but was not able to save his own later in life. (Sad)

After everything was over, I had to stay in the hospital. I had a tubal pregnancy. I lost my right tube and right ovary. I always felt that was my punishment for having that abortion. If I paid an 'eye for an eye' on earth, then I am okay with that.

Bernard looked for Vicenza Giuliano; I kept calling places, but I could not find him. Bernard took Sabrina for the days I was in the hospital. It was the only time he ever really took an interest in his only daughter.

Meanwhile, Vicenza Giuliano came walking in the hospital with flowers. I was so angry with him that I threw the flowers against the wall and broke the vase. He hated scenes and started to leave the room. I cussed him out as he was leaving. When it was time for me to come home, Vicenza Giuliano picked me up.

Later that evening, Bernard brought Sabrina home. I told Vicenza Giuliano, I wanted him out. He told me, he wanted to marry me and to forgive him for not being there for me. He gave me another diamond ring. I tried to question him again, where he was at, but he would not give me an answer. Vicenza Giuliano turned out to be a very secret man about everything in life, especially about himself through our whole marriage.

The next day, he smoothed me over by taking me to Hudson again and bought me a whole new closet of clothes. He knew by doing this I would drop things and get suckered in. He also purchased a beautiful bracelet for me. I always kept things in the back of my mind. I never really let anything go.

Unbelievably, we decided to get married in October. We had a few months before we took that big step. Looking back now, I see that October was a really bad month for me. Vicenza Giuliano wanted to marry me after my birthday. We got married on October 3. October has turned out to be a month of memories for me. Right after we got married, all hell started breaking loose.

I went back to the bar to work. I had gotten a leave of absence when I was in the hospital for that operation of losing my tube and ovary. My boss was so good to me. A few weeks passed and Vicenza Giuliano walked into the bar where I worked.

Vicenza Giuliano had brought a newspaper in with him. He opened it up on the pool table and I walked over. I knew something was wrong by his facial expression. He looked at me, stating there was a lot of crap going down. His boss, (his own words) J.D. Poach, just ended up in the trunk of his Cadillac with his head cut off.

It happens when you promise the union things and they support you and then, you don't pay up. He owned the White Lilly on Main Street in Detroit.

I asked Vicenza Giuliano why his head was cut off. He explained to me that it was to show disrespect. That he had made some promises and did not come through with them. He was involved with some heavy things and he lied and did not show honor as a man of his word. (These were Vicenza Giuliano's words to me.) I remembered calling my brother and telling him what had happened. I told him that I remember seeing that person's name on his apartment building when we were dating.

My brother told me to get out of that relationship. Rip said, Billy Joe, this person is hooked up with people that are big; he is a street hood. However, I would not listen. The more secrets Vicenza Giuliano had, the more I wanted to know about him.

Then one day I was cleaning the house and flipped the mattress in the bedroom. Oh my Lord, I could not believe my eyes. There were at least 20 or 30 oz. of heroin in sealed bags under our mattress. Next, I went into our walk-in closet; in his shoes, in each pair, he had stacks of money. There were hundreds, if not thousands of twenties in piles of five thousand, some had just hundred dollar bills in piles. Each pile had rubber bands around them. I had never seen so much money in my life. I could not believe it. I thought about taking it and running away.

I called Dee and said, "Hey, let's just jump on a plane and take off with all this money."

Dee, aghast, said, "NO! Vicenza Giuliano might come looking for us and you do not know who he knows or who he is connected with."

Then Dee told me, "Hook him up; you know I could sell for him. I need a good hustle right now Billy Joe."

That night, when Vicenza Giuliano got home, I questioned him about everything. I told him I wanted to know what was going on. I was excited but upset at the same time, telling him my daughter was at risk, that it was my townhouse. I had a right to know. He sat me down and told me what he wanted me to hear. My whole behavior changed; I was so happy to be included, then I told him, "I know many people who get high. I can help you sell that stuff faster."

I told him about Dee and all the people he could sell quantity to. I did not even think about my daughter any longer (that is the evil of this lifestyle, you let everything go in life).

I knew he was a big drug dealer and I wanted to be a part of that life. I called Dee over and had him talk to Vicenza Giuliano they discussed it and Vicenza Giuliano told him he would start him out with five oz's and work his way up after that. Not only did Dee get rid of those five oz.' s in one day, but also he came back for five more until he had 20 at a time.

It was great, Dee would get me anything I wanted and my husband Vicenza Giuliano was giving me anything I wanted. Both of them were tearing me apart and I loved it.

I even got deeper into the business but not trusting Vicenza Giuliano any farther than I could throw him. He kept too many secrets but so did I. Vicenza Giuliano sat me down and let me know that he appreciated me giving him Dee but he wanted me out of the game. He told me my place was in the home. Vicenza Giuliano was much older than me; I was twenty years old and Vicenza Giuliano was 49 years old. I was not happy that he was keeping me out of everything but I was happy that Dee was part of it because I knew I would never be left out of the loop.

One night, Vicenza Giuliano left the house with a big dark garbage bag. I looked in the closet and noticed all the money was gone. I followed him and called Dee to meet me. We sat at the bar waiting for Vicenza Giuliano to come out. Then finally, he got into his car and drove way out. We followed him all the way. He parked at an apartment building and got out of his Cadillac looking around and went to the trunk of his car and retrieved that large garbage bag.

He went upstairs to someone's apartment. Later, after being in there for hours, he came out and so did his daughter. He had given that big bag of money to his daughter. I never could understand why. I guess it was to pay on her wedding or wedding gift but then, I realized that he did not trust me either. I never said anything about what I saw that night to Vicenza Giuliano, or that we followed him.

Vicenza Giuliano and I would go out for dining; owners of establishments would find special seating for us. It was nice to be out with Vicenza Giuliano because everyone would make a fuss over him. We would dine either at Carl's Chop House on Main Street or Doug's Body Shop on Woodward.

Doug's Body Shop had a sign in the parking lot stating: **"All Don's park in back"**. When you walked in, there were two levels; on one level, it had old cars for tables. You sat in the car for dinner . . . it was so cool. Then, downstairs was plain tables and live jazz that was played loudly.

I loved going to these places when Vicenza Giuliano would take me. Sometimes we would swing by Baker's Keyboard and Lounge. These were our hang-outs. Vicenza Giuliano would take me out once a week, but mainly I would stay home throughout the week. At home, when people came over to talk business with Vicenza Giuliano, he would make me go upstairs so they could talk real low. Everything he did was very secretive. Yeah I was his wife, but I felt like I was just a cover for him.

Then one night, Vicenza Giuliano asked me to go with him to the bar. I was surprised, because he stopped asking me for a while. We went downtown to the Corner Pub, Cass area. While we were in there, Lori was in there strung out and making an ass out of herself. She wanted Vicenza Giuliano to sell her some more dope. Vicenza Giuliano would not do it because she was now dating Greasy. He was a big drug dealer in the area. Vicenza Giuliano told her no.

She got mad and started calling Vicenza Giuliano a bunch of punks and a cheap trick. Vicenza Giuliano kept playing pool and did not feed into her madness. Then she told him she was going to report him to his parole officer and tell him he was dealing dope. Before Vicenza Giuliano knew what he was doing, he hailed off and slapped her across her face. Then, he apologized to the bartender asking him to give her a drink on him.

Then, Vicenza Giuliano apologized to her and turned to play his game on the pool table. Just as Vicenza Giuliano turned around to play pool again, Lori picked up a beer bottle to hit Vicenza Giuliano with it. I saw the move she was going to make and acted so fast. I grabbed a pool stick and swung it around and hit Lori in the back of the head as she hit the ground. Everyone grabbed me and Lori. They took her in the back and told me and Vicenza Giuliano to get out of there before the police came. We did.

A couple days later, Vicenza Giuliano saw Greasy outside by his car, getting something out of the trunk. Vicenza Giuliano went out there to talk with him explaining the situation out of respect. Greasy was her boyfriend and a large drug dealer. I stood on the porch in case something went down. They talked for a long time and Greasy told Vicenza Giuliano that Lori gave him a different story. However, being that he knew Vicenza Giuliano longer and knew of his reputation, he believed he was telling him the truth.

The guys laughed and said if you are not careful women will cause men to kill each other. Greasy told him he would not do something crazy like hiring a hit man over a slut. Greasy knew, she was a woman that any man could have if the price was right. She was just someone to have fun with, not marriage material and certainly not someone he was serious with. Vicenza Giuliano came back to the townhouse and started watching TV. I asked Vicenza Giuliano what happened even though, I heard everything, but he told me.

So a few weeks went by and Vicenza Giuliano and I went down to the Corner Pub to shoot a few games of pool and have a couple drinks just to get away from the house for a few hours and relax. Everything was fine while we were there at the bar. When we got into the car, Vicenza Giuliano did not feel right about a car sitting down the street. When we left, Vicenza Giuliano told me to take a different side street.

Vicenza Giuliano watched everything. He watched his rear mirrors and taught me to do the same. I kept asking him what was going on but he would not answer me and told me to shut up and drive. I listened to what he said, and did as I was told. I could tell the situation was serious by Vicenza Giuliano's facial expressions and his voice. I just did not realize how serious until later.

I went down different side streets the next thing I know, Vicenza Giuliano was getting excited telling me turn here, turn there. I was trying to figure out what was going on and I looked in the mirror and saw a car following us every direction we took. Then I turned onto the expressway.

I was heading down 94 going toward the suburban area. I saw the car gaining on us and Vicenza Giuliano started yelling, "Slow down", "Go fast", "Keep the pace up", "Do not let this car get on us". As the car approached our car, I looked sideways for a split second and realized these people had a large gun—it was a sawed-off shot gun pointing right at me, or us.

That scared the shit out of me, I slammed on the breaks. They shot ahead and then slowed down to let us catch up. I switched lanes and kept doing what Vicenza Giuliano had told me in the beginning. I knew these people were serious and I was scared wanting to save my life.

This car chase seemed to last for a long time. Vicenza Giuliano was steadily opening the windows throwing Thai-sticks and weed, heroin and cocaine out the window. At first, I did not understand; did he think this was the police, or what was going on? I realized this was someone that was trying to harm us or rob us. Was this someone trying to kill us, and why?

My heart was beating and my hand was nervous as I grabbed tightly the wheel of the car. It seemed like the chase lasted for hours. Finally the people gave up and stopped. Did they turned off at an exit? Vicenza Giuliano did not trust it and told me to continue the same way all the way home. He had me get off on back roads and jumped in the back seat watching the back window. He watched the sides. He was watching many directions.

We finally made it home. Vicenza Giuliano had me go into the house. He stopped me at the door, put up his index finger and told me shhhhhhhhhhhhhhh. Then he took out his gun that I never knew he carried. He walked upstairs slowly and went to each room. Then came back downstairs and told me everything was clear.

I went to turn on a light and he yelled out . . . **"No"**! I asked him about us picking up Sabrina, and he told me, not tonight. He said it wasn't safe and that it wasn't a good idea in having the baby here tonight. He asked me if I know how to shoot a gun. I told him, I went deer hunting with my stepfather and shot before. He explained just point this hammer on top of the gun in the direction, and just fire if you have to. Always look first to see the target clearly before you shoot if possible.

Vicenza Giuliano told me to lie down on the coach and get some sleep. He would take the first watch. He never woke me up to take my watch. Vicenza Giuliano stayed up all night to watch our townhouse.

The next day, our babysitter came over with Sabrina. Vicenza Giuliano saw Greasy over at Lori's again; he was hot with anger; he went over there yelling at him. Greasy kept telling Vicenza Giuliano that he did not have anything to do with it. I stood in the doorway listening to them argue.

Lori came out and Greasy yelled at her and pulled her back into the townhouse. When Vicenza Giuliano came back home, I asked him what was going on? I already knew because I stood at the door listening but I wanted Vicenza Giuliano to tell me anything I did not hear.

He told me it was better if I did not know. I grabbed him by the arm and turned him around. "That's bullshit! I need to know if my life and child's life is in danger. Now, you tell me what the hell is going on and what does Greasy have to do with this?"

Then Vicenza Giuliano told me, that only Greasy would have the funds and connections to hire a hit man to come after us, I asked him why a hit man? He explained that little bar scene caused all of this. Greasy assured Vicenza Giuliano that he was not a part of this. Vicenza Giuliano did not believe him. He felt like he hired someone to kill us both.

I told Vicenza Giuliano, that Lori might have got them. He asked how she could afford that. I told him she screws many people for money. It made Vicenza Giuliano think, but he said that is Greasy's issue. If he cannot control his woman, that is on him. I never saw Vicenza Giuliano so angry. I knew this was not going to be the end of this. I asked Vicenza Giuliano how is he able to control what another human being does? Lori gets thousands of dollars from guys she prostitutes with. Vicenza Giuliano said nothing and left the room. I just stood there in thought.

A few nights later, Henze and Big Mike came over to the house. Big Mike was the person Vicenza Giuliano got his heroin from. He was Italian like Vicenza Giuliano, that was his connection. Henze was a good friend of Vicenza Giuliano and would do anything for Vicenza Giuliano.

Vicenza Giuliano told me to go upstairs because they had business to talk about. I went upstairs but listened at the heat ducts. I heard Vicenza Giuliano tell them that someone tried to kill us on the way home.

I heard him discuss his conversation with Greasy. Then I heard Henze state he would take care of it. Vicenza Giuliano wanted to know if 20,000, thousand would be okay. I heard Vicenza

Giuliano coming upstairs. I lay on the bed as if I was bored. He went into the closet and got a bag out. He went back downstairs and I went to the top of the steps to listen. Henze told Vicenza Giuliano, that he would take care of everything, but he was only going to give the person 10,000.00 thousand smack, and keep the rest for himself.

Vicenza Giuliano told him, "he did not care what he did or how he did it, just makes sure you get Greasy."

Henze told him, "I am going to have my person take a shotgun, go on top of the Red-Dog, and shoot him as he comes out of the bar, right in the street."

Vicenza Giuliano told him "Make sure he wears gloves, no fingerprints not even on the bullets. Tell him to leave the shotgun there; do not carry that thing with him when he leaves".

That is just what happened. They hired Billy to shoot Greasy. He did just that. They shot Greasy twice in the chest and once in the lower stomach. He survived the shooting. I believe Greasy knew who shot him, that is why he left and went to Arizona. He had a bar out there and got out of town. To this day, they never closed the case on this or found the shooter. I knew Vicenza Giuliano was not one to mess with and that included Henze as well.

I called Dee and told him what was up. I was really surprised when he told me he knew Billy and that he was his property owner. I went over to Dee's house. Dee got Billy and we all talked about it. Billy was real open and honest about the whole deal because he trusted Dee. I asked Dee later, why he was telling everything to us. Then Dee told me, that Billy and his girlfriend were one of his best customers, that he trusted him completely. I told Dee to let Billy know that they also cheated him and kept eight thousands of the hit money. I told him that Vicenza Giuliano gave Henze twenty thousand for the hit. Billy did not care, because he said, Henze hooked him up all the time to make lump sums of money like that. He also felt like Henze was going to make him a partner. He thought the world of Henze and you could not tell him anything different.

It was July and Vicenza Giuliano's fiftieth birthday. I rented a hall in our townhouse complex and invited my family, Vicenza Giuliano's family (his brothers and sisters) and many of our friends. It was not a good mix with professional hit men, dope dealers and hustlers and family.

I had a special cake made and ordered caterer food. I had everything decorated and purchased. I also got a very special present for him. Vicenza Giuliano had a special ring that he lost last time he went to the joint. It was not the same ring, I had one made just like he described to me. It was a pinkie ring, weighing in at 28 grams of white gold with the word "VICE" made in diamonds. His name was a couple carrots in diamonds. It was big beautiful and something to be proud of.

We had a personal jeweler on Green Road across the street from the mall in the twin tower building on the fourth floor. There was a whole sale jeweler there named Michael. He would take coke or money for payment. He did all our jewelry unless Vicenza Giuliano picked them up from junkies. Vicenza Giuliano was so surprised by his party but later told me, you don't ever mix family with work, mama. He told me you placed your family in danger. I thought about what we were doing to Sabrina but the thought left as quickly as it came into my head. Vicenza Giuliano and I seemed closer each day.

I started looking at Vicenza Giuliano a lot differently after that. We started going out more often together. I joined the pool team at The Express Bar on Detroit Ave, in Detroit right across from the old stadium. Vicenza Giuliano had a special stick made for me and everything was so great.

To me, we were like Bonnie and Clyde. I was a young girl living a fantasy that was turning into a reality. I just thought Vicenza Giuliano was the toughest person in the whole world. He told me to stop working at the bar that I could stay home with Sabrina. I told my boss T.J. Norton and he was not pleased. He told me, "You do not know this dude, I was in the joint with him."

I was surprised to hear that because I did not even know my boss had been in the joint. He explained to me, that I was going to end up in trouble, that I was a young girl with my whole life ahead of me. He talked about me having a child and how I needed to place her in a safe environment. However, I did not listen to T.J. I quit my job and was a stay-at-home mom. T.J. did tell me I could come back if I needed a job. He was a great guy and I don't care what he did. He did try to turn me around concerning my life; he was a true friend.

I loved every minute of being Mrs. Billy Joe Giuliano. Everyone referred to me as Vicenza Giuliano's wife. They knew he was serious about me and was living with me.

Like Vicenza Giuliano said, they know you are "MY" wife. Vicenza Giuliano would take me to stores in New York and Detroit, letting me try on anything that I wanted and telling them to find the shoe and purse to match and add it up. I had all kinds of suits, with matching purses, undergarments, negligées, shoes and hats that filled a walk-in closet.

I dressed as if I was in Hollywood. My hair was styled, nails done, feet pampered and I always looked my best. One thing Vicenza Giuliano did not like me to wear was blue jeans. He hated them on me and wanted me to always wear suits, dresses and pantsuits. Sometimes, I just wanted to relax and wear them. I liked hot pants and halter tops and wanted to show off my figure. But Vicenza Giuliano did not like me showing anything except to him. He told me I had to carry myself as his wife. Vicenza Giuliano taught me how to talk, walk and molded me into his solider wife.

He showed me how to know when people are following me, never to take the same way home. How to set things in the house to make sure no one has been in it. Vicenza Giuliano would look on the roof and in the car windows before getting in for people in the back seat. He would even check under the car and the engine to make sure bombs were not attached. It became an exhausting life style. Vicenza Giuliano was great with Sabrina, teaching her A, B, C's. I could not ask for a better father for her.

A few days later I found out Vicenza Giuliano's daughter was getting married. He did not want me to go with him. I did not understand why. Then in an argument, he told me in so many words, that he did not want his daughter or his ex-wife to see how young I was.

I was so infuriated; I felt like, I was the one who should be embarrassed. I was only 20 years old when we got together, he was 49. That is a twenty-eight year difference. It really hurt me that he felt like that. I yelled at Vicenza Giuliano, "You don't want me as your wife, I am someone you show off to your street pals; I am your trophy wife but when it comes to real family, you are embarrassed of me."

I got angry and cussed him out. I went out that night and hung out in the bars. I came home late that night and Vicenza Giuliano was waiting up for me. He asked me if I had a good time. Then he told me he wanted me to accompany him to the wedding. We hugged and kissed and I attended the wedding with him. His daughter was not pleased to meet me. Neither was his ex-wife. I felt so out of place and such a little girl next to everyone else. Even his daughter was older than I was.

Now, I knew why he never took me over there to meet her. He always went by himself. He took her shopping by himself too. I was never invited. I think that is why Vicenza Giuliano took that garbage bag of money over to his daughter for her wedding. I started looking at mine and Vicenza Giuliano's relationship more and more as a business relationship rather than as a marriage; I did not feel like his wife anymore. Then, to top things off, I found out an unbelievable secret, he was getting high on heroin.

So many times when I would get high and he found out about it, he would always correct me and tell me that it is for selling, not doing. He would always make me quit. Sometimes when Vicenza Giuliano and I would cut the dope, and weight it, we would wear mask and gloves. I would still get addicted because the powder would go into my pores when you lift the lid from the blender. I would take a shower and get chills and know I got a habit. No matter how careful we were, it would still get into our pores. I would tell Vicenza Giuliano and he would have me lay on the couch and kick it.

What this means is that every time I got a habit through the gloves and mask, he would make me lay on the couch and cover up with blankets. What this does is make one get sick like you have the flu and you wait for it to pass just as if you would the flu. Every time I got a habit from handling the dope, he would go out without me and make me lay on the couch and kick the dope, to go through the sickness until the habit was gone.

One evening, he went to the bathroom downstairs. I could hear him in there snorting through his nose. I looked in the hole that you slide the door open with. He was in there putting water up his nose, trying to clean it. He started to come out of the bathroom and I moved away from the door quickly. He asked if I was ready for dinner.

He took me out to a nice place to eat and some jazz later on that evening. While at the restaurant, sitting at the bar waiting for our table to come up, Vicenza Giuliano saw both of the Giacalone brothers. They were considered the Dons of Detroit (mobsters). He spoke a few words to them. I recognized them by their pictures in the newspapers when they did articles on the Mafia.

When Vicenza Giuliano and I were finally seated, I asked him did he know him. He smiled and said yes. Then I asked him did he know all the people in the Mafia? He told me, he knew every one of them, from the top man down. I then asked him if he was in the Mafia. He smiled and said; "No mama that is not for me, I have done work for them but I am my own person. I like working for me; I am no one's pond. If I screw up, it's my mistake, and I am the only one that suffers from it."

Then Vicenza Giuliano told me; "My father ran numbers for them and carried envelopes of money in New Jersey from point A to point B, but unless you are in the family, and of the family, it's not a good deal. Shit, even being of the family is not safe."

Then he explained to me he used to be a shylock for them in 1974. (A shy-locker is a person who goes to places and collects money owed to the mob and he would take baseball bats and break their knee caps to convince them to pay the money they owe.) Vicenza Giuliano made sure to inform me he does not work or take jobs from them anymore. Vicenza Giuliano stated, "I am my own man."

Vicenza Giuliano just knew if they had knowledge of him getting high, they would kill him. Then he made me promise to never, ever speak to anyone about him chipping. (Chipping is a dealer who is still using drugs like heroin, here and there, but not every day.) He told me that meant life or death because of his relationship with people in the streets. He told me, "I Don't care who it is; keep it a secret, mama."

I had to go to work one evening at the bar in the neighborhood which is where we would go sell our dope. I pinched Vicenza Giuliano's dope all the time and made money on the side, I would stash it without his knowledge. Vicenza Giuliano was not around to watch Sabrina, and I needed a babysitter badly. I never called Bernard but I took the chance and I called Bernard up and asked him if he would watch his daughter. He agreed.

That night, coming home from the bar, I could not get in my townhouse door. Bernard had passed out in the corridor of the apartment door. He must have drunk too much.

It was awful. Then I woke up Sabrina and she came downstairs upset because daddy was passed out and I could not get into the house. I finally got in through the window. The next morning, I had a long talk with Bernard about his behavior.

Vicenza Giuliano was missing all night long; he did not get in until late in the morning. Sometimes I wondered if he was out knocking people off or with another woman. I could never ask him because he would not have answered.

A few months later, Vicenza Giuliano approached me about Sabrina touching his privates and asking for a cookie, stating that she told him daddy did that with her. At the time, I really believed Vicenza Giuliano. I called Sabrina downstairs to ask her if daddy ever touched her inappropriately. She stated that daddy offered her a cookie to touch him.

I called Bernard up and questioned him about the situation. He told me it was lies and he wanted to see Sabrina. I went to his motel with Dee, to tell him I do not think he should ever see Sabrina again in his life. His girlfriend opened the door and she was drunk as a skunk. I asked for Bernard and his girlfriend started telling me I was not wanted there. I pushed her to the side and walked in.

She went to grab me and I beat her down, I punched her in the face several times. Then I pulled out my gun and told Bernard I wanted him to sign paper over to me for our daughter. He told me, he would but he wanted to do it legally. He kept screaming that he did not touch Sabrina. I wanted to believe him but because of his past with me it was hard. As I left the motel, Bernard came running at me and as I got in the car seat and the door was still open, he grabbed me by my hair and started punching me in my face; I knew there was no more love between us.

So I threw the stick in (R) reverse and started backing up as he was hitting me; the car door was still open and as I backed up the open car door pushed Bernard down to the ground. Dee kept yelling, "Billy Joe, stop!"

I shut the door and I ran over him again by backing up the car, and then again by going forward. I could hear Dee yelling and Bernard's girlfriend coming out of the motel screaming, "Help! She is killing him."

I took off, looking in my rear view mirror and saw Bernard just lying on the ground. I never saw him again after that. *In 1989, Bernard passed away at the age of 32 from alcohol. (May he rest in peace.)*

Vicenza Giuliano and I needed to get away from the stress of the streets, so we planned a vacation up north to see my mother, and I allowed her to meet the man I was married to.

On the way up there, I tried to tell Vicenza Giuliano about my mother and that I did not get along with her very well. I told him, I did not want to stay long because the more I am away from her, the better it is. There was a lot of sightseeing up there which was relaxing. I tried to give him a crash course on the abuse I went through with her.

When we got up there, Vicenza Giuliano loved the quiet and the remoteness from everything. He liked my mom too. She always puts on a good act for people until they get to know her. He had never seen a cow up close. I took him around to show him horses and cows. Vicenza Giuliano was blown away. He grew up in New Jersey and then Detroit. He never dealt with the country before and only saw cows and horses from pictures. I was washing dishes after dinner and Tom and Vicenza Giuliano were getting to know each other.

Vicenza Giuliano really liked Tom the most. He came in the house and asked why I was washing the dishes by hand. I told him my mother did not have a dishwasher. He went out and purchased her a dishwasher for her kitchen. Then, we got a few other things like a washer and a dryer for her and some fishing equipment for my step-dad. We sat and talked all night long, then finally went to bed.

Vicenza Giuliano got up and sat in the kitchen for a long time. He sat there talking to himself. I could also hear him sniffing his nose, as if he was snorting something up. I peeked in on him and he was blowing a few lines up his nose. I asked him what the hell he was doing. He jumped up startled and wanted to know how long I had been there. Then, I wanted to know how long he had been doing this behind my back.

I knew by that situation in the bathroom and the comment he made about not letting anyone to know that he chipped that he was a constant user but I wanted him to admit it openly. Come to find out, he had been doing it the whole time we were together. I went to bed and could not sleep thinking about the person I married. I did not want to give up the life style.

What was wrong with me, I could feel this guy was no good for me. He fooled me, thinking he was my prince on a white horse, but in reality, he was the devil in disguise. Finally, I fell to sleep and did not wake up until noon the next day.

Vicenza Giuliano and my mother had been out all day, my stepfather Tom said. I asked where did they go, and he did not know. Then they pulled up in the driveway. Vicenza Giuliano and my mother had went and bought a house for us. I was mad as hell.

We drove over to see the house that my mother and husband picked out for me. This was too much. I could not believe he did this knowing how I felt about my mother and knowing I should be the one picking out my house not my mother.

I did not want to move way up in Mesick, Michigan. I hated it up north when I was a kid and I did not want to move up there for I was a city girl. A few days later, we went back down to Detroit. I contacted my father and told him about the situation. Then my dad talked with Vicenza Giuliano. They had a connection with each other. My dad was a firm, hard type man, and Vicenza Giuliano was very impressed by my father. He also liked the way my father lived on barely anything and always had lots of money. My dad was just down to earth, did not care about money, and always was blessed with it.

He gave a lot of it away, and took care of many people who did not have the same blessing. Dad wanted to go up north to see the house Vicenza Giuliano and my mother put a down payment on. After seeing the home, my father told me, it was a good deal. The house was worth more than what we were paying for it. Vicenza Giuliano was paying cash so the mortgage company brought the price down. Vicenza Giuliano asked my father if we could put it in his name in case something ever happened to him. He also asked my father not let anyone take it from me and the baby. My father agreed.

We went home to pack up and move up north from Detroit. I did not want to go. I was totally against this. I liked hanging out at the bars. When Vicenza Giuliano was out doing whatever, I was doing my thing. I liked going out with people my own age, and getting high behind Vicenza Giuliano's back, receiving gifts from Dee and doing as I pleased when he was not around. This move would take me out of civilization and dump me in the backwoods. I was not a happy camper about this. We would be up north; the closest neighbor was miles away and my mother lived too close for comfort for me. I did not want to go. My father told me that Vicenza Giuliano was my husband and I was to do as my husband wished, and "Billy Joe, you married him for better or for worse. Now you get ready and go on up there."

Vicenza Giuliano paid cash for our house. He put it in my father's name and had my dad sign for everything. Dee assured me that he would come up there all the time and keep me company when Vicenza Giuliano left for trips.

Dee did keep his promise to visit. Then, Big Mike told Vicenza Giuliano he was getting out of the business that he would have to go someplace else for heroin. We had been getting stuff from Big Mike for about three years now though, it would not be hard for Vicenza Giuliano to find other connections. (A connection is the street slang for a supplier.) He was known by everyone; Vicenza Giuliano had a reputation and stood by it. Big Mike made his money and bought a legitimate business and house and got out of the drug business. Vicenza Giuliano told me that is how it should to be done. He was not upset with Big Mike and loved him as a friend and business partner.

Vicenza Giuliano also dealt with a guy named Ruben who lived down in Southwest Detroit. Ruben just purchased a super nice place in the suburban area and he was not pleased when he heard the news. He usually got rid of ten oz's a week for Vicenza Giuliano. He was worried about getting this house and not making the payments on his new house. Ruben was on a mission too. Vicenza Giuliano assured him that he would contact another connects and reconnect with him.

We went down to Brightmoor to see Doodle and Carney. They were also drug dealers. We agreed to hang out for the night with them as Vicenza Giuliano and Doodle talked business. Vicenza Giuliano went to Doodle asking for a connection.

When Doodle got out of prison, he was doing well for himself. He and his woman Carney gave Vicenza Giuliano and me an anniversary party. They paid for dinner and we got high all night long. Vicenza Giuliano and Doodle went and talked business while Carney and I sat and girl talked. She showed me her fur coats, jewelry and sports car Doodle had bought her; we went for a ride.

The next day, the boys were talking and taking care of business. Later on, they took out the bong and cooked up some of the cocaine adding baking soda for us to celebrate and get high on. Back then, it was called freebasing. Now, they call it crack. Except crack now-a-days does not have any real cocaine in it as we had back then. We sat around the kitchen table smoking the pipe. I got sick, and went upstairs to lie down. Doodle brought me up some downers to help bring me down. I took them but I was still very sick, I had gotten too high and my heart was going a thousand miles a minute. I thought I was going to have a heart-attack. We were going to spend the night over their house, but I was too sick to stay.

I begged Vicenza Giuliano to take me home. He was in the bed sound asleep. I was pissed and kept hitting him to let him know I wanted to go home. I kept bugging Vicenza Giuliano to take me home, because I could not sit still, that 'Cain' had got me going, and I could not go to sleep like him. I kept waking him up telling him, I had to move around, to please take me home. Vicenza Giuliano finally agreed to leave.

It was around 3:00 in the morning. I am not sure of the time; I just knew it was early in the morning. We got up and got dressed and Vicenza Giuliano told me I would have to drive, because he was too sleepy. I told him, no problem, because I am wired. He got up and went downstairs to let Doodle know.

We had gotten a kilo of heroin from Doodle. Vicenza Giuliano had taken out a few of the oz's to test it. It was 92%. Doodle had given us some good stuff. Vicenza Giuliano and I would make a lot of money on this; we would be able to put a 24 or a 26 gram cut into it. (All dope has to be cut and depending on what style we wished, we would take two grams of pure dope and cut it with a filler to make a Mexican oz which is 26 grams or an American oz which is 28 grams.)

Vicenza Giuliano laid the two oz's down on the coach in the spare room while we were smoking the pipe. He had forgotten about them as I did too as we were leaving, Vicenza Giuliano looked into his study room and saw a stack of cash on the desk against the wall. He then, told Doodle that's not a good practice to leave money like that out in the open, especially if you got customers coming over. Doodle told Vicenza Giuliano not to worry; it was only three or four thousand dollars.

Vicenza Giuliano told Doodle, "Yeah, three thousand to you, four thousand to me, but to another mother Fu—er, it's a big sting. They will kill you for it."

Doodle agreed with Vicenza Giuliano and stated he would put it away. Then, they walked us out the door and we left for upper Michigan. We both did not know it but it would be the last time we saw Doodle. I remember as we pulled up at the stop sign, I noticed a car pulling into the driveway of Doodle's house.

We went home and Vicenza Giuliano counted his ounces. He had forgotten two of them in the study room when he was talking to Doodle. He called him as soon as we got home. No answer, just the recording on the answering machine. Vicenza Giuliano said he would try him again in the morning, that they must've been tired and went to bed. So, Vicenza Giuliano said, "Let's do the same."

The next day Vicenza Giuliano kept trying to call him without success. Then the following day, Vicenza Giuliano called again and he no longer got the answering machine. He knew something was wrong. He kept trying, and then some person answered the phone. Vicenza Giuliano hung up and told me to get ready for Detroit, something had happened; Vicenza Giuliano had to know what he was dealing with.

We got a babysitter for Sabrina and went back down to Detroit. We went to see Ruben the Spanish man that did business with Vicenza Giuliano. He showed the newspaper account to Vicenza Giuliano where Doodle and Carney had both been shot in the head. Doodle was dead on arrival; Carney was fighting for her life. Doodle was found in the study room area, with a shot in his upper shoulder area, then one to the middle of his head. Carney was found outside on the front yard on the grass with a bullet in her head and most of her hair and brains splattered on the wall in the study. A paperboy found Carney.

Doodle and Carney lived over by Lamphere in Brightmoor, right off from Grandriver and Lasher area. There was blood all over the walls where she had been blinded by the shot in the head. Because of her will to live, she took her hands and felt all around the walls trying to find her way out of the house. When they found her, all she cared about was telling them her husband was still inside. It was a nightmare that night.

179

Vicenza Giuliano would not let me send flowers or card. He told me that the authorities were watching everything.

The newspapers stated that they got 80,000 dollars in cash in a suitcase upstairs and 70,000 dollars in uncut heroin and seized jewelry, fur coats, boats, cars, and everything else. Their house was hot, the hospital was hot, and we could not get anywhere near them without Vicenza Giuliano being known by the Feds.

Then, they found Pep who Doodle and Carney did business with. He had shot both of them in the head for a few thousand dollars and was caught trying to buy a used car. They said, (rumor) that Pep dropped bills with his fingerprints going out the door.

The first thing Vicenza Giuliano said was . . . . I told Doodle to put that money up; Cats will kill you for a few measly dollars. I kept thinking it could have been us; we just left that night and went home in upper Michigan. We could have been with them in the hospital or in the grave. My head was thinking all kinds of stuff and why we were spared. Vicenza Giuliano had to look for other connections now. We had that heroin that we didn't have to make payment on, as well; it is the way of the business. That was all free money because Doodle told Vicenza Giuliano to bring the money the next time he came down; it was all now blood money. But it would not last long. I did not know that heroin would go faster than I thought.

Vicenza Giuliano started calling around to see who was clicking. All he could think about was there went our connection; I cried worrying about my friend Carney. It seemed like it was a chain reaction after that.

We went home and I asked Vicenza Giuliano if he wanted Dee to come pick up to get his load. Vicenza Giuliano did not want to let go any of the stuff because he had a nasty monkey (a heroin addiction) on his back. It would not take long for the truth to surface, one thing lead to another. We were fighting with each other every day about him not selling that stuff and making more money to purchase. He was getting high every day. He was watching our pennies and putting more up his nose than the law allowed.

We were fighting so much, that one night Vicenza Giuliano said, come on, let's get out of here for a while and relax at the bar. Vicenza Giuliano wasn't a drinker and really did not like to drink when he was using because it took his high away. I asked if we were going to Detroit. He stated no, to the bar in town, so I got dressed up and we went down there. We lived in a little out of the way town called Mesick, and boy this town made me sick. I was way over dressed and stuck out like a sore thumb. Everyone out here smelled like cow poop. They wore blue jean coveralls and smelt and looked as if they had been on the farm all day. We went in and played some pool for a while. We did need to relax.

I really loved Vicenza Giuliano, but he had some odd ways that made me not fully trust him. I had a hard time dealing with his habit. I saw some guys in there my age and every time Vicenza Giuliano went to the bathroom they would hit on me. They kept asking me to play pool with them. Sometimes they would ask me when Vicenza Giuliano went to get our drinks. Then finally, I told them that he was my husband. One person responded by saying he looked like he could be my father.

When Vicenza Giuliano came back, they started making remarks about him being pops, and a trick daddy. I told them to leave my husband alone. Vicenza Giuliano told me to be quiet and go to the car.

I did, but I was worried, this was the second time I saw that look in Vicenza Giuliano's eyes. He was so angry I think he could have killed them. Then Vicenza Giuliano came out of the bar, and got into the car and drove me home. He dropped me off and went back to the bar.

I yelled for Vicenza Giuliano not to go, I pleaded with him. He would not listen and his voice got deep. He already sounded like someone on the TV show playing the godfather. I ran over to the bar because it was not far away.

When I opened the door, it was like a freak movie. Vicenza Giuliano had one of the young guys by the neck holding his head to the bar. Everyone else was on the floor at the other end of the bar.

Vicenza Giuliano had a gun to the person's head. Oh my Lord, he was being sloppy with his actions. I yelled and told Vicenza Giuliano . . . . "NO!"

He told me to return to the car, but I told him I would not leave without him. He got angry and told me to go home.

I yelled out, "No Vicenza Giuliano, I will not leave this bar without you."

"Can't you see those guys were just mad because you have a young pretty wife that they could never have?"

Vicenza Giuliano looked at me and pushed the man forward. He backed up and walked out the door with me and we took off. Thank the Holy Father, no one followed us. I never could understand why.

We went back to the house and weeks had passed by; Vicenza Giuliano was not allowing any drugs to be sold. I asked Vicenza Giuliano about our finances, but he told me not to worry. He must have money put away because he hired a couple of men to come in and redo the house upstairs. Vicenza Giuliano put ten thousand dollars in the construction work upstairs. Back in 1980s, ten thousand was a lot of money. I do believe Vicenza Giuliano was keeping the dope for himself and living off the savings he had put up.

He wanted to wait because of his habit, to find another connection. We were fighting every day. To me, he wasn't even looking for one.

Then Dee came over and Vicenza Giuliano asked him to stay and help him kick this heroin habit. So Dee agreed. Vicenza Giuliano was in his 50's and it was too hard for him to quit. His habit was too big, and physically he was unable to take the pain. His heart could not take it. Vicenza Giuliano was doing about two grams a day of uncut dope.

Dee had to come between us every day. We were fighting like cats and dogs. I could not stomach him anymore. He was not the man I thought he was. He was weak and a dope fiend and could not get himself together.

I have quit hundreds of habits and made it. It made me sick he could not get it together. I sat and thought about how Dee and I made all this come true. We made the money; it was us who hustled bringing in most of the income.

All Vicenza Giuliano had, was Ruben and that was it. Vicenza Giuliano had the connections, but Dee and I brought in the money. I had set up dope houses with ten different people I knew from my past. I put dope houses together in Ann Arbor and in Brightmoor Heights. Plus I had a few spoon people that came and got stuff from me every day, when we moved up north, I had Dee give it to them.

Spoon people were nothing but pure profit. Each was selling a couple grams a day, if not more.

Then Dee was selling anywhere from ten to twenty oz's' every other day. Between my little people and Dee, we were the ones that made Vicenza Giuliano. He only had the connections, but we had the resources. The more I thought about it the more I hated him. He moved me up north where I did not want to be. There was no place to go, just woods. I was young and wanted to live in the city and go out on the town. All my outfits could not be worn up there because it was just a bunch of farmers. I was really pissed at Vicenza Giuliano and hated that he placed me up there. What a piece of crap he was to me. I could not see myself living up here for the rest of my life. I went to bed angry and Dee left back for Detroit.

The next day Vicenza Giuliano and I had to go to my mother's house. I went to the store and left Vicenza Giuliano with my mother. I took my step-dad and my little sister and brother with me. When we came back, Vicenza Giuliano and my mother were acting strange. After we left, Vicenza Giuliano told me that my mother sat in front of him without any panties on, and pulled her dress up high. It brought a flash back to my memory of a story I used to hear growing up.

Now, my mother was hitting on my husband because she thinks he had a lot of money. My mother was always money hungry. She even made the deal with my father to allow him to have me if she could have my social security check. All of this was flashing in my head. She had so many boyfriends that I used to get baby sat by different men. Men she brought home wanting to see if I had hairs on my private area. I even flashed back to Mel her boss in the factory who had a wife and seven kids, who my mother was screwing and he came to babysit me while mom was at work. "He was her boss." Mom was a trip with the men. She would screw anything that she thought would give her money.

Now she was up to her old tricks again hitting on Vicenza Giuliano, thinking he had a lot of money. She would always make the comment to me, that he was old enough to be her boyfriend. All this was going through my mind and other things. The more I thought about it, the madder I got at Vicenza Giuliano for moving me up here.

Then I thought about that shooting of Greasy, that is why he moved us up here in the first place, because he knew Greasy would come back on him. Greasy owned a bar out in Arizona, so he went out there.

Vicenza Giuliano used to own the Hello Dena and the Winner's Lounge in Detroit and he lost both of them.

Then, I started getting high myself, just to deaden the pain of being stuck up north, no place to go, neither one of us working, and my husband, a drug addict. I stayed up all night crying and we didn't even sleep together any more. He was always in pain. I was a young woman wanting to make love to my husband. We had sex maybe three times since the shooting of Doodle and Carney.

Dee came back up north with some V's to cut back on the heroin. We were down to ten oz's! Vicenza Giuliano's habit was about 900.00 dollars a day that was uncut heroin. Those oz's weren't going to last long. Vicenza Giuliano was messed up too much to get his shit together to find us another connection. He could not go out like this because no one would have anything to do with him in this kind of shape.

What drugs we had, was it and all of them were free because we got them from Doodle and Carney on consignment. They were shot and Doodle died. Carney went back to the house and stayed until they kicked her out for not paying her bills. Or the fed's took it. I can't even remember.

I stayed up all night getting high and talking with Dee while Vicenza Giuliano slept. When he got up, he would eat a little soup and go right back to sleep as if I did not exist. I was so young to be living like this. I cared for Sabrina in the daytime and Vicenza Giuliano would yell at me to keep her quiet. At nighttime, I would just sit and watch TV. Dee had to go back home to get his bills paid up.

I felt like I was in a prison. I would go into the bedroom and yell at Vicenza Giuliano asking him what was he going to do? He would just lie in bed day after day. We could not keep living like this, him in bed every moment and me taking care of the child and just watching TV. He would yell back telling me to leave him alone and if I was unhappy, go out and find someone to satisfy my needs.

Every day the same ol' crap; this was getting old. I did not know how much more of this segregated treatment I was able to take. I felt like I had no life. We went nowhere, all he did was get high and sleep, and we did not talk, or communicate with one another. I could be by myself with Sabrina and not be miserable. I had someone that I could always enjoy, my daughter but I did not get married to be miserable.

I had all these suits, clothes and items only to be stuck up north away from everyone. I hated the country. The seasons were changing and soon it was winter.

Then Christmas came; it was not like the other past Christmas holidays that we had. This one was dry with no company, no presents, no dinner, and no husband. I had bought Sabrina a couple of items. She and I spent it by ourselves. I got her a puppy dog; she wanted one so bad. He was cute, all black with a little white under his neck. We were up with the puppy all night long.

Finally, I went to bed. I was so tired being up with that dog. I went to lie down on the couch to sleep. Sabrina got up and started running around the house. I got up with her. I was really tired and to my surprise, Vicenza Giuliano was high off the v's, I think. He told me to go back to bed and get some sleep. I was really surprised and took him up on it. I went upstairs and lay down.

I was smiling, because I thought Vicenza Giuliano was coming back to himself. So Vicenza Giuliano went downstairs to give Sabrina her breakfast and spend some time with her.

I guess, when he went downstairs, he told Sabrina to leave the dog in his cage until he was ready to use the bathroom, and then he would take him outside. Sabrina did not listen. She took the dog out of the box we had him in and the dog peed all over the brand new carpet.

Vicenza Giuliano became angry, drew a circle on the wall, and made Sabrina stand there until he dismissed her from the wall. That was a form of punishment we would give her, instead of hitting her as my mother did me.

Hours later, I was awoken by a cry in the distance. It was Sabrina, so I got up to see what she was crying about. She was standing against the wall moving from one leg to the other, trying to keep standing. She had been there so long, that she could hardly stand up any longer, so she would lean on one leg and then the other.

Sweat was all down the wall where she leaned her head and had snot running down the wall and sweat. When I came down the stairs, she called my name right away, "Mommy, Mommy."

I asked her why she was up there, she could hardly talk. She was trying to explain and cry all at the same time. Then, I saw Vicenza Giuliano nodded out on the couch. Vicenza Giuliano had spit hanging down from his mouth, his head all down in his chest. Vicenza Giuliano was slumped over on the couch.

I was so mad at him for leaving Sabrina against the wall, before I even knew what I did, I pulled my fist back and reached down to the floor with all my might and anger that had been building up, and hauled off and hit Vicenza Giuliano in the head with my fist, as hard as I could.

He came out of that slumber madder than hell.

"What the F—is wrong with you?"

I asked him why Sabrina was up against the wall. He told me the story about the puppy dog. I expressed that was not enough reason to leave her up there all this time. He stated he put her against the wall at 9:00am. I looked at the clock and started yelling that it was 12:30pm Vicenza Giuliano!!! That child is only three ½ years old. She did not belong up there all that time. We started fighting about it. He told me my child was too damn spoiled. Then we started fighting about that.

I called him a bunch of names like a dope fiend. I further told him that is why you never got with the Mafia, if they knew what a dope fiend you were, they would have never done any business with you; they would've killed you.

Then, I called my brother and told him I could not live with this man any more. Then Vicenza Giuliano tried to take the phone out of my hand. I tried to beat him in the head with the phone. Vicenza Giuliano pulled out his gun while I was on the phone and hit me. Sabrina started crying and I told her to go upstairs. Vicenza Giuliano went into our small bathroom downstairs and was in there for a long time, pulling something a part.

He finally came out and had a box in his hand. I asked him what that was. He told me it was money and he was taking that and the last of the oz's and leaving. I asked him where he was going.

He told me he was going back to Detroit. I stated to Vicenza Giuliano, I know you are not leaving a little baby and me up here without no food or money. He told me that he did not care how we ate or what we did for money.

I told Vicenza Giuliano, he was a dirty bastard that Dee and I made that money for him, that he was not going to walk out on me and leave me and my baby dry. I tried to stop him from walking out the door. He pushed me and I grabbed him and started hitting him in the head. He took the gun and hit me one time hard in the head and it was enough to make it bleed. I still have the scare to this day.

We were outside arguing and hitting each other in the front yard. I was trying to grab the box of money from Vicenza Giuliano. He put it in his car, and locked the door and then walked over to Sabrina who was witnessing all this; grabbed her puppy out of her hand and broke the dog's neck by snapping it and threw the dog down the front yard.

He just killed that dog in front of her. She was crying and I did not know what to do. I made Sabrina go back into the house.

Vicenza Giuliano and I had lost our minds but I did not see how we were going to repair this, and I could not let that man walk out the door. I had to do something fast to keep that from happening. I had to put my pride to the side for me and Sabrina. I did not want us to be abandoned up there. Someone must have called the police, because they came to the house, as I was pulling on Vicenza Giuliano to keep him from leaving. The police talked with us. After they left, I convinced Vicenza Giuliano to come back in the house.

I cried and told him how much I loved him; I did not feel that way but did not want him to leave me up there like that . . . He came back into the house and lay down. I sat there as he went and lay back down in the bed.

I could not get it out of my head what went on between us. I knew that he did not care about us, because he was going to leave us flat, without anything.

I called my brother Rip and told him, I was going to leave Vicenza Giuliano. He tried to talk me out of it. Then I called Dee and told him I was going to leave Vicenza Giuliano and what he did to Sabrina's dog and me. Dee told me Sabrina and I could come down there with him until I got myself together again. I felt better and we talked all night on the phone.

It was a couple weeks later some men came to the house and wanted to talk to Vicenza Giuliano. I called Vicenza Giuliano to the door. I asked the men for I.D. and they stated they were FBI men and flashed a badge. They took Vicenza Giuliano to the side and spoke to him in private. Something was not right about this situation. Then they asked Vicenza Giuliano to stand up against the wall and hold a sign.

Vicenza Giuliano did, as they took pictures but it still did not seem right. It was as if something else was going on. Was Vicenza Giuliano giving these Fed agents information? Why did they come see him? After they left, Vicenza Giuliano told me that an armored car got knocked off and he was under investigation because one of the guys was described like him. I did not believe him for some odd reason.

After they left Vicenza Giuliano went right back to bed. Unreal to me that he could act normal when they were there at the house but go back to his bull crap. He did nothing but lie in that bed 24/7 and get high.

A few months later, I tried to talk to Vicenza Giuliano about me getting a job, he got upset and stated we were fine. I tried to explain to Vicenza Giuliano that he had been lying in this bed since October and it is now February. He became violently angry and did not want to speak on it. I then asked him why those guys were at our house and what was going on with that? Vicenza Giuliano screamed out, to mind my own business.

As I went out the bedroom door I stated, you are my business. I went to the living room again with Sabrina and watched TV. I started crying and could not believe my life came to a stop like this. I was in prison in my own home and had a husband who existed and was not alive. I cried myself to sleep holding Sabrina in my arms.

Later that night I was awakened by someone throwing a rock at the window; it was late at night time or morning hours. I got scared and ran into the room and told Vicenza Giuliano to get up with fear in my voice. I kept shaking him trying to tell him someone was out there and I was scared. Finally, Vicenza Giuliano heard the noise. He jumped up grabbing his gun. He told me to take the baby upstairs.

He walked outside and looked around. There comes a time in your life when you know things are not going to be the same, when you can tell you have 'Come to a place of NO RETURN'.

Then just as I stood in front of the screen door, I saw Vicenza Giuliano by his car and he waved at me to go in the house. I heard a large noise and saw Vicenza Giuliano go down to the ground. It was like a dream. I could see it happening but it looked so unreal. I could hear him in pain as he laid there.

At first I ran inside out of fear then I ran outside turning on the flood lights screaming his name.

I felt so confused inside and knew this was the day I would die.

What was going on?

I realized right then, that I loved him and did not want him to die. What was wrong with my thinking?

Was it the drugs that made me have bad feelings toward my husband over an argument? I heard a car take off down the street. Many things were going through my head but the most important thought was to get him to the hospital and save his life.

I ran into the house and called 911.

Then I got two pillows off the bed downstairs (we had one master bedroom downstairs with a connected bathroom to it and two bedrooms and a playroom upstairs). Our bedroom was the master bedroom adjacent off from the living room. As I got the pillows, I also grabbed a blanket. There was snow on the ground and it got very cold up north this time of the season.

I ran outside and put one pillow under my husband's head and the other one up against his wound. Blood was everywhere! I then placed the blanket over him to keep him warm.

It was taking the ambulance a long to get there, I was afraid Vicenza Giuliano was going to die before it got there. We lived in a small town very far from the main city of Cadillac. We lived right next door to this big white church; our house used to be the preacher's and the town was behind our house. The town consisted of a food store, gas station, two bars and a small restaurant. There was no police station, fire department or hospital in the area. This was a bad situation to get shot in.

There were no more shots; no one attacked me so that the car I heard, must have been the shooters.

Sabrina came to the door, and I told her to get back into the house and away from the door now! So she did. I could tell that Vicenza Giuliano was going into shock. He was shaking and losing color.

I leaned down and told him to hang on and please do not die. I told him how much I loved him and how sorry I was for us fighting.

I yelled at him, "Please fight for life . . . Vicenza Giuliano, Don't give up on me, I love you."

He scared me by grabbing me and holding on to me with a lot of strength stating, "Don't say anything to the rollers when they get here. ***Keep your mouth shut and go clean out the house now, while they are not here yet; get my gun and hide it.***"

I started crying and could not believe he was staying strong like that. Was I wrong, thinking he wasn't a punk? Was I being selfish with my own loneliness and saw what I wanted to believe about him?

I had been sneaking and getting high behind his back for some months now to be able to put up with his bullshit; could it have been the drugs talking to me or motivating me to hate my husband? I began to hate him for his addiction to and what it did to him turning him into a bum. It is funny, you can do things in your life that at the time seems to be what you want but, then, when it really happens, you realize that is not at all, what you wanted. In other words, be careful for what you wish for, because if you get it, it might not be what you really wanted . . . . life has a way of coming back and haunting you for what you wish for.

What drove us to do things like this and then after something happens, you realize the arguments meant nothing. How can you love someone, hate him or her, and still claim that you love him

193

or her? What kind of sick love is that, or am I sick? Lord knows, I did not want to lose Vicenza Giuliano he was all I had in my life besides Sabrina.

Finally, an hour later the ambulance came and took him to the hospital. I cannot believe that man lived. He was shot eight feet away with a 12 gauge shotgun with buck shot. What a will to live.

I stayed by his side all the time he was in the hospital. I wanted him to get out of surgery. I was doing heroin and cocaine, back to back. Sabrina went to my mom's house and I left the lock box over there with the money and Vicenza Giuliano's gun. I told her to hide it.

She asked me what was going on and I told her about the two men. I expressed that Vicenza Giuliano sold drugs for a living. I told her that he had Greasy shot and that's why we moved up north. I also told her about Doodle and Carney getting shot. Tom and my mom took precautions in hiding the money and I went back to the hospital to be by Vicenza Giuliano's side.

I could not sleep, the nurses kept telling me to lie down and get some rest. That they would inform me the minute he came out of surgery and just how well he was doing. However, I could not rest. The guilt alone of our fights was keeping me up. I would hate myself if he died because I wished it so many times. I would never forgive myself.

How did this all get so out of hand? How would I be able to tell him, I did not mean to fight with him? I never thought we would be in this kind of situation. How would I explain that I was lonely and he never paid attention to me anymore? How would I explain that I felt like my life was ending at such a young age because we never spent time together anymore? How would

I explain, that other men paid attention to me at grocery stores, but all I ever wanted, was his attention.

How I wanted to have sex, make love, to him but he was unable to because of the drugs. How do you tell your husband, that inside you felt as if you were dying because there was no more spark and romance? Or that you never went out together anymore or had those romantic dinners. Or went on vacations, or places together anymore, because he was always lying around, getting high to stay normal. That the heroin made his body dead, and he had become an addict. That his desires were so low because of the drugs and you just felt as if your life was being wasted.

I was only 21 years old not ready to sit all day in a house and never talking to anyone, or having anyone to share with; no one to make me feel pretty or to make love to me. No one to take me out, or makes me feel alive. The drugs ruled our life and destroyed what we had. It almost felt like torture having a husband and never being able to enjoy him. It was as if, you could see me, desire me, but you cannot have me or touch me.

I hated we had an argument and he had been shot now, and I am unable to tell him how much I do care. Vicenza Giuliano was in his fifties why did this have to happen now?

I walked around the hospital at night staring at the statues. Sometimes, I think I was tripping because they seemed to be talking to me. I called my brother and told him I was tripping and that the statues were talking to me and they looked like Vicenza Giuliano. My brother told me, I was just having a reaction to the drugs I was on, and to get some sleep and leave the drugs alone. I was hallucinating; I had been up for seven days and seven nights, waiting for him to come out of the coma.

Finally, a breakthrough, the nurse came and told me, he was talking, but they think he was talking in Italian. I ran into his room but he seemed to be very disturbed by my presence when he looked at me entering the room.

I leaned over to hear what he was saying, and he grabbed me by my neck, with a death grip and started choking me, telling me to confess. It took nine doctors and nurses to pull him off me. He pulled his tubes out of his arm trying to choke me.

He felt that I had Dee do this to him. He hated me and there was no way he was going to believe me. He thought because we had that fight I did this to him. It took nine doctors and nurses to pull him off me. I was so upset and could not believe he felt that way. Then I got mad at him and yelled at him, "After all I went through for you and now you are trying to kill me? Are you kidding me?"

The doctors and nurses asked me to leave the room and not to return until they talked with the police department. I was so embarrassed. I went back to the house, got a few items, cried my heart out and went back down to the Detroit area, to my father's house in Farmington Hills. I left Sabrina with my mom and Tom. She was safe there.

My father would know what to do. As I was driving down 94 I nodded off and ran off the road into the gravel. There were a bunch of road block wooden stands with flashers on them. I ran into four of them and one of them ripped off the top of our car. I called a tow truck and had the car picked up. Then I called my brother to assist me. Rip came to my rescue. We went down and got a rent-a-car. My day sucked.

Later I went to Dee's house and Billy started flipping out about someone seeing me there like Henze. I told Billy I did not care if Henze saw me what was the big deal? Billy told me, that Henze had been keeping an eye on the situation with Vicenza Giuliano and he was told by someone that they think it was you.

They have you in the newspaper. I was totally out done and started getting upset stating, "What about Greasy, the one you supposedly shot for Vicenza Giuliano? Why doesn't anyone think he had something to do with it? What about the FBI men that came to the house and talked to Vicenza Giuliano? Why me?"

"Why does the wife always have to do it?"

I only stayed for a moment. Dee asked me where Sabrina was, I told him I left her with my mom for a few days. I told him I had been doing cocaine and heroin back to back and had not slept in seven days.

I expressed to him I was going crazy and what Vicenza did to me in the hospital in front of all the staff. I expressed that Vicenza and I had a fight just a few days before this happened. Dee stated he remembers. I let Dee know that I beat Vicenza Giuliano in the head with the phone and then showed him my cut on my head where Vicenza Giuliano hit me with his gun splitting my head open.

Dee said, "Just calm down, and go to your father's house and get some sleep Billy Joe. Your dad will talk to Vicenza Giuliano."

I expressed to Dee that my heart was hurting because I would have never fought with Vicenza if I knew this was going to happen to him, that I am sick to my stomach wondering if I was going to lose him. I told him it was pissing me off that everyone is blaming me. Dee comforted me and told me to go to my father's.

I left his house and went to a phone booth to make a phone call. As I picked up the phone, someone shot at the phone booth and the glass shattered a crack but it did not hit me. I did not get hurt only a few pieces of glass in my face and hair. I jumped into the car and tried to drive off. I laid down real low in the car and tried to drive out of the parking lot. I felt like that had to be Henze trying to kill me because of Vicenza Giuliano. I didn't know, just wanted to get out of there.

I went to dad's place and told dad what had happen. My brother came over and the three of us talked about what happen. My father said he was going to go talk to Vicenza Giuliano, man to man.

We got in the car and drove up north, my father and me. It was a three hour ride. We got there really late at night. Dad said let's get some sleep and go to the hospital in the morning. While we watched TV, that night, I kept thinking of everything Vicenza Giuliano and I had been through. Where were we going from here and what did the future hold.

Vicenza Giuliano had not been a perfect husband to me. Yeah, I cooked and kept the house clean, did the laundry and raised my child. However, I had been unfaithful and took money out of piles he had stacked up in the closet in his shoes. I would take hundred out of each pile; I took bags of dope he had. I stole a lot from Vicenza Giuliano and lied about where I went, whom I saw. I know that Vicenza Giuliano was not faithful either, and he was doing dope behind my back. He hides money at his daughter's apartment thinking I did not know about it. So as I looked at the whole picture, neither one of us had been very truthful in the relationship or faithful.

Vicenza Giuliano would sell prostitutes spoon and meet them in the bathroom at the Red Dog Bar and have them suck his dick for the spoon of dope. I did not do it for him; I had a big hang up about sucking men's dicks. I just wasn't into that in my young life. I felt like I was enough; I did not have to put my mouth on his private areas, where he peed.

It is funny now, what you felt was nasty as a young girl, changes when you get older. Maybe, you just meet the right one when you are older. (Smile)

Dad slept well I stayed up getting high. I still had not been to bed in eight days now. The next morning we got some coffee and I purchased a pack of Newport cigarettes, and we went up there. Dad went in first; they would not allow me too. The staff at the hospital did not want me to go in and they had a guard at his door. They also notified the police department that I was there.

To my surprise, my mother was in there with Vicenza Giuliano and holding his hand as she talked to him. Dad asked her to give him some private time and then she could come back. Mom tried to tell dad that Vicenza Giuliano felt I did this to him, and she believed it too. Dad did not comment on the issue and just asked her again to excuse him for just a few minutes.

Mom left and started telling me how many days she had been there for Vicenza Giuliano. I told her that was not true because I just left his side yesterday. She walked away as if I had said nothing. She was in the hospital trying to convince Vicenza Giuliano that I did it. She was a trip.

Dad started to talk to Vicenza Giuliano and told him, that (if) I did this, there was no excuse. (If) I was guilty then let him deal with me. My father told him that someone tried to kill me.

He told Vicenza Giuliano, "I know you love her. I also know you love Sabrina so out of the respect of love, which you shared with both, and the respect that you have for me as the father, I am asking that you do not let anyone hurt my baby and let her live. She has a baby to think about Vicenza Giuliano. Who will care for that child? I am too old; her brother is not married. Her sister has her own family. Her mother did not do such a good job with her or she would not have all the issues that she has. I am asking you as man-to-man and father-to-father, do not let anyone kill or harm my daughter."

"I love her more than life itself; she has always been sickly and then her mother wronged her growing up. She has had a hard life, Vicenza Giuliano, and does not know about honor and trust. I am asking you as a man and father, I love my daughter no matter what; don't ever take her life, and promise me you will not. If you want someone to pay, then take my life instead of hers."

Vicenza Giuliano told him that no one would touch me. He promised that.

Then Vicenza Giuliano told my dad to hand him the phone and he called someone and told them no one is to touch his wife. That he would deal with his wife himself. My father thanked him and left the room.

It was all over the newspaper and guess who was behind it, giving the press and police information . . . . yeah you guessed it . . . . my mother. She was right in the middle of all the information they were getting. My mother did not say two words to me in the hallway waiting to go back in. When dad came out, mom went in and the guard would not let me go in. I went to the bathroom and did up some more dope for the ride home.

Dad got all his items together and we rode out. I told dad I did not want to stay in that house. My father said there is nothing wrong with the house Billy Joe. I told him, it just did not feel right and I want to move back home to Detroit.

I spoke on my mother and her hanging under my husband. She has her own husband. Why she is up here with Vicenza Giuliano and what is she doing? Turning him against me? Why? Because she thinks he will have her? So we drove back down to the city.

We were on the highway now, going down on I75. I could hardly keep my eyes open. I kept dosing off. The car ride and no sleep were finally getting to me. I guess, I went off the road too many times and went into the gravel. Dad got scared and grabbed the wheel, which woke me up. I also grabbed the wheel out of reaction.

With us both doing it at the same time, it caused the car to flip off into the middle of the road where the grass was. We tumbled like a weed; it was deep and the car flipped over and started rolling. It was just a little Honda I had rented and it hit something and flew up in the air high above everyone, on the other side of the expressway. As the car flew up in the air, I fell out the door onto the expressway with the other cars coming at me at high speed.

You did not have to wear seatbelts back then; it was not a law yet. I came down on the road and it was as if spiritually someone put their hand out there and scooped me up and pushed me forward. I did not have a scratch on me. I was not even thinking as I got up running after my father; he was still in it, rolling. The car finally stopped and I could see the windshield was busted where my father's head went into it.

My dad's head was bleeding and he was not awake. I started shaking the car, yelling dad, dad, wake up!! Some people stopped to help us. One man stated he was a doctor. Then a nurse stopped, then the fire department got there, and they had to break dad out of the car. He was stuck in there. It was only a little brown Honda and it was banged up on all four sides.

They got dad out, they had to cut him out of there and they dragged him over to the grass to lay him down. They ask him how many fingers were they holding up and what time of the day was it, the year, and who was the president.

Well, dad not only answered all the questions, but he was right on the nose with every answer . . . even the time. Dad did pretty good to be 72 years old. My father was like a Diehard battery.

We had to go to the hospital to make sure everything was okay, a routine checkup after an accident that serious. I just fell out on the ground after knowing my dad was alright.

As we were getting into the ambulance, a man came up to me and said, "Man oh man, I never saw anything like that before, you were flying through the air like superman and landed on your back, and got straight up without a scratch. Girl, God is with you."

It was funny he said that, because I was not a religious/spiritual person but I have to admit, it did feel like someone's hands did touch me and push me up. That feeling haunted me for the rest of my life to believe something was there for me. I can't explain it; I can only know it. I was kind of tripping about that feeling. Was it the drugs or did someone push me up?

We then went to the hospital. My brother was called to the accident; it did not take him any time whatsoever to get up there. My brother must have flown up there. I did not think about dad having flashbacks about Pegleg and him getting into that accident and him dying. But Dad did not want to drive with me any more after that day. The doctor told my brother I was lucky or blessed or both, that the cars coming down the expressway could have smashed me, an article of clothing could have been caught on the car dragging me with it, or the car could have landed on me crushing me. I could have split my head wide open flying like that and landing on the expressway with that much force. He looked at my brother and me, and shook his head saying, "You are one lucky lady. I think the only thing that kept you alive was all the drugs in your system. It kept you from tightening up your muscles and causing you to flow freely. Other than that, I have no other logical reason how you made it out of this."

It was not reported to the police that I was high. I did have to make the police report for the accident. I asked Rip if he would get me another rent-a-car. My brother laughed and said, "Hell NO!"

My dad started telling my brother that he did not want to ride with me anymore. That he felt like I was trying to kill myself because I knew too much and that is how those Mafia women are if they know too much, they kill themselves. My brother tried to tell my dad that wasn't true. However, dad gets something in his head and you cannot convince him otherwise. Dad never did get back into a car with me after that accident either. If he needed to go to the store, he would have one of the other siblings take him.

After my brother dropped dad and I off, I went to get my husband's car out of the shop. It was there being repaired for when I nodded off on Hwy 94 and drove off the side into some wooden roadblocks which then tore the roof off. I can't believe that I had two car accidents within a week's time. By this time, it was repaired and I had Dee take me over there. I got the car and rode back up north after I got some sleep.

Vicenza Giuliano had a setback. His artery busted; he turned all white and the bed turned all red with blood. They would not let me in to see him. While I was in the waiting room, waiting for him to come out of surgery again, a homicide detective came to me wanting to ask a bunch of questions.

I told him to arrest me if he felt I did it or leave me the "F" alone, and walked away. I got into the elevator, went downstairs, and called Dee. I cried to him on the phone and told him Vicenza Giuliano needed arteries. He asked me what he could do to help.

I asked him would he donate some to him. I did not know at that time you could not donate arteries to someone; I was so naive.

Dee came up north to the hospital. When I saw him, I gave him a big hug. I told him I needed a pack of cigarettes.

Dee went downstairs and got a pack for me out of the machine. Two cops arrested him while he was down there. Some witness claimed they saw his car at the scene of the crime the night Vicenza Giuliano was shot. His bail was set at 50,000.00 dollars, 10%. It was 5,000.00 dollars to get him out.

I could not get him out, because he was in there for shooting my husband. How would that look? I went down to Detroit and got a Greek couple that I knew. I asked them to go in the station and get Dee out. I had to keep his wife in the car with me while he went in. To dope fiends, $5,000 dollars was a lot of money. I did not want him trying anything. I kept a gun on his wife. He went in and got Dee. The bad part was, I used the $5,000 that was in Vicenza pocket, with all the blood on it and bullet holes.

They, the cops, knew something was up because they must have known we were riding out of town together. Not to mention I used the money with the blood on it from Vicenza's pocket. I did not care, because we were not guilty.

They had a squad car right outside of town waiting to see if we were leaving together. I did not feel Dee did that to Vicenza Giuliano. We had been friends for a long time and I knew him well. I told Dee that we could set everything straight with Vicenza Giuliano when he got out and his head was clear.

Dee said, "Vicenza Giuliano felt that way about you because of all the arguments you two have been having and that he trained you well, Billy Joe, as a solider in the street life. VG knows you are not to be trusted because you have had a taste of the street life and you are good at it. He does not know you any more as a person because before you depended on VG to survive but he knows you could survive on your own now. So he is insecure with you. He knows you are becoming stronger than him. He knows your survival instinct has kicked in and you don't trust anyone including him, the teacher. He also knows, you will take them out if they get in your way or try to harm you. He is scared of you. VG knows he turned you into a monster, kind of like Frankenstein. I was not to be trusted, because I had gotten a taste of the other side of the fence."

Vicenza Giuliano knew once people got a taste of the power and money, that they would turn against their own mother. Vicenza Giuliano and I was making close to 70,000.00 a month. There was diamonds, cars, motorcycles, toys, any restaurants, furs, furniture, whatever we wanted was at our finger tips. Once you get a taste of that you know the addiction to the life style, you will get rid of anyone in your way. The power of it makes you feel you are untouchable. You become untrustworthy. You do things you normally would not do. Everyone including Vicenza Giuliano was not to be trusted. I slept with Vicenza Giuliano and did not know who I was sleeping next too. He was a man of many secrets. It is a cutthroat world within a cutthroat world.

We got back to the Detroit area, and I let Dee know I was going back in the morning. That night I was blowing some heroin and the Greek man said, "Why are you wasting all that dope? You could just shoot up and save."

I told him I had rhematentic fever when I was younger and I was afraid to have something like that run through my heart. He told me it makes no difference. He showed me how to shoot up. He was right, here I was, blowing enough to fit in the palm of my hand and now I was only using enough to fit on my thumbnail.

I left the next morning for up north. When I got up there, I found my mother sitting with my husband. I do not know why it surprised me that my mother had been sitting up there with Vicenza Giuliano as much as she could.

She now ran an adult foster home in Cadillac on 34 mile road. The police approached me again, trying to ask me more questions.

I finally got them, the police and the hospital staff, to agree to allow me to see Vicenza Giuliano. I sat in the room with him until he woke up. He was surprised to see me. He kept telling me in Italian to get his shoes and money. Vicenza Giuliano had some more money stashed and wanted me to give it to his brother and sisters.

His daughter would not come to see him. She also told me on the phone she felt I was responsible. She stated that her father had put her through so much in life, she was not coming any more. Vicenza's brothers and sisters came up. Acting just like an Italian family, hiding things and making sure no one knew they had his money.

If the cops knew I was doing everything my husband said, how could they think it was me, but I could not tell them our business; how could they think it was me who was trying to kill him. I was caught between a rock and a hard place.

Vicenza Giuliano asked me to get him some V's (valium); he felt he was still kicking. And again, Vicenza had another setback and they found the V's. They found the v's under his pillow and blamed me. They said I was trying to overdose him. I would not have covered him up and put a pillow to his wound, cover him with a blanket if I wanted him to die. With me placing that pillow there, the EMS stated I saved his life. If I wanted him to die I would not have tried to keep him alive.

My mother was talking to the cops every chance she got. Vicenza Giuliano was claiming he was still bogus, meaning he was still withdrawing from the habit. (Being "bogus' is still kicking and being sick from the drug.)

They had given him morphine for the pain, so he might have been having withdrawals. He talked me into getting him some more v's to take, to ease the discomfort. I did and Vicenza Giuliano had another setback with his arteries. I went and talked to the doctor to see why his arteries kept busting. He told me that this hospital was not equipped to handle long-term bullet wounds, that he needed a specialist. I made the arrangements and paid an ambulance to take Vicenza Giuliano down to Ford Hospital in Detroit. They charged me fifty dollars per-mile. They would not allow me to ride with him in the ambulance and when I got down to the Hospital, his brother met Vicenza Giuliano down there. He told them at the nurses' desk that I was not allowed to see him.

I was hurt that Vicenza Giuliano felt this way about me. I just tried to keep the business going and waited until Vicenza Giuliano's health was better so he would have his mind together. Didn't Vicenza Giuliano know, it was me that covered him up with a blanket and put a pillow in his stomach to stop the blood? It was me who paid to send him to Ford Hospital. If I tried to kill him, why would I do everything to save him?

I got an apartment in Escorse, Detroit. I gathered some people together and moved all the furniture down there. I closed out the house and paid a person to winterize the pipes. Vicenza Giuliano was in the hospital for a long time. I worked and put Sabrina in pre-school. I sold drugs on the side. I made ends meet. When Vicenza Giuliano was ready to come home, I was surprised when his brother called and told me Vicenza Giuliano wanted me to pick him up.

I went as fast as I could to the hospital and I was very excited. I kept thinking he forgave me for the fight and we were going to be a family.

He was shot down in the lower abdomen and his left leg. The wound on the left leg was from his knee to his groin. It was about five inches wide and about a foot and a half long. He wore a colostomy bag. He had buckshot's coming out of his penis when he went to the bathroom. Sex was hard for him to perform. His penis could never get completely hard any more. I did not care; I was going to stay with him regardless. The sex was no longer an issue, because of the situation. I cleaned his incisions and colostomy bag. I took care of his every need. I helped him to get up every day and walked with him to bring his strength back. Vicenza Giuliano was getting better each day and was even getting around to more places.

We had got him some crutches and I cleaned out his wounds every day and night. Sometimes, when I went to change the colostomy bag, feces would go everywhere because he was not able to control it. The doctor stated he would not have to keep it forever.

We got ourselves together again. We received a call about going up north for a preliminary hearing. Dee's case came up and they wanted Vicenza Giuliano to sign an affidavit concerning me. We went up north and my mother was there with the Giuliano and the Chief of Police. The Chief of Police approached me stating I may be next. I looked over at my mother and knew she had told them something.

I walked over to my mother and asked her what she told them. She fumbled with her words stating I had to tell them the box you hide at my house. I expressed, "You don't even know what was in there. The box was locked, so what the f—did you say?"

My mother assured me she had to look inside to make sure what I had in their home. She told me, "We broke into it. Billy Joe, there was a gun and money in that box. I told them I believe you were hiding the evidence there."

I got so angry with her I could not see straight.

"Mother! You, senseless woman! Vicenza Giuliano was shot with a shotgun! Not a 38!"

I then looked my mother in the eye and told her, "If you are their witness and you testify to this shit, you better hope to God I don't get my hands on you because for sure I'll be going to prison for life after I tear you from limb to limb before they carry me out of this courtroom. You have opposed me and beaten me my whole life. You will not manipulate this situation or me anymore."

Everyone got on the stand and stated the same thing, "Lack of memory" including my mother.

Vicenza Giuliano signed an affidavit that I did not have anything to do with the shooting of him. That was the end of their case. I still have that paper to this day.

Vicenza Giuliano and I left for our Escorse apartment and Vicenza Giuliano said nothing to Dee. I tried to talk to Vicenza Giuliano on the way home but he would not talk. He was not ready. We went home and Vicenza Giuliano got another connection with Ju-Ju Bean in Hamtramck. They referred to him as Big Bowie. He was a big man with a bald head, living with his mother. He also wore a colostomy bag. Big Bowie was a Polish man and could be mean as hell; he was no one to play around with.

Someone blew his car up with him in it a long time ago, and he had worn a bag ever since. He also kept a pre-starter for his car. He never started his car up after that. He had a person working for him named Blackie. They called him that because he had really white hair and he had no tan at all.

Meanwhile back at our apartment, Eddy (the one I had the blind date with when I met Vicenza Giuliano) was just released from the joint and called wanting to do some business. I did it with him, but he kept coming back wanting a larger amount. Vicenza Giuliano knew he was working for the man (DEA), but he did not tell me. I invited Eddy over to talk with Vicenza Giuliano about more weight.

When they went into the bedroom and discussed it, Vicenza Giuliano kept telling him he had to go through me. He stated that he did not know what he was talking about. I did not know it at the time, but Vicenza Giuliano was setting me up to take a fall. Eddy was wired and bought from me several times. Vicenza Giuliano would not have anything to do with him, so because of that, I would not sell him the weight. The DEA does not want to mess with small amounts nor do they want the middle man, they wanted the head honchos. Something was not right and it was strange that Vicenza Giuliano would pass up a weight sale. Eddy was in jail on a couple robbery charges, and I think pending murder cases. The Feds wanted a few people so they released Eddy to make those deals with the ones they wanted. They were going to drop charges against Eddy if he turned state's evidence.

Vicenza Giuliano was getting ready to go out and the phone rang. I answered it and it was Danny a guy I knew from school. He told me he was with Alan and they wanted to come over to get some weed. I asked Vicenza Giuliano if we had any to give them and he told me yeah about a quarter bag. I let them know on the phone. It was great seeing Alan; he had his wife with him. He got married to a pretty young girl. Danny had a girl with him. I was not sure if it was his wife or not. Alan asked me why I was with this hood. I told him he was good to me. Alan told me I could do better and he only wanted me to be happy. It was great to see

Danny and Alan from my past but that was the last time I saw either one of them.

Vicenza Giuliano left to go take care of business. He would go to the bars and do his regular routine. He'd call me when he was ready to come home. I just could not believe that if Vicenza Giuliano felt I was guilty of that shooting, why he was staying with me. We slept together and we were sort of back like a family again. You could tell things were different between us now but we were a family again. Vicenza Giuliano was still using but his habit was not as bad as before.

Later that evening Vicenza Giuliano called home, I told him I was waiting. When he knocked on the door, I looked out the peek hole and opened the door when I felt it was safe for him. Just as I opened the door, someone came running down the hallway and pushed Vicenza Giuliano into the house onto the floor. My husband's stitches broke open and the intruder had a gun.

I jumped behind the kitchen table out of fear and realized that I left Sabrina up there in the living room. I slowly got up and kept telling the person to be cool, that we would do whatever he wanted just let me get my daughter. My heart was going so fast, I could feel my body shaking.

I walked slowly over to Sabrina with my hands in his eye sight and stood in front of her. She was standing up with her hands in a tight fist position. She did not move an inch the whole time that person was there. He had a nine-millimeter gun on us with a silencer. He kicked Vicenza Giuliano telling him to get up. He prodded us to go into the bedroom where we kept our stuff.

I kept thinking this was life as I knew it, Sabrina would see me get shot. Vicenza Giuliano told me to get the stuff out of the closet and give it to him. Then he gave him what money he had in his pocket.

When I went to the closet, I saw our gun up there. The person still had the gun on Vicenza Giuliano. I went to pick up our gun but realized it did not have any bullets in it. Vicenza Giuliano kept them separate because of Sabrina being in the house.

I looked at Vicenza Giuliano and he told me no by shaking his head. The person saw him, started to go crazy with excitement, and wanted me to come on and get the stuff NOW. He told me to put it in his pocket. I could not fit the entire bottles in his pocket.

We kept our dope in small dark brown bottles to allow it to breathe better. So I laid them on the bed. Then he told me to stand over there by Vicenza Giuliano. I did.

He yelled at Vicenza Giuliano, "I know you have more money than that."

Vicenza Giuliano told him he could search, but he just got out of the hospital and we were not yet on our feet.

The person picked up the bottles, backed up and left the house without harming us. I just knew I was going to die that night. I was scared as he went out the door. I wasn't scared while it was going on.

As soon as he left, Vicenza Giuliano grabbed the gun and loaded it with bullets and told me to lock the door and do not let anyone in, no matter what. If he was not back within twenty minutes, to call the police for protection for me and the baby and do not come looking for him. I did as he asked.

As soon as the robber left, Sabrina flew through the hallway into her room, covered up her head, and would not come out. All she kept saying was Uncle Dee was out there. I asked out where? She stated outside the window.

Later when Vicenza Giuliano came back, I told him what Sabrina kept saying. He questioned her in addition, about what she saw outside the window. I could not believe that Dee was a part of that. That person could have gotten scared and shot us. I was angry with Dee and wanted to talk with him concerning this. Vicenza Giuliano did not see any one out there, but he did spot some Fed's in a car watching our apartment.

He took me outside and we talked, he told me to get everything ready to move by Sunday. I asked him why Sunday? He told me that Fed's do not work Sundays. I went back in and started packing.

I could not believe Dee was a part of this! Was Dee part of that crap up north? Was I blind to who Dee was when drugs were involved? Many questions were going through my head.

We found a nice house in Wyandotte to rent with a backyard and basement. We moved in that Sunday. We still paid our taxes on the house up north every year. Everything was going back to normal; at least I thought it was.

One night when I was shooting up some dope, I felt like I had been given a hot shot. I jumped into the shower and turned on cold water. Vicenza Giuliano asked me what I was doing. I asked him was he trying to give me a hot shot. If he was, I was not going to go down like that. I told him, you would never tell my father and child that I O.D. on drugs. Vicenza Giuliano sat on the toilet crying stating he would not kill me. He wondered why I felt that way.

I told him because you believe I shot you.

Vicenza Giuliano became emotional and stated, "I believe that dirt rat Dee—." He shut up and did not finish his statement. We did not talk about it again.

Life went on and I was beginning to feel like I was an awful mother. I did so many things I wish I had not of done. After we got robbed, Sabrina was scarred by that situation. I did not make things any better for her. I would yell at Sabrina for no reason. One time, she woke up and was entering my room to tell me she was hungry when I unleashed on her. Addiction will turn you into a person you do not know. I cussed her out for coming in my room without permission. I only did that because I was shooting up and did not want her to see me.

I was doing uncut dope so I was really flying. Back then they referred to it as China White. We were able to take two grams and place 26 grams of mostly lactose and sometimes other things to cut the purity down giving us 28 grams for an oz. Sometimes we would only do 26 grams called a Mexican oz.

Anyways, Sabrina got hurt feelings by the way I responded to her and went into the kitchen and tried to make herself something to eat. She made a mess in there; milk, cereal, eggs were all on the floor. I punished her for it and screamed at her at the top of my lungs. She just stood there shaking. I knew then, I needed to quit drugs but mentally I was not ready to leave dope alone.

My older sister called up wanting to know if Sabrina could come to a family outing with her. She agreed to pick her up and asked for me to get a beach bag ready for her.

I put a few things in a see-through beach bag as I got Sabrina together. Then, my sister Paula called stating she would be there in five minutes. They picked Sabrina up and spent hours at the beach with her. My sister Paula was pissed because she found my bloody needles in the beach bag. That was surprising, because I don't ever remember putting them in there. This incident always made me wonder if Sabrina was grabbing my needles and hiding them from me.

I was surprised that Paula even picked Sabrina up because usually they did not even allow me over at their house. I was just flabbergasted that she called asking for my daughter to go with them. Vicenza knew I was doing dope but not shooting up. I really don't ever remember placing it in a beach bag. You know how some kids will hide their parents cigarettes, well may be that is what Sabrina was doing.

I was such a dope fiend I was ashamed of myself. There were times I did not even want to take a shower. My body was dead inside, but it also kept my sex drive down, so that I did not bother Vicenza. He would still perform oral sex with me to keep me satisfied. I did not want him to feel he had to do that.

The next day, I took myself to a couple of methadone clinics to clean myself up. I choose two of them, because one was not enough for my habit. I was tired of being a dope fiend. I was going to clinic every day and cutting five milligrams every week from my dose myself. I would wake up sick and go to bed sick. I took a needle and drew out 5ml. every two weeks.

It would take my body three days to even feel the amount gone. Then it would take another four days or so to balance my system out. I was determined to get off the drugs. Vicenza Giuliano was still struggling with his, but he was not as bad as he was up north. He was healing very well; he was no longer using the crutches.

One night when Vicenza Giuliano and I went to bed, I woke up full of sweat and screamed out. Vicenza Giuliano woke up too and asked me what was wrong? I told him I had a nightmare and it was about Sabrina. I told him, that we were going to the methadone clinic and as we were crossing the street, Sabrina got away from me and was hit by a car. I told Vicenza Giuliano, I could see her bouncing around under the car and then getting thrown out from underneath to the street curb. I expressed how panicked I felt not being able to help her, while she was trapped under that car. I told Vicenza Giuliano it was so real, that I could actually feel myself there.

Vicenza Giuliano tried to calm me down and to go back to bed. I did, but I could not stop thinking about that dream. Many times my dreams have come true, sometimes not exactly like I dreamt it. I took them as a warning.

Vicenza Giuliano and I went to the methadone clinic. I would hold Sabrina's hand tight crossing the street as we went into the clinic. When we got there, Vicenza Giuliano stood in the lobby with Sabrina while I was buzzed in at the door to approach the window where they kept the medication (methadone). I was behind bullet proof glass and you had to be buzzed into the room. Once you were in you could not open the door, you had to be buzzed in and out for security reasons.

While I was getting my medication, I heard a noise and looked out the window and saw Vicenza Giuliano standing there with Sabrina as a man came rushing in and bumped into Sabina and Vicenza knocking them over.

Sabrina fell to the ground and Vicenza Giuliano fell on top of her. Then the man fell on top of Vicenza Giuliano and he was holding a cue stick in his hands while another man charged right behind them with a gun. The man with the gun followed so closely on the heels of the man with the cue stick, that when they entered through the door simultaneously the man with the cue stick fell on Sabrina and my husband.

The other man with the gun hit the man with the pool stick in the head, and he fell when he opened the door to get away from him. The pool stick man began bleeding profusely.

Sabrina was trapped on the bottom of the floor with Vicenza Giuliano on top and that man on top of Vicenza Giuliano. I tried to get out the door but the woman behind the bullet proof window was scared and would not buzz me out to get to my daughter. I kept pulling on the door while cussing the lady out, telling her to let me out. After the man with the gun left and Vicenza Giuliano got the other man off of him, the lady finally let me out.

I did not even think about the consequences, I ran after the dude with the gun, cussing him out down the street about fighting in front of my daughter and almost killing her. He was almost two blocks down when I started chasing after him. Vicenza Giuliano ran after me, yelling at me that the guy I'm running after has a gun. I tell you when it is mother's love, a mother does not care what someone has; she is about taking care of her baby. The man turned around and looked at me and yelled out, "Sorry, lady", but he kept traveling so I could not catch up to him.

Vicenza Giuliano jumped in the car with Sabrina and came after me. Vicenza Giuliano was yelling, "Get in this car." So I did and we went home. Vicenza Giuliano kept telling me on the way home;

"What is wrong with you Billy Joe? You can't beat up the whole world. Sometimes you can't stop destiny."

I repeated over and over to Vicenza Giuliano that incident was my dream. I kept having flash backs of that dream when that happen. In the dream, I could not get to Sabrina under you and that guy she was under, was that car. It was weird because it was my dream.

Vicenza Giuliano went down and purchased another car from the police pound. In order to purchase a car from the police pound, you had to have license as a car dealer. Vicenza knew a guy that ran and owned a used car lot. They went to a police pound auction to get it. He got a really great deal. He brought home a beautiful 89 Oldsmobile car, fully loaded with crushed velvet seats.

Vicenza Giuliano ran into one of our customers who revealed that his girl threw him out and Vicenza Giuliano stated he could stay with us. Vicenza only agreed with this to get all of his money from this guy who had a game hustling hub caps off cars for money.

He brought us a lot of money. His name was Aaron and he stole hub caps from cars. He sometimes, would make anywhere from three to four hundred dollars a night. Vicenza Giuliano only allowed him to stay, because he did not want to lose that spoon action.

Aaron was around 6'2 tall, very skinny, dark black hair with a pointy nose, brown eyes and black mustache with gave him a cartoon look. He was a weak man with a lot of insecurities, and very sneaky. I really never cared for him but would not go against Vicenza about his decision to allow him to stay. What Aaron spent on spoons from us, we made three or four times over what we made selling lids. So I understood Vicenza's reason but something did not seem right to me. It was all profit when we sold spoons. I knew Vicenza's greediness; he only did that to get more from him.

I hated that Aaron was sleeping on the couch. I could never walk in the kitchen wearing my exotic lingerie. I loved looking good all the time. It was a big inconvenience to have him there as far as I was concerned.

A few weeks went by and we were in bed sleeping and the next thing I know we had four men in our bedroom. They were U.S. Feds. They had a warrant for both of us and our car. We had five oz's of cocaine in the window to stay cold as it was winter time. We were buying the coke from my old boss T.J. Norton that owned the bar where I worked at. Years later, T. J. Norton got busted under the Rico Law and did time until 1996.

I started yelling I needed to get dressed and while I was yelling about the issue, I made my way over to the window ledge and grabbed the cocaine and shoved it down in my panties. They were all men and I did not know it at that time but there was no woman with them which was required if I was to be searched. They let me go into the bathroom and get dressed. I was surprised when I came out because Vicenza Giuliano was sitting at the kitchen table eating breakfast with the U.S. Marshalls. They were just sitting there talking to him as if they were old friends. I had dumped all the cocaine in the toilet and flushed it down washing the toilet out with bleach to take the smell out. They did not even search the house, so that wasn't even necessary.

I found out later that they had gotten in because Aaron let them in. He said, he thought they were somebody else. The DEA's were dressed like gangsters, one even had long hair. They did not look like officers. We went downtown to the federal building and got booked in. They let me go on a personal bond and let Vicenza Giuliano out on cash bond. It is funny that they never took Aaron with us or arrested him but he was in the dope house with us.

A month later, they took Vicenza Giuliano in for a parole violation. Vicenza Giuliano had called all his connections and asked them to do business with me. He referred to me as the "Ice Maiden." (I did not know this until later.) He assured them that I was a stand-up woman, that I took care of business and that I was not afraid of anyone. He also told them that I was so mean, that I could look someone in the eye and shoot them and think nothing of it and then care for their wounds later.

Of course, this was not true, but for some odd reason, that is how Vicenza Giuliano and his friends saw me. Vicenza Giuliano told me where all the money was hidden in the house. I sent him a few hundred and purchased a nice car. I started taking care of business for us. I dealt with Bowie in East Garfield Park until things got too hot over there. Bowie liked me because Vicenza Giuliano owed him thousands of dollars from our last pick up. Bowie stated he would get it from Vicenza Giuliano. I told him I was Vicenza Giuliano's wife and I would take care of the bill. So I did. And that gained me a lot of credibility with the people on the streets.

One day when I went over there, I was not able to use the front door. I went to the back and parked my car down the alley because I knew Bowie was hot. I had on 3" high heels, which was a normal thing for me. They usually were 3 to 4 inches high along with either suits, pantsuits, or dresses.

I tried to get in the back gate because I knew Bowie's house was being watched. Then out of nowhere, I saw a car coming toward me. It looked like a fed car. It had four people in the car. I was not going to take any chances, so I started walking fast, back down the alley toward my car. The faster I walked, the faster the car kept coming up on me. I started running, and the car speed up. So I leapt a fence about four feet high, high heels and all.

The next thing I know, I heard someone calling out my name. It was Bowie in someone else's car. He laughed and so did the guys he was with. He told me that he never would have believed that I could run and jump a fence like that. He was impressed. We did business and Bowie told me he was getting ready to shut down. His main person was busted a couple weekends ago. His main person got into an argument and shot this person in a bar called the Corner Pub, in East Garfield Park. Then his boy was riding down the street and a cop pulled him over for a backlight being inoperable.

The officer told him that something was stuck and if he opened the trunk, that he would check it out for him. His main man did not want to open the trunk. The officer could tell that something was not right and told him to open it. When he did, there was the shotgun used in the shooting and a bunch of lids of heroin in the truck. When they arrested him, they took the oz's and checked them for fingerprints and traced it back to Big Bowie.

Bowie told me that when they questioned him, he told them, someone came over and borrowed some baggies, he counted each one out to them, and that must be why his prints are on them. From then on, the feds placed Big Bowie under investigation. That is why there so much heat over here.

I went down to Fort Street in Detroit to see Benny. He was a big wheel in the Detroit area, and used to be one of the biggest dealers a long time ago in the Cass Corridor area.

They referred to him as King of Cass Corridor. He was now hanging around John's Pop Top Bar on Fort Street in Detroit. I believed that Benny owned it and just let Henze run it for him. I went there and asked if he would help me out and let him know I was Vicenza Giuliano's wife. I had met him before but wanted to remind him who I was. He told me to have my husband call him from the joint.

When I told Vicenza Giuliano the next time he called, he told me not to worry about that petty crab because he had someone that was bigger. He stated that Benny's days were numbered because he had beat a cat named Donny the Greek out of some dough.

I went over to Blair and Denise's house. They lived on the Southside of Detroit. They were a couple whom we sold to and did business with here and there. Blair was an idiot, and looked like a weasel that no one liked. Denise was dizzy as hell. Both of them would sell heroin to pay for their own habits.

I walked up to the door and it looked as if someone kicked it in. I still knocked on the door. Denise answered in her night clothes. I walked in and the kitchen and house looked like a dive. I asked her what the Fu—happened in here? She stated that the DEA and Feds busted in and went through their house.

I looked at her and stated, "Dammit, I am out of here. I am on bond with the fed's."

It was not long after this that Denise was found by the police at the Crestwood Hotel parking lot in Detroit all shot up. The police went to her house to notify relatives and found her husband Blair, her brother and children were taken out too. Only one child, I believe, was left alive because that child was too young to testify. That child was in the closet. Not sure where the child was at the time of the shooting but the kid did know what went down. So I knew I had to look for something else. Blair & Denise were snitches on our federal case and everyone else's.

Vicenza Giuliano had an associate that was of Greek descent and doing financially well for himself with narcotics and other businesses he invested in. He agreed to work with me. His name was Acacius. He did not want me dealing with Benny because he had heard in the joint Benny was a dead man walking.

I met Acacius once in a while back before Vicenza Giuliano went to prison. He walked around the yard with Vicenza Giuliano and talked. Acacius was a few years older than Vicenza, a short man with a full head of gray hair. He was only 5'4 and was mean as hell. He was full-blooded Greek and lived down the street from his mother's house. She knew what he did for a living and she was a bit of a gangster herself. The first time she met me, she kept telling Acacius something about me in Greek. I could tell the way she was saying it, it was not good or nice. (Smile)

Everyone called him Cassius. Sometimes I called him Cassius or Acacius. Cassius was very strange and did not trust anyone but his mother. He worried about me when he first started doing business with me. He had me met him at places, but when I arrived, I would have to call him. Then he would tell me to put the money in different locations. Then leave, and go to another area, and pick up the dope. This was a pain in the butt but I did it because he had the best dope in town and everyone wanted it. Finally, he started coming around and dealing with me little by little. I was glad when he just started dealing with me on the up-n-up and on a personal level.

I remember one time, he told me to meet him at the K Mart parking lot over on Main Street. I was driving like crazy to get there because I had a customer I had to deal with before I went, so it caused me to be a bit late. He could not stand it if anyone was late. If one was late, he would just up and leave. I drove like a mad woman. Then as I was going down the road, shit . . . . the traffic was congested. I got mad and started driving the side of the road on the shoulder around all the traffic. Oh course, I was pulled over by the police and got a ticket for reckless driving on Main Street.

I got to the parking lot and sat there for a few minutes. I did not know that Cassius was off somewhere watching to see if anyone drove up with me, or if I was alone. He pulled up and told me to get in his car, and then as I was pulling the door shut, I heard a click.

He had a gun pointing at me asking why I was so late. I told him, I had a ticket in my pocket. He had me pull it out slowly. After he read the ticket and saw the date and time, he un-cocked the gun and put it away. I was sweating my butt off thinking . . . . What kind of weirdo am I mixed up with?

As time went on, we became good friends and I made him a lot of money, enough, where he was able to buy a couple of new houses in Dearborn. I did more business than anyone that worked with him.

I rode down and see Vicenza Giuliano for three days every other week. He was at Springfield Mo., at a federal prison. It was a convict medical facility. He was first locked up at Detroit Federal Joint where I was able to bring him packages, like cocaine, weed, money and methadone pills. Frank was up there too. On the street, they called him The Head Chopper. Everyone in Detroit knew the Head Chopper. He and Vicenza Giuliano knew each other, and when I would visit sometimes. I would meet Frank's wife and children. I visited Vicenza as much as possible in Detroit.

One day when I left the Detroit facility they did a shake down on Vicenza. Vicenza was caught sneaking a package in. They did not even let Vicenza's feet hit the compound. They sent him directly to Springfield, Mo. That is how he ended up down there.

That guy Aaron who stayed with my husband and I, was still living at the house in Wyandotte. Vicenza allowed this man Aaron to stay there after he went to the joint. I really did not like him living at the house but allowed it. Aaron had a 300 dollar habit a day. So that was 2100.00 dollars a week that Vicenza Giuliano made off from him. He wanted him right there in the house to get that money. So when they took Vicenza Giuliano to prison for that parole violation. (They did it because of having guns in the house.) They also took our car because they believed it was used in the commission of a felony of selling drugs . . . . Aaron stayed there with me and Sabrina regardless of Vicenza going to prison. I agreed with Vicenza and allowed Aaron to stay there because now I was getting that 2100.00 a week from his drug habit.

I made plans to visit with Vicenza so Sabrina and I went to see Vicenza in Springfield Mo. I would give my dope to Dee or Gene my friend from the Marlow House. Yes, I was back doing business with Dee behind Vicenza's back. He told me he did not rob us or shoot Vicenza. I wanted to believe him and did.

Sometimes I would leave Sabrina with Gene and Kathy his wife. They had three children. They lived in the Brightmoor area. Gene used to work for the Motor Car Industry. They were doing well until he got laid off and he started selling dope for me to make ends meet. One time Gene and Kathy wasn't able to watch Sabrina, so I asked Aaron to look after the business for me. Sabrina and I made a vacation out of it. Aaron never did me wrong before, but there is always a first time for everything.

In the conduct of my drug business, I would wrap each amount of dope, for each house, in cocaine paper, which was bought at head shops. It keeps the dope from losing potency. If you wrap it in aluminum fold, it loses strength. I would take a box of matches, and open them up. I would then slide the wrapped dope in the back of the matches and close them back up. Then take tape and wrap each one. This way, the tape would not rip the dope open. I gave Aaron a couple of packs for himself as a gratuity and he had the run of the house while I was gone. I had about seven dope houses in Brightmoor and a couple in Detroit to supply.

Sabrina and I packed up as always. I threw the unused matches on top of the dining room China cabinet. We got into the car and left for Springfield, Mo. It was a long trip, but we stopped and did a lot of sightseeing. We were gone for a whole week. We went to the Jessie Tom Wax Museum and many other places. We had a great time. We also visited Chucky Cheese. It was a place for kids to play and order food, have parties and just express their selves. I would take Sabrina in with me to see Vicenza Giuliano.

The first day I went, I attended a hearing for Vicenza Giuliano to state on record that the guns found in the house were mine. That was to clear Vicenza Giuliano of all charges. However, it did not work out that well, because he still had to do his parole violation; he was not allowed to be around guns. We enjoyed our visit but it had been a week living in a hotel it was time to go back home.

We loaded the car and headed home. We stopped on the way at many other locations for sightseeing. Sabina and I were bonding, enjoying the time away from the rat race. When I arrived home, it felt great to unwind. Dee came over with some steaks and began to start the barbeque outside; Dee asked me for some matches. I jumped up on the chair to get some and saw many ripped up matches on top of the cabinet.

I looked at them very closely. You could tell that I had dope wrapped in them and someone pulled the wrapping off and rewrapped it with a new match book. I looked outside watching Aaron helping Dee and knew in my heart, that he had opened all the packs of dope pinched out of them and rewrapped them. Immediately, I started calling my customers to see if there were any complaints. Many of the customers did, stating that the dope was weak and not enough of it. It all came together when we arrived home.

I could tell Aaron did not feel well, he looked sick. I asked him if he was okay, he told me he had caught a cold. I looked at his hair and knew it looked really greasy. All of this started running through my head and I became outraged.

I called Aaron in the house. I showed him the matches that I had found tampered with. I asked him for the truth. He started lying to me. That just pissed me off even more. I don't know where it came from, maybe it was out of pure anger. I took my fist while standing on the chair and hit Aaron dead in his face. I jumped down off the chair; I busted his nose on the first hit and the blood went everywhere, it scared him and he grabbed his nose. I took advantage of his surprise and kept hitting him, repeatedly, one punch after another. Maybe it was his guilt too that made him stand there and take it. He stood about, 6'1 about 155lbs, and skinny because of the drugs.

I kept hitting him until he fell against the stove, hitting his face and stomach area; it's called a beat down. When he bent over, I used both hands and clasped them together and hit Aaron on the back of his head, while he was bent over. He went down to the ground. Then I started kicking Tommy with my foot, I kicked him in the ribs several times. He just balled up in a fetal position. Dee came in the back door. He was very surprised; he started laughing while pulling me off Tommy; he stated he wished he could have witnessed all of it.

Dee was a fool with a weird sense of humor. He knew I had a bad temper and I was a fighter but him seeing me beat up a man, that just put things over the fence for him. Well Aaron was so embarrassed he grabbed his things and left. What I did not know was he went downstairs and grabbed my lockbox and took that with him. It had my pearl handle .38 short nose gun in it, a couple thousand in cash and about a half an oz of dope.

After he left the house, I tried to run after him to keep him from going worried that he might go to the police. Dee went downstairs and realized that Tommy took the lock box. We went everywhere we knew he hung out; we could not find him anywhere. We checked with people, we both knew, checked at places he sold his hubcaps to. He kept a very low profile.

I left a few messages for him to get in touch with me before I caught up with him. (I cannot answer **what** I would have done if I had caught up with him. Either I was going to beat him down again or have him 'check out' to make an example out of him. In my mind frame, I cannot answer that because I was becoming the role I was playing. My conscience was leaving and my attitude was becoming cold.)

I had to get some work done on my car so I placed it in the shop. They set up a rent-a-car for me. Dee and I had to go down to Detroit to make a sale on Fort Street, and Green area. The person I was supposed to meet was to be in front of this store. He was not there. Dee and I always arrived early to case the joint out. Something was not right; I felt it deep down in my gut. I asked Dee to go stand in front of the store to see if that would make a difference.

They did not want Dee they were waiting for me. After about 30 minutes, Dee flagged me to pick him up. As I pulled up to get Dee, I leaned over to open his passenger door and just as I leaned down, a car came fast around the corner and shot at the driver's side.

I was very lucky; the angels of the Lord were with me that day. Dee jumped in the car hollering at me, while hitting the dashboard of the car to take off as he was jumping in. The door was not even shut. As I left the area, the car followed me, trying to get to the side of us to shoot. I kept putting on the brake and speeding up to keep them from getting parallel to us. It reminded me mentally of that night Vicenza and I got chased home.

I knew they were trying to come along the side of us—to kill us. My heart was beating with shock and fear. My hand was shaking on the wheel, it was uncontrollable. I felt more secure when it had happened with Vicenza. I was feeling as if I was in a movie but the only difference was . . . . this was real life, and I could not turn off the channel.

This might have been my destiny, the end of my existence. They tried to push us off the road several times trying to kill Dee and myself. As I said before, the angels were with us. We drove up on a few lawns pulling wheelies on the Southwest Side of Detroit. We tried to get away from them. I am not sure, but I think the people in the houses, whose lawns we drove up on, called the police.

When the other car heard the police coming, they went down another street; we went through the alley. We had a few dents on the rental car; the damage occurring when they smashed into us a few times. Dee and I slowed the car down and rode under the speed limit to keep the police from thinking it was us. They followed us for a minute on the next street. Finally, they turned off and went the other way. Dee and I were able to breathe again.

I went to a phone booth and called Joe up, the guy I was meeting to do business with. He had been to Vietnam during the war and had become a heroin addict over there and remained one after he got out. He hung out at the Carnival Bar by Clark Park off Vernon Highway in Detroit.

I lived down there with my first husband for several years. He tried to tell me he had nothing to do with that situation. I knew that was bullsh—. He tried to tell me people he owed did that. I figured then he was selling me out to cash in his debt. I never saw Joe after that. I went into the Carnival a few times but never saw him.

The last time Dee and I were in the Carnival, we sat down, ordered a drink and some guy fell on me. I thought he was drunk. I pushed him off as a reaction and when I turned around on my bar stool, another guy came running at the man who fell on me. With a thrust, he stabbed the person again, (the one who fell on me). His guts' were hanging out. The person behind the bar, started pushing everyone out of the bar and calling the police. I drank my drink down and left out of there as well.

Clark Park was across the street, kitty corner. It was getting to be a bad area then. Sabrina's father belonged to the Clark Park gang. He wore a tattoo cross on his left hand with three dots above the cross. That was their little sign.

As the excitement was over, we rode back to the house; Dee and I had to make up the thousand dollars that Aaron took out of the packaged dope. You just cannot tell the dope man, that you got robbed. He doesn't care, just get his freaken' money.

We fixed all the packages of dope up. Usually, I would cut the dope for my extra earnings. Not this time. This time, I left it open for them to get some Mac attack dope. I knew in the beginning I would come out ahead, because once they got hooked on that good dope, I could put my cut on it later by bringing it down a bit. They would just assume that they were getting used to it and just had to do more; every dope dealer does that.

I just needed to get my clientele happy again. Little by little, everyone would be satisfied and things could go back to normal. I would have to take a little cut on my intake of income, but in the end; I would come out smelling like a rose.

This black chick I knew called me up wanting some cocaine. I invited her over which I don't usually do. She came in and wanted some shake. (Just the powder of the cocaine). I pulled out an oz and showed it to her. She asked if I had some rubber gloves. You never want to touch the dope because of the oils in your hand. I turned around and heard a sniff. Turned back around and saw white powder on her nose and a white streak on her black shirt, going to her pocket.

I am thinking to myself; "Are you kidding me bitch? How are you going to play me in my own house."

I was pissed off. I just shook my head and laughed. She looked at me with puzzled.

I walked over to the bed and grabbed her pocket and asked her what the fuck is this? As she was trying to explain, I pulled my gun out from under my arm. I told her to give me the rock back NOW. She did and asked if she could leave. I walked her out of the house with the gun on her. This was just another day at work. That was my fault; you never let an addict come to your crib. You never hang with an addict or make them your friend. They are the customer. You are a different caliber than them.

Dee and I took care of all the clientele and they were happy. I saved my business. Life in the underworld but real life still goes on.

Sabrina's birthday was coming up. Dee and I went to a parade with Sabrina and she fell in love with the horses. She must have had it in her blood, because my father loved horses, and so did I. There were quarter horses and ponies. Sabrina became so excited by this that it made me run up to the guy and ask what he charged for a birthday party. He gave me some prices and I made a deal with him to bring the ponies and quarter horses to my house. This parade was in Wyandotte, Detroit. They had one every year.

I went down to the bakery to order a cake for her birthday. They had the best cakes ever made. (I wish I could remember their name. I want to say it was Continental Cakes.) They made a regular round bottom cake, and a bear that sat up in the middle of it. The bear was filled with crème filling like a Twinkie. The bear stood about 10 inches high and about five by five inches across.

Sabrina liked strawberry short cake items. I bought a whole swing seat set, etc. Dee put it up in the back yard.

We went around to all the neighbors and asked if their children could participate. We bought great gifts for each child to win and made sure each one would leave with a gift. Back then, I believe we spent a couple thousand dollars on just gifts for everyone.

Sabrina had the perfect birthday; she went to sleep that night holding her plastic doll horse.

With us dealing drugs it was not safe to have kids over the house. We tried to keep from socializing with neighbors and only dealing with people that we knew from the business. The only ones allowed over the house were dealers like me. My husband allowed that rat to come live with us, and I was foolish to allow that girl to come over. Other than that, it was only dealers allowed to the main house. You were not even friends with them either. You kept it brief and as much as you could about business.

I loved it when my daughter had fun and had people to play with. She would look so happy and contented but I created such a lonely life for her. I lived such a dangerous life style that she was never allowed to have other children over the house for fear we could get robbed or gunned down, or the police would come in and arrest us. So it was safer for other children not to come over for fear they may see something and report it to their parents, police or DEA. So because of that, Sabrina was a lonely child and I created a lonely life style for her because of what I was doing for a living.

So when it came to her birthday, I went around the whole neighborhood and invited kids and bought toys to entice them and the parents. I also rented a clown to come to the party. That one time of seeing her run and have fun was worth all the money in the world. She was so scared in the beginning of the horses, but by the end of the night, she loved them. I loved my daughter so much, but I knew in my heart I was not giving her the right kind of life. How do you turn back when you are so deep?

I was so deep into it. I really did not know how to live any other way. I knew, they could bust into the house, and take me away or worse, someone could kill us. I would look at her sleeping and just wonder how I could change this for the both of us. I decided to start saving money so we could have a legal business.

The party was over and everything was quiet. Dee kept looking out the window that evening. I asked him what was wrong. Dee wanted me to look at something. I went to the window and saw something strange. That night Dee and I went across the street to see what was really going on. We took flash lights and checked out the area. It was a building that was directly across from us. The funny thing was, there was an area that had a telescope in a window with just a small rip in the curtain. Dee and I believed that the Feds were watching me across the street.

I decided it was time to move. I was still on personal bond with them. In this kind of business, you have to move every few months. I found a nice apartment in Winchester, Detroit. It was called Global Woods Apartments. It was a nice apartment and just perfect for Sabrina and me. My brother had to sign the lease for me, because I did not have a history of employment. I had not worked since the bar, which was in 1979. Rip came down and signed.

We moved in that weekend and I was on the top floor with four neighbors on the top floor with me. One wall was brick in a large living room with a terrace and sliding doors to go out. We had two big bedrooms with walk-in closets and one large bathroom, dining room and kitchen. We moved all the furniture in and I set up house. That rat that stole my dope might have as well went to the fed's too. It did not matter; it was a must to move.

I went out and purchased a motorcycle for myself. I loved it. I learned to ride when I was 14 years old when I stole my neighbors' bike and rode it to Clarenceville High School. Now, I had one of my own.

I was enjoying life with just Sabrina and me. We did everything together, but I also took time out for my business. I would try to take care of business when Sabrina was in school or in bed.

While she was at home, I would not go out; I would spend family time with her. When she went to bed, I would have Gene or Dee watch her while I went to the bars hustling my business. It was hard in the morning because the majority of the time, I did not get in the house until 3 or 3:30 am. Sabrina would get up for breakfast, bathe, dress and go off to school. A lot of times, I took the little girl down the hall to school too. So I would have to wait until she was in school before I was able to sleep. It was a strain on me but I had to keep up both life styles.

With my dope houses and Dee selling, I was doing well. Dee became my bodyguard also. I usually took him everywhere I went. Dee stood about six-two and was built. I knew without a shadow of a doubt that Dee would never allow anyone to hurt me. Dee did not live with us, but he was over every day. Many times, we would go out at night to take care of business. I also had a babysitter in the apartment building for Sabrina and the nights I did not get Gene to babysit, Karen would watch her.

Gene and Karen were the same people I hung around with when I was fourteen years old. We stayed in contact with each other since then. They got dope from me and Mike (the man who claimed I had crabs) who ran a dope house too for me. A different Eddy (Kathy's brother) ran dope from me. Winchester Ted ran a house; Shawn ran a house; Happy bought from me; and Tweedy bought from me.

Joey, who ran a pawn shop on Finke in Brightmoor area, would get stuff from me. I had a lot of clientele and a lot of houses. I was making about nine to ten thousand dollars a week. That was 36,000 a month and 432,000 a year. With all that money, I spent a lot on Vicenza, making sure he had what he needed in prison. I was spending lots on gifts for Sabrina, clothes, shoes and toys that were collector items. I was putting a few thousand away to get a business and investing some at Vicenza's family's house for when he gets out of prison. I spent a lot on the kids in the neighborhood going to carnivals, park picnics, and giving a lot away to people who did not have food, or stuff.

We purchased a bird for Sabrina; his name was Papeto. He was baby blue and he had the run of the house. I would let him fly all over and only place him in his cage at night. He did pretty well not making a mess. Sometimes he did and I would have to clean it up. I purchased mirrors to place on the wall in the dining room. The whole wall was a designed with mirrors from the floor to the ceiling. It made the apartment very nice. Our bird loved it. He could go to the mirrors and sing to himself all day. I still owned the house up north. I just paid the taxes on it every year. I hardly went up there any more after Vicenza was shot.

I would still go and visit with Vicenza Giuliano in the federal joint, at least every month. Each time I went, the trip would cost me about 1,000 dollars or sometimes more. I would take drugs and weed to him. I would either pay for a babysitter or take Sabrina with me and make it a vacation.

When Sabrina was in school it was hard to go but Vicenza understood. I left my answering machine with a tape stating, "If there are any collect calls from Vicenza Giuliano they are accepted."

I wanted to own my own bar as Vicenza did. He owned the Hello Dolly and Loser's Lounge in Detroit. I wanted my own so that Sabrina and I could take care of ourselves and get out of this life style. I had saved up 20,000.00 so far but needed a lot more.

There was this one guy I dealt with named Winchester Ted, who was a paraplegic bound to a wheelchair. Mike my childhood friend introduced him to me. He had a nice apartment full of art and knick knacks. His furniture was nice and looked like a bachelor's pad. Sometimes I wondered how he was able to keep everything so nice. His apartment was neat and very clean. He introduced me to a girl named Tweedy, who could not be trusted any further than you could throw her. He purchased dope from me all the time and was a very good customer.

Tommy was another person I met over there that sold drugs on the side, from his business and spent cash with me daily for his habit. He always picked up a few grams daily. This was a little clique that hung out together at Winchester Ted's apartment. I met Tweedy there, her brother who I really did not deal with a lot, a person named Shawn, and Jimmy who later became a nightmare for me.

Once I started going over to Ted's place, all of his people kept approaching me trying to deal with me directly. Winchester Ted would put a cut on the dope so bad that they wanted it straight from me. This business is dirty because there is no real loyalty. I had them come to me direct because I could make more selling them spoons or grams than I made selling Ted a couple grams at one time, cuz Ted would mercilessly cut the dope so a couple grams would turn into four grams.

Ted would purchase from me no matter what because he had a habit. I could pick up his clientele and keep him purchasing a couple grams a day. I was on it and making my dirty moves. That is what this business is. Stabbing each other in the back and smile in their face while you are doing it.

Dee was always by my side; he was my body guard and made sure I was well protected. In Detroit, I had many people I dealt with.

I could not even list everyone. There were a few regulars that I dealt with personally.

Gene and his lovely wife Karen would watch my daughter for me all the time. I felt comfortable with them. Sabrina liked it because they had kids to play with. She would spend the night sometimes so I did not have to drag her out to go home in the early morning hours. When she was not in school and it was summer, this worked out for me. When Sabrina came home, I would try to spend quality time with her.

Sometimes I felt tired of this life style, I was not a religious person but I do remember lying in my bed at times and telling God or whatever was over us human beings, how tired I was inside. I had a hard time believing that when we died, we went to heaven. I felt like we just went to the ground, it was over. At other times, I always felt like a spirit was watching me. I had a lot of conflicted feelings inside about this because my mother was very religious. I felt if she was religious I did not want anything to do with it. I know when I got into that car accident. It sure felt like a hand came down from heaven and scooped me up. I have a hard time getting that thought out of my head, because it was almost as if I could really feel someone's hands.

Things were not perfect and at times, I could not picture me being with Sabrina throughout her whole life. I kept thinking I was going to die. I also felt it would be better for Sabrina because I was not a very good mother exposing her to this life style.

I was at home one night and Tweedy had some guy come to my house. I know it was her. They were out in the parking lot and they tried to come to the door and rob me. I got my gun and answered the door with it. I would try to keep people from knowing where I lived but I did allow Tweedy to know. When she saw me with the gun, she asked me what I was doing. She told me I was tripping. I told her I did not trust anyone. I continued to ask her who was in the car. I told her I was too busy for company. When she left, they stayed out there for a long time. I am talking about hours. I finally got pissed and ran outside with my gun shot one bullet in the air and told them to get the F—away from my home.

They finally left. I knew Tweedy was up to no good. I could feel it in my gut. That feeling you get when you can feel something is not right. I could not prove it but I still hung around with her.

I went back into my apartment and the cops soon circled the apartment complex. They never came to my door so they must not have known it was me.

"Whew! I was Happy about that." (I stated out loud)

People were always trying to rob me or take my spot. Better yet, trying to play me and work me out of money. Many used me or tried to make me feel sorry for them. The street life is a trip and no one is to be trusted, not family, not your so-called friends, or the people you are dealing with or the police; so where do you turn, how do you deal with the stress of the game. You become as phony as them and trust no one.

Just for an example, I went to the bar a couple times with Tweedy. I thought she was so beautiful. I wish I had her looks. Anyways, a few times, we would go out and she would lay up with anyone for money, or do things that could jeopardize my freedom even more. We went to Center Stage Bar, which was located off of Highway 275. It was a main nightlife spot. Tweedy and I started drinking. Then we kind of split up and went our own way inside the bar but would meet back with each other. I was talking with this person and Tweedy came running up anxious telling me she needed my assistance. I thought she had gotten herself into trouble so I went with her.

She led me into the bathroom and told me not to let anyone get past that bathroom door for a few minutes. I stood firm as she asked me, only to be surprised. Tweedy leaned over, grabbed this woman's purse from under the stall, and ran out the door.

The woman came out of the stall mad as a bull. She was big, maybe around 250lbs. Her pants were down to her knees and she was pulling them up as she was coming out. I stood by the door as I told Tweedy I would.

This girl, that approached me, was African American with a very pretty face. She had to weigh around 250 lbs., stood about 5' 10" and was very big boned.

"What the hell did I get myself into?" (Was my thought.)

As she was trying to get out of the door, my 5'6 body, 110 lbs., and only a size 5 was not any match for her. I played stupid and every time she tried to get out the door, I acted as if I was trying to get out of her way, but would get in her way on purpose.

She finally got fed up with me and stood with her feet firmly on the ground and took her hands and pushed me out of the way. I fell sideways toward the wall and she flew out the bathroom to see if she could catch this person.

I took this opportunity to leave myself. I, of course, went a different direction. I went out the back door and went out to my car. I did not see Tweedy right away. I was wondering if that girl caught up with her. If she did, I know she would've stomped Tweedy to pieces.

Tweedy was small like me and did not fight at all. Tweedy did not care, she was crying for death. She was on a mission to hell. She would trick people, steal purses, do robberies, steal anything she could get her hands on as long as she could sell it and get dope.

Or sell her ass for money. She told me once she wanted to be like me so bad, that she tried to clean up her life once and get her daughter back from her man "Blue."

Her daughter was very pretty, African American and white. Tweedy got an apartment and I helped her to get a television and other things to go in it. She lived over by the University of Michigan in Ann Arbor. The apartment complex was mainly gay couples. I helped her to move in, get her daughter from Detroit and hung around Tweedy so as to share some of my good-natured techniques of raising Sabrina on her.

She loved the relationship my daughter had with me. I had quit using dope in 1979 and went into a rehab outpatient clinic for methadone. Tweedy would see me with nice cars, my relationship with my daughter and our apartment and she wanted the same thing. I just did not know it back then, but all that I did have, would cost me my life and many other things.

I would lose the biggest gift that life has to offer. I would lose the ability to raise my daughter myself, watch her develop into a woman. Life is funny; you cannot do it over. This is not a stage where the curtain closes and you can do a retake. Your life choices affect you and your future but it also affects everyone around you. My lifestyle and actions affected my daughter, my sister, her children, her husband, my father, brother, the man that died on my case . . . . his family and loved ones. One's life choices affect people around you and your destiny. I learned that lesson the hard way.

Tweedy stole that woman's purse but she did not stop there. She ripped off at least seven purses that night. She threw all of them in a field next to my car. That was all I could see on the other side of my car, was purses laying everywhere. That scene of the purses will bring back memories to me later on down the road, but at this time, I just wanted to get Tweedy and split.

I saw Tweedy and flagged her down to come on. She got into the passenger's side of the car and started telling me the night was young. I told her it was over for me and I did not want to be a part of this bull crap again. She pulled out some of the money she got that night and gave me fifty bucks. I asked her what this was for. She told me she needed some dope. I gave her a pack and we started back toward my apartment. I told her not to do it in the car with me.

Tweedy changed her mind and asked to be dropped off at her own apartment. I drove her home. When she got out of the car, I couldn't help to think to myself, what a waste and knew, sooner or later Tweedy would meet her destiny, but what I did not think about, was I was about to meet mine too.

I went home and Dee was there with Sabrina. I lay in her bed and thanked my lucky stars that I had her, and how peaceful she looked. When the street life was crazy, the look of her brought me back to sanity. I patted her head and kissed her. I felt that if no one else loved me, she did and always would. She was so smart and I was glad I did have her. I did not want children, even though I had lost a couple children and aborted one.

I never wanted kids growing up. I always felt I would be a child abuser. I did not hit her, but I destroyed her emotions with my lifestyle. I look at her with love but was unable to see our future together. I did not know what was going to happen to us. I kept having heavy thoughts about me dying; actually, inside, I was.

Dee was so good with Sabrina; I thanked him for watching her. We had a drink together and watched cable television, back then there was a box that went on top of your TV with pushed in buttons. I started drinking a lot when I got off heroin. I became cross-addicted. I went from heroin to methadone, to Percodan's to codeines to alcohol. To me, I was clean because I was not on heroin anymore. Every addict feels that way.

241

I finally went to bed and Dee left. No matter what time I went to bed, somehow Sabrina would end up in my bed in the morning. This never failed. (Smile)

Sabrina wanted me to spend the day with her so I did. She wanted to go to the carnival that was in Winchester town. So I started to load up the car when I saw the man that lived kiddy corner to me.

He was raising two twin daughter of his own. So I invited them to come with us. He stated he did not have the funds. I told him they did not need any funds, it was my treat. Then the little girl that lived down the hall from us was standing there and asked if she could go too. What did I get myself into?

I went to ask her mother. I loaded the kids up; Sabrina, the two twin girls and the girl down the hall.

We had a blast and the children rode everything they could a couple times. They got my car so dirty I had to have it detailed. I dropped a couple hundred on these kids but it was worth it to see their faces and to see Sabrina so happy.

A few days later, Vicenza Giuliano called on the phone and asked if I would bring him some packages down. I got my things ready to travel and asked Gene and Kathy to watch Sabrina. Sabrina wanted to go with me, but I explained to her, that this would be a quick trip. I asked Tweedy if she wanted to go for the ride. We packed up and went down to Springfield, Mo.

Vicenza Giuliano was in the federal joint down there. I sent Vicenza 200 to 500 hundred dollars weekly. Whatever he wanted I got it and sent it or snuck it in.

It was a mistake to bring Tweedy; she was turning tricks in the bathrooms at gas station stops, and talking people's money. I was very embarrassed of her. We went down and got a room. I came back one night from seeing Vicenza and Tweedy had a man in my room. She was stretched out on the bed, with this person kneeing down giving her some head. I shut the door and was pissed that I had to wait to come into my own room that I was paying for.

When they were done, I cussed Tweedy out and we packed to leave the next morning. I saw Vicenza Giuliano before I left and told him I had to go back. After we got home, Tweedy kept apologizing telling me how highly she thought of me, and asked me to forgive her. I ended up forgiving Tweedy and went out to the bar with her again once we had been back home for a while.

I felt so sorry for Tweedy and wanted to help her but she was pulling me down. We went out to a bar in Ann Arbor off Main Street. It was called "Second Chance." We were dancing and having fun.

This one man would not leave me alone. He kept following me around, putting his hands on me. I told him several times to stop. The asshole would not stop.

So I pulled open my jacket so he could see the gun under my arm. The man backed up and left me alone. But to my surprise, he told the bouncer.

They threw me out because I would not allow them to shake me down. Tweedy was up to her same-old' tricks again and started an argument with these two chicks. They accused her of stealing their purse. Somehow, I believed them over Tweedy. She was my friend and I stood up for her. She could not fight.

As I was walking out of the bar, she ran over to me for assistance. I hung back and let Tweedy argue with them for a minute. As long as the fight was fair I was not going to get involved.

Then this man got involved with the argument. I pulled out the gun and told the man to stay out of the argument that it was between the ladies.

The one girl grabs Tweedy by her hair while the other kicked her. I ran up to her and busted her in the face and told her to leave Tweedy alone.

"One on one bitch!", I sighed and stood strong.

The girl yelled out that I busted her nose. The other girl ran up on me and said;

"Pick on someone your own size"

I do not know why she said that to me, because she was about two times bigger than me. She grabbed me by my hair and swung me around. I had three inch heels on and could not get my balance. She tossed me left and right and then left and right again. She was flipping me like a rag-doll. She flipped me once too many times because I was able to get my balance back and grabbed her.

I latched my hands around her neck and did not let go. I hung on to her neck so tight like I did that girl in high school. I left hickies around her neck where my grip was so hard. I started to bang her head against the cement in the parking lot across from the bar. There was a bank or something there and a curb in the parking lot. I kept banging her head against that curb until she did not move any more.

When she was getting the best of me, no one said anything or tried to stop the fight. Now that I was getting the best of her, they tried to pull me off her.

I would not stop; I was so angry and afraid to let go, that I would not stop.

Finally a couple guys pulled me off her stating I was killing her. I snapped out of it and got up, looked around at the crowd and walked back to my car. They were all booing me for what I did. One person in the crowd stated I had a gun under my arm. I knew it was time to go.

Tweedy got into the car with me. I asked Tweedy where my purse was. Tweedy tried to say she did not know. That was when I was through with Tweedy. I knew she took my purse because of the money and drugs that I had on me. I cussed Tweedy out and asked her to get out of my car. I did not speak to Tweedy any longer.

I went home pissed, my outfit got dirty, and so I jumped in the shower. I am fighting for her ass and she steals my purse. I was the only one helping her; that was the street life.

The phone rang. It was Tweedy. She told me to please forgive her that she was in her addiction and she really did not take my purse. That was her M.O. I did not want to mess with Tweedy anymore. She was a lost cause to me. She was a waste of a cum drop as far as I was concerned.

I did get my purse back from the police a few months later. It was found in a person's yard next to the bar. Someone had thrown it over the wall. Nothing was in it but my paper work, driver's license, and empty cigarette case. I smoked two packs of cigarettes a day, Newport's. I saw that purse lying on those people's grass. The police took pictures of it, the way it was found.

I went home and was relaxing. Sabrina was with Gene and Kathy. She loved it over there because they had children. I needed a break from all the bull, but to my surprise, it did not turn out to be a restful night.

245

My brother came over and asked what I was doing. I told him nothing and he wanted to hang out and talk. So I took Rip over to Center Stage and we had a few drinks. Rip was digging on this girl he met. I gave Rip a few dollars to entertain her. He was having fun bull crapping around with her. I was enjoying the music.

The bouncer would talk to me every time I came into that bar, but because I was married to Vicenza I would not do anything with him. We kicked it but nothing solid was between us. I wasn't sure if I wanted to stay with Vicenza Giuliano.

I had 3,000.00 dollars saved up for him. I had 20,000.00 dollars saved up for myself. I was really confused because I wanted to get out of the drug business, but I knew I would have to own a business to make the kind of money I needed to take care of Sabrina and myself. So the Bouncer would always talk to me when I would come in there. I talked to him for a moment and this other guy was watching us talk. After the bouncer left, the man came up to talk with me.

I was standing leaning against the wall. I had a nice suit and large black velvet hat on that covered one of my eyes. I am looking at him from underneath the hat. He approached saying

"Oh, what are you, a model, a gangster, a mystery woman, or what?"

When he stated mystery woman, he bent down looking under my hat. I did not say anything at first. I felt he was a drunken asshole. Finally, I pulled my head back and looked at the man and played the cool gangster roll by opening up my suit jacket.

I was wearing a three-piece suit set. When I opened my jacket, I slowly told the person, "Get lost loser, you don't need my trouble."

The man looked at my gun. He backed away and looked at me as if I was nuts. As he was walking away, he said, "Fine, I don't want to talk to you anyways, You're too skinny."

I stood there for a minute and then found another spot in case he got the police involved. My brother told me to stop doing that to people because one day they might take me up on it.

As I was walking down the hallway, the guy spotted me and told this girl he was hanging out with about me. The girl was drunk and started cussing me out, telling me you think you are big stuff with that gun; let's see how tough you are without it bitch!

That was my cue. I stood there and said nothing. She ran her mouth and then walked out of the bar talking crap, stating, "She's a punk. She has to have a gun because she can't fight with her skinny ass."

I went and got my brother and told him I had to go out and dust this bitch—off.

My brother followed me and left the girl there. I saw the girl that was berating me get into a car. I walked up to the car. There was one man driving and the girl was in the middle and a man on the passenger side. They all looked at me and did not move or do anything. I pulled open the passenger's side of the door and reached over the man and grabbed the girl by her throat. I was good about grabbing people by the throat or breaking their nose.

That is how my brother taught me to fight. I grabbed her and pulled her toward the door, the man sitting in the passenger side took his fist and started hitting me in the face then tried to hit me with his knee.

My brother came over to the car just as he was doing that. My brother grabbed the man on his shoulder and told him to stop, this is not your fight buddy.

He kept doing it while I was beating the girl's face in with my fist. My brother got pissed and drew his hand back and busted the dude in his cheek. My brother busted his cheek bone and blood went all over me. I could feel it in my hair and face. The dude's bone stuck out of his face.

The driver got scared and put the car in reverse. He was trying to back up with the door open and it would have caused Rip and me to fall. I yelled out to Rip to let him know that the door was pushing me and him down. We were trying to hold our feet firm on the ground to keep from falling.

Rip hauled off and kicked the door. The driver really got scared now, all the time this was going on, I was still holding on to the girl and choking her and punching her in the face.

Rip and I got out of there and took off. We went back through the bar and those people came back to the bar too telling the owners. The bouncer found Rip and I and helped us to sneak out the back way. I had to go around and get the car. Rip waited out in the back until I could pull around to get him.

Rip had already gotten into trouble about his karate before and lost his license to teach. I could not allow my brother to go to jail. We got into the car and home we went. Boy that night was something else. I told Rip, every time I go out, I get into a fight. Rip and I stayed up a long time and talked about life and what I wanted. That was a night to remember that dude's bone was sticking up and a big piece of his skin was just hanging. Rip did some damage to that dude.

The next day Rip had some things to do and told me he would be back later. Then a couple hours later Gene came over with a few friends and Sabrina, asking if I had any stuff. I told him no, I had to go and do a pick up. I took Sabrina with me. I called Cassius and told him I needed to pick up a load. Cassius asked when I wanted to meet him. I carried a beeper and so did Cassius. I told him I wanted to get my hair done first. I told Gene to wait at my house that I would be back later.

Gene was sitting at the house and my brother came back. Gene would not let him in. He did not believe it was my brother. My brother became angry and told him to open the door.

Rip called me, and I did not answer my beeper. I was getting a perm in my hair and it was down to the middle of my back. So it took a few hours. When I finally got home, Gene and my brother were going back and forth with their argument. Gene did let my brother in. Gene pulled a pistol on my brother and my brother wanted to beat Gene's butt. So I came into a very heated argument. You could cut the air with a knife.

I walked in the door like nothing was going on and said, hey, what's up? My brother and Gene started telling their side of the story simultaneously. Finally, I got everyone to calm down and had one person at a time explained what was going on. When I found out that Gene did not know who my brother was, I started seeing the issue at hand.

Gene only knew of my father and me, he never knew about any of my brothers or sisters. I started to explain to Gene that he was my brother. Gene was really hurt that he had known me for over six years and never knew I had a mother or siblings. We all sat down and had a good laugh once everything was cleared up. So I took care of Gene and my brother and I chilled at the house for a while. He was getting my bird high on alcohol. My bird was flying into the walls and Rip thought it was funny.

We went to bed that night and the next day, Joey, wanted to come over and get some personal stuff. I asked him to bring his selection over. Joey had a pawn shop and sometimes had a good selection of jewelry. Once in a while, I would do a trade with him, bartering dope for jewelry instead of money.

He brought over a few nice items and I was impressed with a stone he had called the Alexander stone. It was quiet beautiful. I told Joey that I would take that stone. I warned him that the dope was strong and he needed to be careful with the amount. Joey felt like he could handle it and shot the whole thing up. I watched Joey nod in and out. The bird flew down on his baseball hat. It was so funny; I could not keep myself from laughing.

It was astonishing to watch this bird sit on the rim of Joey's baseball hat. Watching the bird sit on his hat peaking over and look down at Joey sleeping. Then he would jump down on his pocket where his cigarettes where and pick them out one by one.

Then the bird picked behind the pack of cigarettes and pulled out a five dollar bill. The bird struggled until it was removed and flew away with it. The bird would then fly over to the curtain with the money in his beak and put the money behind the window curtains on my sliding doors to the balcony.

I was totally amazed at this bird. He would then fly back and get back on Joey's rim on his hat and do it all over again. Rip asked me if I trained the bird to do that. I told him no, I did not even know the bird could do that. Papeto was a trip.

He did this until he had almost fifty dollars or more over there. Then he started to peck his cigarettes until he pulled them all out. We sat there and sniggered so hard and Joey never woke up. That was the funniest crap to us.

We finally woke Joey up and told him what the bird did. I don't think Joey believed us totally. I think, he thought we were trying to rip him off. I tried to tell Joey, I don't need to rip anyone off. Joey left and we laughed about that for weeks.

Tweedy calls and asked if she could come over and talk with me. I agreed and Tweedy came to the house asking me to help her with something and to forgive her. My brother split from the house and I did not see Rip for a few days. He wanted to take a girl out that he felt was special. I gave him a thousand dollars. He was on his way to get laid.

I always felt I owed it to him, because when Vicenza Giuliano got out of the hospital, Rip gave us 5,000 or more to get started again, when that man robbed us, Rip lost out too. Vicenza never got him straight. I don't really think he cared because Rip was family.

Tweedy was mad at her ex-boyfriend and wanted to get her stuff back. She said he would not give it to her. I listened to all she had to say and agreed to get her stuff back. I had a soft spot for Tweedy; I felt she was an okay person. She just had a drug issue. Also, I just hate it when men try to get over on women and play them.

We went to his house in Ann Arbor and Tweedy tried to get in the door, thru windows or whatever she could find that would open. Finally, I came up to the door, wrapped my hand in a coat, and busted the window out. Tweedy took her hand and unlocked the door as we walked in.

There was a big dog coming at us and it did not look friendly. I pulled out my gun and Tweedy yelled out . . . . "NO, he is my dog too". She grabbed the dog and placed him in a room so he could not get out. I went and backed the car to the house and we started carrying out TVs, stereos, scales to measure dope with, and I saw a nice gun in there.

It was an AR-15 paratrooper carbine. We loaded the back seat and trunk. I moved so fast that Tweedy could not keep up with me. Then we took off.

Tweedy kept laughing in the car saying, "I cannot believe how fast you did that".

I told her that I used to do them all the time, but I got out of that crap. Tweedy only took what belonged to her and allowed me to have the rest of the items for helping her out.

I dropped Tweedy off and went back home. I was proud of my gun and placed it with the rest of my collection. I had a 12 gauge shotgun, an AR-15 paratrooper carbine, pearl handled 38 short noses, .25 Berretta, and a 22 magnum pen gun shaped as a ball point pen. Vicenza Giuliano got those for me, a box of them some dude made.

If I went on a dope deal and it turned sour, I would hold that .22 magnum pen gun in my hand pull back the trigger and fire in the person's face so I could get away. (They placed that information in my Federal file). These little things were one shot wonders, once you shot it, you had to unscrew the top and throw it away then the gun was no good anymore. So he got me a box of them in case I needed more than one.

So I added the items to my collection. I told Cassius, my dope man, about the break in. He told me to be cool and not get involved with dumb-shi#$. He told me that many people would love to take my place, that the word on the streets was that I am the toughest woman out there.

He said, "I am not telling you how to live your life, but within a few years you will be able to retire if you keep this up."

I was making Cassius about 5-8 thousand a day. I was making myself about 9 thousand a week. Cassius was right, that was dumb of me to do that. I went around checking on my dope houses. I never got involved in dumb crap like that anymore.

I was still dealing with Winchester Ted and a few of others. I went to Ted's house to drop off his package and he had not seen me in a couple of weeks. When I got to Ted house, he told me he heard about my incident at the bar.

He told me, "I thought you were all talk. I thought that was why you carried that gun, because you could not really kick ass. I really thought you talked tough, but I did not know you were tough."

"Boy, oh, boy," he said, "You are my new hero, I like people who can talk it and walk it."

I just looked at him and did not comment on the subject, and asked him if a gram would do him? He laughed and stated yeah. We sat and kicked it a little and then I left. Later on that week, Winchester Ted called me and told me he had some people who wanted more, and he had some sweet deals for me.

I went and got Winchester Ted and placed his wheelchair in my truck. We rode off together and picked up some jerk friends of his. I told Winchester Ted I would not give him any dope in front of his friends. I let Winchester Ted know he had to do the deal without me being a part of it. I do not want anything from your friend's hands. He agreed and we rode on.

I had to make a few stops throughout the night to take care of some business.

We picked up his friend and then I went to a bar to drop off some dope to a customer. As I got out of the car, I told everyone in the car not to shoot up in my car. I expressed it in an aggressive way. I was not for any kind of nonsense. They agreed not to do that. I went into the bar and conducted my business when I came back outside to my surprise, the dude in the back seat had shot up some dope.

I was so fu—pissed off. I tried to get his attention and all Winchester Ted could say, "I told him not to do it that you were no one to play with."

I opened the car door and kept trying to wake this fool up out of his nod. The dope was too strong for him, he was nodded out. I was hoping the dude did not die in my car was all I could think inside. I pulled the seat back and took the needle out of his arm and started to stab him in his leg with his needle.

The dude jumped up yelling . . . . "What are you doing you crazy bit—!!"

"I told you not to shoot up in my Fu—car, I told you this was my car and no activities like that will occur in my car. Now, if you don't like it punk, then walk! Now, listen with your punk ass when I tell you I am not playing, that is just what the fu—I meant."

I shot my gun in the air to let him know to cool out with his yelling and calling me names. I gave him the choice to either go by my rules or get the Fu—out! Winchester Ted talked to him and told him, don't play with her. The dude got back into the car and kept his mouth shut all the way back.

When I dropped them off, he mumbled under his breath that I took his high away and he felt like I should replace it. I shut the door as if I did not even hear his cry. I said to myself, "Dope fiend, move."

If the asshole would have listened to my words in the first place, the asshole would not have lost his high.

I went home that night; Dee was laid out on the coach. He was babysitting Sabrina. I laid back realizing how everyone was in this world. I was so tired inside, I just wanted to be normal again. But the snowball keeps growing to where you lose control of your own life. Either people were trying to rob me, or they wanted something from me because I was the dope man. Sometimes I would just lie down on my bed looking out the window or look at Sabrina and ask myself if it is all worth it. People were afraid of me on the streets. I had gained my own reputation. Even guys that had been in the business heard about me and knew I was crazy and was nothing to play with. Finally, I was able to fall asleep.

The next day I got Sabrina ready to go to Detroit at Gene and Kathy's house. This particular day Sabrina went outside and played with their children, while we talked in the living room.

I remember my baby coming into the house crying that this little boy hit her over the head with a thick steel chain. Her head had blood on it. I jumped up, and Gene tried to tell me to leave it alone and let Sabrina learn to fight her own battles. I just could not, she was not tough and she did not like to fight. I ran outside and Gene followed me.

I saw the little boy outside and grabbed him by his shoulders and shook him, asking him, "Why did he do that?"

He started crying and pulled away from me and ran home to his mother. Gene, stated, "Oh no, we are going to have trouble now; his mother is a bit—."

I started telling Gene, "I don't care, what the Fu—she is and her fuc—bad ass kid."

Gene then stated, "Billy Joe you have to let kids fight their own battles, parents do not belong in the battles because then it causes more problems."

Just as Gene stated that, sure-enough, here she came, yelling you white bit—from across the street. Of course that did not sit right with me, so I started calling her black bit—back as she was approaching the area.

She jumped up on the porch and started to run her mouth and I just was not in the mood for this, so I pushed her off the porch and pulled my gun out and told her to get on to her house and to take her fuc—ass bratty kid with her.

That did not sit well. She left but like Gene said, parents should not get involved. When we went back into the house, Gene told me, you need to leave out of here now before the police get here.

I looked at him puzzled.

Gene said, "She is going to call the heat, you need to get out of here as soon as possible, and let me hang on to any dope you have on you. They are coming after you."

I told Gene, I could handle it and grabbed Sabrina and went to leave. Gene told me, "And you need to leave her here, in case they pull you over",

I agreed and gave him the dope and told him to please don't let anything happen to her.

I drove the opposite way. It was not long before I got up the street that the big four pulled in front of me and blocked my way. They asked me to step out of the car. I did . . . . They asked to search my purse, I told them no, unless you have a search warrant . . . The one cop grabbed my purse yelling, we don't need any search warrant.

I would not let go, he stated he did not need a stinking search warrant that his badge was a search warrant. We both struggled holding the purse and then the strap finally broke and the cop went flying across the yard.

Of course, my gun flew out of the purse.

They threw me up against the car and kept poking at me with their night sticks. I protested and told them that weren't necessary, the cop told me to shut my mouth and save it for the judge.

They threw me in the car and left my car on the street. They started laughing, stating your car will stay there and there is no bail for CCW charges. Then another cop stated, yeah, your car will be there when you get out, but there might not be nothing left of it when you get there, they will strip that car down to the frame. They all started laughing, thinking it was a big joke. I was in the back seat between two stinky cops and tried to move to make myself more comfortable because of the handcuffs.

As I moved, the one cop pushed me over with his body stating, "Don't touch me, you might be full of crabs or lice."

Then they all started laughing. I told him, "I am sure you already have every disease out there, with your crooked butt."

He pushed me again with his body and told me to shut up that he had ways to make trash like me shut up. I had heard about this group of cops they called Starsky &Hutch. I knew to keep my mouth shut.

I sat there knowing I was handcuffed and out of my territory. When we got down to the police station I requested to make a phone call. I called Dee to get my car and to call my attorney O'Connell out of Detroit. Dee did that for me. I never had to worry because Dee was like the best friend I could have on my side. Late that night, they transferred me downtown to 1300 Bovina Police Department at twelve midnight.

They also fingerprinted me. The police station that I was at, did not have accommodations for female prisoners. I had to hand over all my jewelry and personal items. Then, I had to take off all my clothes and bend over to let them check me out, looking inside my butt. Then they stuck me in a cell that had no heat, and a plastic mattress that had no sheets.

I asked the officer who let me in the cell if I could get some sheets and a blanket.

She laughed at me stating, "This is no Hyatt Regency, honey. So just lay your butt down and don't do anything wrong in the future to end up in places like this."

So, I layed down and fell asleep.

The next morning, they did not give me anything to wash up with, brush my teeth, or anything. My clothes were wrinkled and my hair was not combed, teeth not brushed. I felt like a mess but my attorney was there at the courtroom. He told me, you look bad Billy Joe, but I know you are a strong woman and you were able to handle the situation. When Vicenza Giuliano went to the federal prison, he still owed O'Connell some money. Vicenza used to deal with his dad when his father was an attorney. I tried my best to finish paying him off. So he was right there for me when I needed him.

I had a large black hat on that was gangster style, black dress pants on, and a black and gold top, with 3 ½ inch high heels shoes on; but was wrinkled from one end to the other. My attorney told me not to say anything and don't wear the hat.

He had worked out a deal with the prosecutor. Even though I was not 18 but 21, he made a deal for a pre-division program for me. That was a program for first time offenders, if you stayed out of trouble for a year, they would wipe it off your record.

I went to court a few times for this case, and on the last day that we got everything into writing, they finally gave me the plea agreement.

That was the happiest day of my life, but soon, it would become the worst day of my life. I still had to go to court a few more times on this case before it would become final. So Dee and I left court and took care of business. I needed to pay Mike a visit for he was overdue on his bill like 1,000.00 dollars. So we got into the car and went over to Mike's house to collect my money.

He didn't have it. I told Mike the next time I come over, he better be straight. Of course I had a soft spot for Michael. I went with him when I was 14 years old. He was dark complexioned Indian with long hair. He was the only man that hung out at the Marlow House that had a job. Now he was a big bum.

I really thought he was going to grow up with great expectations. Everyone in the neighborhood hated him because he had it together so well and was not much of a street man. His parents still lived together and were not divorced. I believed some of that peer pressure pushed Mike down sometimes, so I did have a soft spot for Mike.

But I could not let him get away with murder so-to-speak. I would have Mike roughed up in a flat second, nothing drastic, just maybe a baseball bat to his knee caps. It was through Mike that I met Shawn and Jimmy (the two that were on my case that turned state's evidence against me). I also met Tweedy and Winchester Ted through him too.

Mike did not have my money. I pushed Mike physically backwards, and hit him in his chest, telling him he was going to make me do something to him. Mike just kept telling his lies like he always had. He had become such a bum and liar.

As I was pushing him, Dee, standing 6'2", was standing in the background with his arms folded, waiting for Mike to respond.

I then pulled out my gun and told Mike, "Don't make me shoot you Mike." "You are going to force me to hurt you, and I don't want to do that. I like you Mike, but business is business."

There was a girl there that kept trying to see who I was. I told Mike to make sure that Bit—stays behind that door. I did not want anyone to see my face. Mike told her to shut the door and not to look out. Dee and I left to get something to eat and collect other money.

When Dee and I returned to Mike's house later that evening everything was cleaned out of the house. Nothing was left but dirty items and newspapers were all over the floor. I must have scared him, because he and his girl, the kids and everything were totally gone. The house was bare and empty. I had known this man since I was fourteen years old. That was the last time I ever saw Mike.

I had been stashing money away for me and Sabrina to get my own business. I was also sending money over to Vicenza Giuliano's family house for him when he got out of prison. I knew I would never be with Vicenza Giuliano ever again. I loved him and thought he was a wonderful man but there were things about Vicenza that no one knew. Unless you were right there up under him, you would not have seen it.

I had about 3,000.00 dollars over at his brother's house saved up for him. I did not want him to get out and not have any money to start off with. I was fair, and down for whoever I was with. I was going to divorce Vicenza Giuliano when he got out. I would of never of did that while he was in. That was not my style to kick someone while they were down.

There was too much pain between us, from his drug use, to his lies and deceit. Then with the shooting up north. The police trying to arrest me for it. Him grabbing me by my neck. Him asking me to confess. Him killing my daughter's puppy. All the whores he had sucking his dick when I was not around. He would sneak to do everything. The shooting and killings he was involved with. He placed Sabrina and I in jeopardy. I felt like I slept next to a stranger sometimes.

Something was going on inside of me. I couldn't quiet explain it but it felt as if I was going to die. I kept getting strong feelings inside that something bad was going to happen. I was going over my life inside my head, but I could not understand why I was feeling this way. I knew after that shooting up north with Vicenza that we would never be able to trust each other again.

The love that we shared was over, the respect was gone. I didn't want to call my sister Paula, but I did. I had not talked to her since they took Vicenza and me to the federal building when they arrested us for drugs back in 1980. They had a warrant out for our car. I had no way to get to the methadone clinic, and she had driven me down there for that.

It's funny now, but back then it wasn't. Paula did not even want to stop and let me out of the car. She was scared of the neighborhood in Detroit. She kept driving and slowed down and told me to get out while the car was still rolling.

I felt sorry for my sister, no matter how scared she was, she still took me and stood strong, just like a Key. (That was my maiden name.)

She kept driving around the block until I came out. I had to jump in the car while it was still going. I could not blame the way Paula felt because I thought about one time when Vicenza and I went there and those men that were fighting crashed thru the front door and fell on Sabrina. Anyways, Paula and I really had not been talking to each other because I made it a habit of not talking to my family when I was out doing wrong. I was always living on the wrong side of the fence.

I called her, sometimes when I was at the end of my rope, I would call Paula, or my brother Rip. They were the ones I always leaned on. I always thought they had their shit together.

When I got Paula on the phone, I made small talk with her. I just was talking about everything going on in my life. Then I popped up and asked Paula to make me a promise that if I ever died, don't let mom have Sabrina. My sister kept asking if I was in trouble. I told her no, but I felt like something was going to happen and I was going to die. I kept telling her all the crazy dreams I was having. I just felt something was going to happen. Paula asked me what kind of dreams I was having. I told Paula that it was a couple dreams. She wanted me to give her an example.

So I did, I told her one was me getting in a car with three guys and one man was driving and two guys were sitting in the back with me. There was one on each side of me. As we were driving down the street, I kept asking where we were going. The driver told me not to worry about it. Then he turned around and took a gun and shot me in my head. I could see the bullet hole in my forehead. My head went backwards and then frontwards. I could see the blood dripping from my head. The guys on each side of me were laughing. I could see them, but could not do anything. I woke up.

I kept having this dream over and over. I just worried about Sabrina if anything should happen to me. I told Paula I feared Sabrina being raised by mom, because I did not want her to be screwed up like me. I wanted her to have a chance at life.

Not realizing I was not giving her a life. Sabrina was in danger being with me.

Finally Paula told me she would talk to George and see what he would say. I told her to promise me to talk George into it please, don't let her be raised by the state, nor by mom.

My sister asked about our sister Lilly, who lived down in Alabama. I told her no, that I did not want Sabrina raised out of Detroit or in the country like that. I had other reasons too, but did not go into the other issues with Paula. My sister stated, "Okay Billy Joe, I will see what I can do." I hung up the phone.

Lena my girlfriend came over later on that day. I had not seen her in a while. The last time I saw Lena, she was dating John C. Holmes the porn star. It was funny; she told me they would get a motel just to play board games because he had sex for a living. They were cute together. Now she was dating a dude named Leon. She was in love with this guy but really angry with him because he was an alcoholic. He was a substance abuse counselor too. Lena wanted someone to talk with. I was there with all ears.

Then she jumped up trying to talk me into selling her some blow, or 'boy' (both slang for heroin). I told her NO! We argued about it for 30 minutes. I told her I loved her and would not introduce anyone to this crap. She threw it up in my face saying I did it.

I told her I had been clean for two-half-years now. I would never touch that crap again in my life.

Lena bounced up saying, "I will just go buy it somewhere else."

I told her GOOD! That is your choice but you won't buy it here, my friend. She left the house upset with me.

It had been a long evening. I sat home watching TV with Sabrina.

Later that evening I put Sabina to bed and then went to bed myself. I laid there asking God, if you exist, what is going to happen to Sabrina and me? I could not even cry back then. Soon I fell asleep.

The next day Dee and I went to court and I received the pre-division program. I offered to take my attorney out to eat but he declined. It was 3:30 pm and we headed back home.

Dee and I were invited to a Halloween party. I let Cassius know I was going to a party that night. I hung up the phone and it rang again, it was Shawn. He wanted to know if I could get some more stuff on consignment. I asked Shawn, how are you going to pay me back the couple hundred you already owe me? Shawn told me that when he sold all of it he would have my money and what he owed me. He told me that a dude is willing to front him the money if the stuff is good. So I asked him if this dude is going to front you the money, then you will have my cash right away . . . . Right?

Shawn stated, "Yes."

Then, he asked when I was bringing the stuff. He stated he would have the cash within hours. I told him, yeah and hung up the phone.

A little bit later, Shawn called again . . . . This time he told me everything was straight and asked if I would meet him on Lots Road. I did not know where that location was. Shawn told me how to get there. I asked him why Lots Road? He stated that they usually do some deals out at that area. They felt it was familiar to them. So I did not think anything of it, got off the phone and told Dee what was going on.

Dee wanted to go with me. He never trusted Shawn and Andrew. Shawn owned a carpet company and ran it into the ground with his heroin habit. Dee always called them slime-balls. Dee kept insisting to go with me. He was like my bodyguard. He went with me everywhere in case someone tried to overpower me. I told Dee that it was stupid for him to go. I was only going to be gone a few minutes. I would meet him at the party.

Of course, Dee was not pleased with my decision, but did as I asked of him. I got ready and put on all black that night. A black pair of blue jeans, black leather jacket, black leather boots, that went up to my knee caps, and a chain to wrap across my shoulder. I was going to the Halloween party as a motorcycle babe. So I decided to get dressed now and go see Shawn and afterwards, fly straight to the party.

I did not know that dream was about to become more of a reality tonight. The Lord will give you signs, but sometimes we do not listen to our inner spirit. I got ready that night, saw Acacius to get some more stuff, because after I dropped this load off to Shawn, I would be at the end of my stash.

I met Acacius and rapped to him for a while. I told him what I had going on business wise. I told him about Shawn and what he wanted to do. Acacius might be my dope man but he was also my friend. We connected really well. I told him everything. As always, he told me to be careful and told me to call if I needed anything. Acacius told me that evening that sometimes the small stuff is not worth sweating over. Then he got into his car and drove away.

I went out that night driving out of frustration. I went to the liquor store and picked up a fifth of Peppermint Schnapps. The clerk watched me as I pulled 5,000 dollars out of my pocket fumbling through hundreds looking for a twenty. I was frustrated because I had been sitting at the location waiting for them for over 15 minutes. I returned back after the store. I saw a van coming down the road. I stepped out of my car to let them see me.

Out of respect for the family, I will not go into details but give a general outline. I was supposed to meet two men to sell them some drugs. When they got to the location there was a third man. I reneged because of the third man showing up. One thing lead to another and a disagreement occurred and I got frightened. A struggle then ensued and a gun was accidently discharged, hitting one of the men at the location. Once the gun discharged, the two guys took off and left me there with the man on the ground bleeding. I should have called the police and reported the incident. I was scared. How was I going to tell the police that I was selling drugs and the deal went sour? As a result, someone was shot. Many thoughts went through my head but my own survival instincts kicked in and overcame my morals.

It was a drug deal that went bad and an accidental death occurred out of those results. All my confessions about the situation have gone to God. It was an accident and not done in malice.

The night this occurred I did not know or understand that this tragedy was going to bring a new beginning to my life. I thank the family for their forgiveness for my part in this incident. On the day of my trial, his parents forgave me.

There is not a day that goes by, that I don't think about him or count the years he would have been now. This was a drug deal that went sour.

After the situation went down, I was driving down the road. My brain was going crazy, first with wanting to call the police but knowing I could not place myself at the scene. Survival kicked in wanting to save myself too.

I thought to myself that I could call them and say, "Hey I am a drug dealer and during the commission of a drug deal, it went bad."

And then again, I thought, "Yeah, that would go over real well."

Damn it; I was out of court at 3:30 pm for a pre-division program for the CCW charge and on the lam for murder at 7:30 pm. This is not going to look good. So I drove home and started cleaning out my house, to cover myself.

I walked into the apartment. It felt empty to me, knowing this was the last time I would ever walk into this apartment. The red light on the answer machine was flashing on and off. So I took a moment to go over and listen to what was on there. There was about three or four messages from Acacius, wanting to know if everything was okay. There was also a call from Vicenza Giuliano from the joint.

I called Acacius and the first thing he stated to me was . . . . "Are you alright?"

I said yes, and then he replied, "Are you hot, and is the car hot?"

I told him, not yet but I will be. He told me to clean out the house and I will be there to pick you up. I asked him, "What about the car?"

He told me not to worry, he would take care of everything. Then he told me, "Better yet, meet me at that bank down the street from your house."

I told him, okay that I would be there in twenty minutes. I tried to clean out the house to the best of my abilities. I also grabbed as many items and clothes for Sabrina that I could possibly grab. I took all the guns out of the house, the AR-15 paratrooper carbine, the 12 gauge shotgun, the .25 Berretta and those .22 magnate pen guns. I forgot about one of the .22 guns that I left above the door ledge of my bedroom. I did get all the other guns out including a .38 pearl handle gun that I had.

I hid dope all around the edge of the apartment building in packages. I went out in the hallway and made sure no one was coming. I lifted up the carpet on the side of the walls of the hallway and took out each package that I had stashed. Then, I went back in the apartment and gathered the rest of my items.

I went down to the parking lot and pulled off the Italian Stallion on the front plate just in case someone had seen it. I threw everything in the trunk of the car and drove to the bank parking lot.

My heart was beating and I was sick to my stomach wondering about that man left lying on the ground. I kept thinking that was someone's child. I tried to shake my thoughts before I drove myself crazy.

I waited there a few minutes and Acacius drove up. He had a big, tall man in the car with him. The man got out with Acacius and said hello. Acacius asked for the keys, and I told him what was in the truck. He got the keys from me and tossed them to the large dude. The man got into the car and took off. I did not even see what he really looked like.

I got into Acacius's car with him. As I got into the car, Acacius's handed me a box. I opened the box up and saw it was a golden whistle with white mother pearl decorations on it. It was connected to a long gold chain, trimmed in gold.

It was beautiful and it had a note connected to it stating, "Whenever you are in trouble, just whistle."

I read the note and picked up the whistle and blew it. Acacius looked at me stating, don't worry, we will fix it. I told him what was going on, and he placed his index finger up to my lips and told me to save it until we get somewhere we can talk. We went to the lake and talked outside late that night.

My beeper kept going off, all kind of people calling me wanting stuff, but most importantly, Dee kept calling wanting to know what was going on. I did not answer anyone, on the advice of Acacius.

He told me we needed to figure out what was going on with the man who got shot first.

I knew Sabrina was safe; she was with Gene and his wife.

Acacius and I went down to a Greek restaurant on Jefferson Rd, in Escorse. We sat in there and ordered some food and Acacius got on the phone calling hospitals near the area where we were at. He finally got a hold of one hospital that had a report of a shooting on Lots Road. Acacius told them he was some kind of relative and wanted to know what was going on.

Somehow with people Acacius knew or connections he had, he got the man's name and what was going on with him. Acacius had underground connections. He was either connected with the Greek Mafia or the Mafia. He also knew the moment he died. Don't ask me how.

When he sat down the last time from talking on the phone, he told me that the man died.

I could feel my whole existence came to an end.

I looked up at Acacius and tried to play the gangster I was supposed to be.

Acacius told me, "Hey, I remember the first time I killed someone."

I know he was talking but I did not hear anything he said. I thought about that guy dying out there alone. I just left him and only cared about myself.

I thought about my daughter and how I messed up her life.

I thought about my mother stating I was nothing in life.

I thought about how my whole life had been full of misery and now it was a nightmare.

Then I thought about my daughter being better off without me causing her more issues growing up.

I fell into self petty and the victim's role again.

I thought about not being there for my father, knowing he was getting older.

I responded, "It was an accident Acacius, I did not mean for him to die, I will go to the police and tell them the truth. It was an accident."

Acacius responded by telling me, "Ain't any cops going to look at this as an accident. Plus with my record, if they tie us together, they are going to wonder if you are a professional."

My heart sunk, I was no professional and it was an accident how he died.

I knew without a doubt my life as I knew it was over.

My life was affected, and everyone else who had any encounter with me.

"So what do I do now Acacius, where does this leave me and my daughter?"

Acacius paid for the bill and left the money on the table. His cousin owned the restaurant.

We left and rode to a hotel. Acacius told me I needed to stay there until he talked to a friend of his that owned a house on the lake up in Canada. I stayed at a hotel on Southfield Road by Ecorse. I got bored after a few days. I wanted to see Sabrina.

I went out one evening even though Acacius told me not to. I went down to the bar and had a few drinks. I played pool with this guy who kept coming on to me. I told him I was not looking for company. He would not leave me alone.

With the game was over, I snuck out of the bar and started walking home. The man followed me and I started running to my hotel. He kept following me. When I got to the door, he started coming toward me. I pulled out a knife. When he saw the knife, he turned around and left. I went into the hotel and did not go out again.

I would have killed that man out of fear. I was in the room wondering if I was turning into a killer now. They state, once you kill it is easy to kill again. Now my head was going crazy wondering if I was a killer inside.

The next day, I told Acacius that I needed to get Sabrina; she had been at Gene's house for a couple days.

I finally called Gene and Karen; they were always there for me. They did not worry about me picking her up, for them, it was just one more kid in the house. I have bought groceries for them several times because they took care of Sabrina a lot. They were always thankful for whatever I did. I thought very highly of both. I told Acacius I needed to go pick up Sabrina. I was missing her.

I talked to Gene and told him I was in trouble. I made some type of arrangement to pick Sabrina up.

Acacius had an idea in case the fed's or state cops were watching. He wanted us to go in several cars. I told him that was not necessary. I did not want to scare Sabrina. So I rode over there to get her. I talked to Gene and Karen. Both of them was tripped out and wondering what I was going to do. I told Gene, I wanted him to have my motorcycle. He told me, "Hey, you will be alright. Don't give up your stuff so fast."

I grabbed Sabrina and took her with me.

I told him, I knew I was going away for a long time. I had told Gene about my dream a few weeks before and he reminded me of that situation. I was tripped out, and did not remember telling him that. I told them I was going to miss them and was grateful for our friendship. They offered to let Sabrina stay there, but I told them I wanted her with me.

A few weeks went by and I was on the lam hiding from the law. Acaciuss wanted to handle everything and fix it where I could come out of hiding. Except Acaciuss's way of fixing things was to off the people on my case to keep them from talking.

I really did not interfere with whatever he was doing. My only concern was spending as much time with Sabrina as possible before they take me away. I was having to wash Sabrina's and my clothes out nightly. I went to Acaciuss and expressed I either needed someone to go shopping and get her some items or I needed to get her items. They had my apartment locked down like Fort Knox . . . .

Acaciuss did not care about the rollers and them having my apartment under watch. He stated when you do things under their nose they don't know you are there. Acaciuss and I drove to my apartment building and we grabbed some clothes for Sabrina. There was yellow tape all over the apartment building. I used my key and we both went in and grabbed what I could. I felt on top of the doorway of my old bedroom door for that .22 pen gun. I would take it to help me get out of a situation if something went wrong. It was gone—so I told Acaciuss. I had a couple more but that was my favorite one.

I got Sabrina's stuff and a few items for me. We snuck back out without moving the yellow tape. We went to the same hotel and stayed there for a few days.

I started tripping and kept seeing shadows. I would sit on the bed watching T.V. and knew, there was no one in that hotel with me, besides Sabrina, and she was sleeping. I would see something on the side of my eye and look really quick, but then I would not see anything. It kept happening all night long. I felt like there was some thing or someone in the room with me. Almost like a spirit, but the spirit felt evil. I tried to put it out of my head and go to sleep.

The next day, Acacius's girlfriend babysat for me because the walls were climbing in on me. Acacius told me to just go to a place within walking distance. He stated that more people get busted driving. I went walking down by the river on Jefferson in Ecorse. I sat down and watched the water and thought about my life and where I was going from here.

I had five thousand dollars on me but that was not going to take care of me forever. I went back to the hotel and called Acacius and asked him to talk with me. He rushed over to the hotel. I told him I was out walking and my head was going crazy with thoughts. I was expressing my thoughts about where my life is going from here.

He told me that every cop in the city is looking for you. We need to get you out of here but you can't take your daughter with you. I told him I would not leave without her. So I packed up everything in the room and Acacius took me to his house. I stayed with him and his girlfriend. At least Sabrina and I were together and we had a backyard to play in.

Acacius was around 52 and had a girlfriend 21 years old. It was like me and Vicenza Giuliano. I would call my brother ever night from Acacius's house, talking to him about the situation.

I called other people like Winchester Ted and some other's. I felt comfortable there but I knew that Sabrina and I would not be able to stay together long. I could feel it in my soul that I was not going to raise Sabrina. I knew I would have to give her up.

My brother Rip stated to me, that I needed to let Sabina go. He stated, "If the police come in to get you Billy Joe, they are coming in to shoot."

"You need to let Paula have Sabrina. Billy Joe, she is in danger. If you want to live like this that is your choice. Allow Sabrina to have a normal life style," Rip said.

"If the cops and fed's came in to get you right now, you need to strip down nude and come out with your hands on top of your head. They will shot you Billy Joe and say they thought you were carrying a gun or you were going for it."

"To the cop's you are a scum ball, they don't care about you. You have chosen your life, let Sabrina have a fair shake."

I was hurt by my brother's words but knew he was telling the truth. So I agreed to send her to Paula's. The next day when Acacius got up, which was noon, I told him what Rip and I talked about. He agreed and stated I needed to leave the United States.

So I told Sabrina she was going to Aunt Paula's house. She did not take it well; kids are smarter than you think.

Sabrina cut into my heart with her actions and words. She started crying and told me, without me even saying anything . . . .

"Mommy, I don't want to go to Aunt Paula's house."

"I want to stay with you even if it means dying."

I asked Sabrina were did she get that from? She told me.

"I know the police man is after you mommy, I heard you talking. I rather die with you than go to Aunt Paula's house."

I was so hurt inside to let her go, after she showed me so much love and wanting to stay with me no matter what. Of course, she did not understand what she was saying concerning death but it was so cute, and it touched my heart, that it brought tears to my eyes.

When I had to let Sabrina go . . . . by giving her to Acacius to meet my brother and then take her to my sister's house, it killed me.

She screamed bloody murder. She kept repeating herself saying.

*"No mommy, no, let me die with you, I don't want to live without you mommy."*

*"Please mommy, don't send me away to protect me let me be with you, I want to be with you."*

Those words rang in my ear for years to come. It still bothers me to even write them. An innocent child only five and half years old wanting to die with her mother, not knowing what is going on. She just did not want to be without their mother. I did not know that this was going to screw up everything in Sabrina's life either. She had trust issues, abandonment issues, and attachment issues; she was not able to allow anyone to get close to her.

So Acacius took my daughter to a friend, that friend, met Rip, my brother, at a restaurant. Then Rip took her to Paula. It was a sad day and I missed her a lot. We did everything together. But like my brother said, if you want to be on the lam Billy Joe, fine, do as you need to do, but don't screw up your daughter's future because yours is.

Rip was worried that they would try to shoot me while Sabrina was with me, or she would see them place me in handcuffs. Rip was worried they would try to take her to foster care home. The state would try to step in, we would have a long battle to fight. I agreed with him and it was the safest and smartest thing to do no matter how much it hurt to listen to her scream as she left.

In this life style, you have to be able to leave everything and anything including your family and loved ones go within five minutes. I was trained well for the streets. I had to let her go and get my act together for survival.

Well, that day I felt depressed, hearing Sabrina's cry but Acacius told me he had a place in Canada for me to go to. He had a friend that owned a nice home up there on the lake. So I went to Canada.

We stopped off to get some groceries and some personal items for me. I had gotten clothes for Sabrina but not myself when we returned earlier to that old apartment but didn't get stuff I needed so I needed some stuff. I told Acacius about Dee and how much he would sell in a day for me. I told him as long as Dee was out there, money would still come in.

Yeah, my dope man was helping me, but I knew that was so I would not tell on him. It was only a matter of time before he would get tired if I became a burden and maybe even kill me to end this. If he felt he could help for a minute he would but then his survival instincts would kick in. I was on a time game and I knew it.

Dee took over selling and supplying my customers. That way, Acacius would have a reason to continue to assist me. So there was still money coming in. I had nine thousand out there on the streets when I got caught up in this situation so I had Dee collect it for me. Plus I talked Acacius into giving him more drugs to sell as my co-partner.

Acacius and his girl argued all the time. I later found out later that Acacius was using too. Damn, no one was who they claim to be. He wanted to kill me thinking I was using. I was out done! First Vicenza Giuliano was a fake and now Acacius. I had to jump in a fight between him and his girl. He pulled out two knifes from his pocket.

I was crazy so I grabbed Acacius and tried to get his head together. Later that day, my brother came over to the house. He and Acacius were talking when there was a knock at the door. It was Benny and a couple other hoods. They brought the newspaper over and told Acacius I was HOT. Benny also stated that he believed that Henze had a 10,000 dollar hit on me. Benny stated that Henze was his boy but Henze thought I was the one who shot Vicenza Giuliano.

They all sat around the table talking about motherfuckers that were dirty rats and did not have a right to live.

I introduced my brother Rip. When Benny asked who that motherfucker is, I told Rip not to say anything out of the way to these guys because they are killers.

So what did my stupid brother say with his weird sense of humor?

Rip looked around the table and started laughing out loud, the hoods all looked at each other wondering what the fuck was so funny.

Then my brother said, "You guys don't keep friends long do you?"

It went right over their heads but I kicked Rip under the table. Thank God, they continued talking like my brother did not say anything.

Acacius and I were concentrating on keeping the business going. Dee was a great hustler, and he knew how to get rid of that powder. He knew all my customers, plus his own. Dee would run into people all the time who were off into heroin or coke. Dee hung in those places to hook up with new business. So Dee met Acacius's and me at restaurants throughout Detroit. We talked and ate, and caught up on old times. It was great every time I would see Dee.

I missed him a great deal. No matter what, Dee and I were the best of friends. I had talked to him about that robbery when Vicenza Giuliano, Sabrina and I were in that apartment that time. I let it go but always believed Dee set that up. I would dismiss it saying Dee did not like Vicenza Giuliano and it wasn't to harm Sabrina and me. Now that I look back at everything in my life, I saw myself mentally sick back then. I could count on him, just like he knew he could count on me.

Acacius gave him a gram then I told Acacius the more you give him the less he has to meet with us. Acacius thought about what I said . . . He agreed with me and gave Dee an ounce. Dee got rid of that within the hour.

I said to Acacius, "I told you Dee was a hustler. He knows who to go to."

Acacius was impressed, and gave Dee two ounces. Dee brought all the money, plus other money that was owed to me.

That was considered back collection. That was all profit for me, cuz Acacius was paid for my last load. It was cool and made me feel like I was still doing something even though I was not able to be out there physically.

I was staying in Canada and started to go a little crazy. I thought about killing someone and smashing their teeth in with a sledge hammer then burning their body up and placing my ID next to them.

So when Acacius came over I brought it up to him. He totally disagreed and told me I was going stir crazy being in that cabin. He stated for me to stop watching TV. He told me to get out more and take in some fresh air. There was a lake right outside the door but it was October and it was too cold to be on the lake.

If it had been summer I would have just swam and enjoyed the warm weather. When you get caught up in this lifestyle, you stop enjoying what life has to offer.

Acacius was starting to worry about me and thinking the ordeal was getting to me. I begged him to let me call Sabrina, but we would have to go all the way to America to make the phone call. Acacius did not want to take the chance of them tracing the call to Canada. So finally, he agreed and thought it would make me stop thinking of crazy ideas.

So we got into the car and drove to the bridge. We went into the Detroit area so if they traced the call, we would have enough time to escape back across the bridge leading into Canada. The Feds would not even think I was in Canada.

I talked to Paula and she told me that the FBI was parked across the street from her house. She then told me that one of them talked to Sabrina and asked her some questions. I asked her **WHY** she would let Sabrina talk to them. She told me she was not going to stop them from talking to Sabrina that I was the person who had something to hide, not them. I asked what they said to Sabrina. She told me that one of them told my baby if your mom was not guilty she would turn herself in and come home to you.

My daughter stuck up for my welfare but I was angry that they even talked to her. After I talked to Paula and my daughter I called Rip and told him what Paula said and how mad I was.

Rip told me, "Billy Joe look, Paula does not live like that. You have chosen to live this way. Don't expect her to know how to respond to the FBI or any police. Paula is a good girl and does not know that she is hurting you."

"Look Billy Joe, if you chose to live out there on the lam from the police that is your business and I am with you 100%. But don't expect us to know what to say or do. I know what to say, but I am different Billy Joe, your sister is taking on your child. She and George are taking on a whole new responsibility, don't say things or hurt Paula. She is trying to help you out so Sabrina does not have to go to a foster care home. So give her a break, and if you want to be out on the lam . . . . go but cut your ties here."

"Go live your life until you get caught if you ever do. I love you and I am with you no matter what your decision is. But don't drag us down with you. You have never involved your family before why involved us now! Go on with your life and don't turn back."

"Stay gone Billy Joe and live life to the fullest. I am not going to hate you for it. I don't want to see you, baby sister, locked up like an animal. But you must let Paula raise Sabrina, you must stay out of it and leave them alone so the FBI can move on. They are parked outside my house too Billy Joe."

"They are always parked outside Paula's house. They are watching our every move listening to our phone calls. We can't live our lives! We have done nothing wrong, but we have the police and Fed's camped out in our front yards. You are the only one who screwed up and the only one not under surveillance."

"Do what you have to do Billy Joe or **turn yourself in**. You are the strongest, toughest woman I know sis. You can face anything that comes your way, turning yourself in will allow you to see Sabina on regular basis. You say it was an accident, so let the truth come out. You claim to be a stand up person."

"Then stand up!!"

"But with you on the lam you need to go on and not turn back. Allow us to get back to our normal life. You have to make the decision Billy Joe. I can't make it for you and neither can Paula or anyone else. Now, don't get mad just know I told you this with great love and I stand behind any choice you make. I love you Billy Joe, you were always my favorite sista'."

I hung up the phone and thought about what my brother said but part of me did not want to give up my freedom. I was not ready.

But then I thought did I really have freedom? I did tell Acacius's that I wanted to get a job or do something. Acacius told me it was a bad idea. He said they can extradite you back to America because it was an M-1 case. My picture was in the news daily. I saved all the newspaper clippings. That meant there was no statute of limitations.

I really hated being in Canada. So Acacius agreed to bring me back to the states and hide me. He wanted to wait until the snitches were killed. He had been working on that issue trying to catch them. Every time he tried to put something under one of their cars it would fall out.

Every time he went after them, he could not get them in a position to have them alone. Something kept going wrong; to me it was Providence that was stepping in.

So he took me out of Canada, brought me to this house in Evanston, IL with a family that could not speak English. Their son was able to speak, but they spoke broken English. They were a Greek family and was willing to do anything for Acacius and his mother. They told the family I had a miscarriage and needed to lay and rest. He told them I needed a place to recuperate. He also told them, the man I was pregnant by, took off on me and left me to deal with this on my own. Being ol' school, they wanted to help. So I stayed there with them.

Their son came home from Greece. He had been there for three years. His green card ran out after three years. After three years, you would have to go into their army. In Greece, they have a mandatory draft; he was trying to get out of it.

Their son was coming up to see me every day. Acacius did not like this at all. He felt like it was damaging to me because of me being on the run from the police. Acacius kept going on and on about this issue. So I finally told him that I would act as if I was sick to keep him from coming upstairs. It was nice to have company but Acacius been also worried that him being close to my age would be trouble.

Acacius's mother would come every day to visit with me. We would weave Afghans and talk all day. She was such a wonderful woman and she loved her son very much. They had a strange relationship because she leaned on Acacius's more than she did her own husband. They had a special bond that any parent would dream of with their own child. I learned a lot from her. She had so much knowledge and was just a delight to conversate with. I thought very highly of her and grateful she allowed me in her presence because she was not a woman that dealt with many people at all.

Weeks had gone by and I was done with my afghan for my father. I wanted him to see my talent. I was so proud of it. I had gotten tired of staying in the house so I went for a walk. Acacius's mother came to the house and did not see me. Later I showed up and she questioned me where I was at.

I told her I went for a walk. She did not yell or tell me I could not go. She only told me if I slip up and get caught, I will bring so much heat to her son and family. She went on about what a risk that her family was taking to care for my needs and if they get caught or I get caught that her whole family is in jeopardy of going to prison just because of conspiracy.

She also told me, "I am not saying this because I want you to turn yourself in or I want you to leave and go on your own. I am telling you this to keep in mind next time you take a walk and place everyone at stake."

I heard what she said even though she stated she did not want me to go. I knew in my heart that she stated the same thing my brother had pleaded. They wanted to get back to their own lives. After she left that day, I sat and drank some peppermint schnapps. Matter of fact, I drank a lot of peppermint schnapps.

I drank and my thoughts were driving me crazy. I could hear my brother and her talking, then my sister, then Sabrina. I started elaborating on the circumstances and wondering if I was being selfish. Only thinking of my issues and not what could happen to everyone else. I also thought strongly about my brother's words, stating, "Be the woman you claim you are you state you are a stand up person then hold true to its Billy Joe."

So I sat on the back part of the couch in the apartment and drank myself silly.

Acacius had to take care of some business that night and came late. I was still sitting on the couch drunk waiting for him to walk in the door. He brought me a bunch of groceries and started talking about how he came close to getting one of the snitches on my case. When he walked in the living room and saw me perched on the back side of the couch he was looking at me crazy wondering if I had lost my mind. I told Acacius I had something very important to discuss with him. He stood there wondering what I was going to say. He never entertained the subject I was about to speak on.

I told him, I was going to turn myself in and stand up to this crap and be the woman I claim I am.

I told him what my brother had told me and what his mom had to say. I told him being pissy drunk what I had been thinking all day and where my head was at. I had absolutely made up my mind and was not going to let anyone talk me out of it. Acacius did not think it was a good idea. He felt like I should wait until we could get the charge dropped down to a lower charge. He called an attorney and asked him to see if they could talk with the prosecutor's office on another charge.

The only other charge they wanted to give me was murder in the second degree but both Acacius and I knew that was a bunch of crap and it would lock me in by taking that plea deal. They wanted me to admit to something I did not do out of malice. (I always stated that I went to prison for all the things I did and never got caught for.)

Then Dee got busted doing an armed robbery. Dee started sneaking and using the dope behind our back. Once he started using, he was using up a lot of his profits and then got a bigger habit and started dipping into the money he owed us on consignment. It was getting so out of hand, that Dee started to do arm robberies to pay us back and he was using all the dope for his personal use. He had a gorilla on his back. He got out of control. He was using the dope and got caught up. He wanted to get mine and Acacius's money so he did a couple armed robbery jobs.

The rollers ran Dee down during a heist and busted out his front plate with a gun by sticking it in his mouth. When Fly (a guy that we knew, got busted and tried to make a deal for a lesser sentence by turning Dee and me in.) told the cops to watch Dee and they would find me. They staked Dee out. During the stake out, Dee did an arm robbery job. The police followed him. After Dee robbed an establishment, the cops waited for him to come back to his car with the money and as Dee was leaving the building they announced they were cops and told Dee to get on the ground with his hands up above his head. Dee did not move fast enough for them, so the cop came up to Dee and put the gun in his face. When the cop did that, he was so close to Dee's mouth that he cracked Dee's plate his false teeth in the front part of his mouth. Dee lay-ed on the ground. The cop flipped Dee over and hand cuffed him.

When they placed him in custody, they told him they knew he knew my where-about. This dude named Fly who was going with Carney after her husband died, knew Dee and I was a team. He got busted and agreed to give them information on me to get out of his sentence. He told them to stake Dee out and you surely will find Billy Joe. So they did except Dee would not give me up. They placed a bunch of armed robberies on Dee that did not even belong to him.

Dee took a plea deal for a 10 year sentence. Then, I really knew it was time for me to go. I called the police and told them I was going to turn myself in. But later that night, Acacius's and I went out partying. I had a great time.

I called them back and told them I would be there the next day. Acacius said, "Have your lawyer turn you in."

Then I called my attorney O'Connell he was an attorney down in Detroit and had been with me and Vicenza Giuliano for a few situations. Acacius's wanted me to hire Bufalino. I told him

I wanted to turn myself in to O'Connell who I trusted. So we called O'Connell and he told me to meet him at McDees on Woodward in Detroit. So I did, but of course I was so drunk and disgusting. I am glad I will never see those folks again, because I was an embarrassment that day.

I was falling all over the establishment, asking people what the Fu—they were looking at. I dropped my hamburger on the floor, picked it up, blew it off and started to eat it. Poor O'Connell had to be out there with me, but he knew I was drunk and understood. I was turning myself into the authorities for a murder charge.

He drove me down there and told me to be strong and he would have an arraignment right away. They took me into the city jail and snuck me down at the Winchester police station. I had to sober up during the ride and my attorney helped with that. Once we arrived I was able to adapt my personality.

The officers kept saying; I was not what they expected at all. I was nice and polite. I might have been drunk earlier, but I knew when to act right in front of the right people. They took my photo and fingerprinted me.

While they were fingerprinting me the officer stepped to the next room for a second to get something. While he was gone, a man in the jail cell called out to me, "Hey baby, do you have a comb or pick I can use?"

I looked at the man as if I could snap his neck within seconds and stated in a harsh low voice, "Fu—you mother Fu—er; write your Mamie for a pick, what do I look like your freakin' best friend?"

Just as I was stating those words to the man, the officer came into the room and heard me. He turned and told the other officer; I guess we do have the right person that is just how they describe her. So they placed me in a holding tank until Detroit Sheriff's Department came and got me.

I was still very drunk and was like that when I went downtown to the county jail which was the biggest piece of crap sh—hole I ever laid eyes on. I have seen shit houses that looked better and cleaner than the Detroit county jail. The staff was mean and loved to abuse their authority. There were no civil rights like in prison so they would treat you anyway they pleased and then some.

The officers stuck together so they covered each other's butts. I went in and they stripped searched me.

They wanted to take away my religious emblem, obviously I was not a religious person, but I had a gold bar on that necklace and a few other items all on one chain. It was worth maybe around 1000.00 dollars or more back in 1982. That was a lot of money. I had to strip down totally naked and bend over spreading my cheeks, and cough. Of course, one cough was not enough. I had to spread more and cough louder because they knew they had the power to make me do it.

I refused and the one big female officer that looked like a dyke told me, "Look sister we can do this the easy way or the hard way . . . it's up to you."

So I gave them my necklace and bent over spread my cheeks as far apart as I possibly could and bent over so they could get the treat to look all up inside me. It was embarrassing and degrading. If I could have blew a stinky fart, I would have.

Then they gave me some greens as they called them, county jail clothes. They took me to the rock called Rock 4-11. I was put in a cell where there were no whites on the rock at all. I was the only one. I did not really have an issue because I had been around blacks all my life, but for some odd reason, I felt it was going to be a bit different.

I went into my cell and it was not much later may be 15 minutes and a girl called Militia came to my cell with a girl called Sara. She came into my cell and asked me my name. I told her I did not feel like being bothered.

She kept questioning me, and then started calling me white girl and told me, "I can make you suck my friends Sara's pussy."

I looked up at her and told her to exit my cell. I did not want any trouble. I was going up for M-1. I did not want the court system to think I was a violent person, or a trouble maker.

She just was not listening. Militia walked right up to me and slapped the dog sh—out of my face.

I bounced back from the slap and looked up at her and told her . . .

"Look, I am going to pretend you did not just do that and ask that you leave my cell now before I really get pissed off."

She drew her hand back as if she was going to slap me again and I grab her wrist as it came close to my face and jumped up and started knocking her head against the wall. I hit her respectively in the face and pounding her head against the wall. I had a death grip on her neck (that was my M-O to grab the neck). The other girl Sara decided that she would gang up on me too and jumped on my back.

I threw her off me and she landed in the bunk bed across the cell and ran out of my cell without her slipper, scared like a real punk. I was pissed now and had to make a name for myself.

The goon squad came rushing in and tried to pull me off Militia. Every time they pulled, I would pull her by her neck and pull away and hit her head hard against the wall where there was a metal strip that divided the steal wall into sections.

It took about four or five officers to pull me off Militia. When they finally got us separated they striped me down nude and placed me in what they call a bam-bam dress. It was a white quilted material that was designed like a dress but it was thick and could not be torn off.

You could tell the staff was a bit biased and there were not many whites in jail at that time. I would not tell the staff what the fight was about and that is why they put me in that dress. They kept me on suicide precaution. I was not trying to commit suicide, I was trying to beat the Fu—out of that bitch for slapping me and not respecting my space.

I was on it for something like 10 days or less. I can't quit remember how many days I was like that. Of course, they only locked Militia down in a lock up for two days and Sara received nothing. I realized then and there, that it was not going to be easy to do this time.

Later they finally allowed me to go back to the cell they gave me, but I was still on lock down because I had a hearing and was found guilty of fighting. (That was a surprise.)

So I tried to sleep as much as possible. I could hear the ladies talking on the cat walk. One of the ladies' another girl named Sara C. I could hear her tell the rest of the ladies, "Yeah, well this time they found the wrong white girl to mess with; am I glad; they always think they can run that game on everyone. She just wasn't the right one to run it on." (The girl was stating it to the others on the cat walk)

I took it by that statement, that they had messed with many of the Caucasians that ran thru here.

Then Militia knocked on my cell wall, she was in the next cell to me. I did not answer. She did it again, and again. Still no answer . . . she finally asked what is your name white girl. I really did not answer that statement. She stated it several times . . . finally I got tired of her mouth. So I finally said what the Fu—do you want? She stated I just want to know your name.

I told her it is not Fu—white girl, bit—and don't call me that no more, it is Giuliano, and it is Ms. Giuliano to you.

A few minutes later she called out again, "Giulianka, I mean, Ms. Giulianka, yo' al 'right. I like you."

I waited a few minutes and said, "Yeah, I guess I am, I put about seven knots on your head. I guess I am alright."

Then I rolled over and tried to go back to sleep and forget where I was at.

Every day was a trip. I mentally withdrew from everyone and everything. I did not trust anyone as it was but I really did not trust my surroundings. Everyone was always asking you what your case is about so they could contact the prosecutor to get a cut on their sentence. They use your information to cut a deal. It was a real cut throat situation in here.

The trashy people coming in there were off the hook. I was constantly engaged in fights while I was in the county jail. I stayed in the county jail for almost a full year somewhere around 335 days or something like that. I am not totally sure of the exact days. I could look it up on my paper work but I am sure it is close.

I did all I could to fight that M-1 case. I am not going to go through every single detail of the county jail. I am sure when this book is published many will come forward to tell their stories. The ones that are true, I will stand up to them. I will be totally honest and tell the truth.

I got into thirty-six fights while incarcerated in the county jail. It was awful sometimes in the county. One time, this girl wanted me to be her woman and I told her, I was not into that. She had HIV but back then we did not know too much about it.

One night when they locked our cells. I was talking on the vent to Dwight. We could yell to the guys through the vents. It was a way to entertain ourselves.

Anyways, this girl yelled out on the cat walk, that she wanted me off that vent and told the dude she was my woman. I told her, she was not my woman and to get out of my business. She demanded me to get off the vent and stop talking to the dude. Really? You have to be kidding. These hoes were off their rocker.

Dwight yelled down on the vent and asked me, "Are you going to let her talk to you like that?"

I kept talking to Dwight and told him to ignore her and I would handle my own business in the morning. I did not want him instigating shit but was pissed off with this bit—; she thought she could rule me. I was not a punk but these hoes would try you in a minute.

When morning broke and the cell doors were opened, I ran into the girl's cell and fought her. I broke my hand hitting her. They had to take me out and put a cast on my hand and I had to go to court like that. When I went to hit her, she moved her head and I hit the bars. Anyways, she left me alone after that. I just did not like people trying to rule me and I was going up for life.

I was laying in my bunk and could hear the men upstairs. They were yelling about something. Either a fight or raping someone. At night time you could hear those guys on the vent attacking other men as they came in. You could hear them scream like a cat that was being killed by a slow death. They were screwing the new guys coming in, raping them. They would gang up on them and many of them would hold one dude down while the others took turns screwing the new guys in the butt. The officers knew this was happening and would hear the screams just like we did downstairs but never did anything about it.

I believed many of the staff were getting payoffs to allow it.

There was a man upstairs in a cell that knew of me and when one of the snitches on my case came in he was mouthing off stating I was the real snitch. He was talking about me like a dog trying to look good to all the other guys up there. One of the guys up there screamed down the vent calling my name, and stated that the sound that you hear tonight will be dedicated to Giuliano because she is a real one.

That night, you could hear screaming through the vents like murder was taking place. Even the strongest person would be sickened by this sound.

The next day in court, the prosecutor approached me and asked me about one of the guys on my case, that was there that night of the shooting. He had been raped.

I got mad and on the defensive and asked them, "Why are you asking me? Does it look like I have dick and balls between my legs? You're crazy asking me what happens in the men's joint!"

I could not believe they felt like I had that much power that I controlled what happened in the men's joint. I told him to ask the men in the men's division, don't ask me, because I don't have anything swinging from my legs.

My brother told me to watch my mouth because I had not gotten sentenced yet.

They took me back to my cell in the county and I received a visit that week. It was my dope man Acacius. I had told Acacius not to come around during my trial because I did not want them to associate him with me.

He had my brother out with him one night. He wanted me to know what happened to my brother. I told Acacius to please leave my brother out of this. Then Acacius told me there was something he must tell me. I knew something was wrong. I could see the look on his face.

I looked through the double plated glass window and picked up the phone to talk. Acacius would not pick up the phone. He started to write on a piece of paper. My heart started to pound with fear. He wrote that he asked my brother to build something for him. He did not tell my brother what it was or for, but told him how to put it together. He told me that something went awry and my brother along with a friend got blown up by a chemical reaction. I looked at him wondering if I heard what he was saying. He told me my brother was in the hospital. That a piece of metal went into his chest.

My brother saved his friend from burning up and put out the fire before the fire truck got there. His lung was in danger. I could not believe what was being said . . . . I started to pound on the window and told Acacius to stop.

I said, "Let me go to prison, no more death. If my brother does not live I don't care if I rot in here."

The guard came to see what all the noise was about. I walked out and went back to my cell crying. My whole world had fallen apart.

Later that week I heard from Acacius that my brother was going to be alright. I heard my brother saved his friend's life, put out the fire and cleaned up the scene before the rollers arrived. Wow, my brother was something else but I did not want him involved.

I did not want Acacius to come around and see me anymore either. During my last court date, they took photos of Acacius. He placed his coat over his head and they did not get a great shot of him but I was worried he would get pulled in.

Afterwards, I was laying in my cell and the staff told me that I had a visitor. I was wondering who it was. I entered the visiting window and saw that my mother had come to see me. I was wondering why.

She told me that she loved me. I asked her why she waited until I had a life sentence hanging over my head before she wanted to tell me she loved me. I looked at her through the double glass and told her she was twenty years too late. I needed you when I was a kid not now that I am facing two life sentences.

I did not want any more visits and asked them at the county to place that down on my paper. I just wanted to finish this trial and hopefully get through all of this with a will to stand strong no matter what the outcome.

The trial was two weeks long.

My trial was a kangaroo court led by my lawyers, the prosecutor and the judge. The prosecutor and the judge both disliked me without even knowing me. They had dealt with so many criminals in their lifetime that I was just one more scumbag off the streets to them. They were jaded by their constant immersion in criminal prosecutions. On the government side, it wasn't so much justice for the man that was killed, but a scheme of revenge against me, "Put her away for good just because we have her and she is a drug dealer."

As to my lawyers, my first lawyer was always late for court. Cassius (aka Acacius) let O'Connell go and hired a second lawyer that was worthless as far as I was concerned. I paid my first lawyer a 9,000 dollar down payment. The second attorney I paid him 20,000 dollars and he got me 20 years for every thousand I spent on him.

I believe my second lawyer did not know what he was doing. I believed he even told them I was guilty. I can't prove it, but I do believe he turned on me at the end. He even asked Cassius if he could get some cocaine from him. I told Cassius I did not trust him. I believed right after that he sold me out to the judge and prosecutor. (I want everyone to know this is my opinion.) He also tried to get me to turn evidence in my federal case. Cassius & my brother paid him a visit to convince him to stop pressing me.

I was not going to take anyone down because I got myself caught up in some crap. My destiny was ahead. I was going to be the "Stand-up Lady".

After numerous preliminary hearings, rescheduled court times both by the Feds and the State, my trial finally began. Both of my state and federal charges were conducted at the same time. When I turned myself in, federal authorities stepped in as well. The State began my trial by accusing me of 1st Degree Murder. I had also many underlining charges under that. They bootstrapped my state's charge meaning that they added all sorts of charges in order to make sure I was found guilty of something. The Feds piggybacked onto the State's case and piled on their charge. My federal charge was for Possession and Distributing Heroin and Flight to Avoid Prosecution. I was looking at 5-7 years.

In the matter of the shooting, because I was on a drug deal, I was committing a felony so I wasn't able to claim self-defense. Therefore, they charged me with 1st Degree Murder.

During my State trial, the officials took me back and forth between the Federal Courts and State Courts. I went to downtown Detroit for the State and Federal trials. At the Federal hearing, the person that was the informant did not have to show their face. They did not have their name anywhere on any of the documents. This was to protect the informant. This was the way the Fed's did it with a drug case. When the Fed's took me, the authorities would chain my wrist to a long chain to my feet. Then they would put what they called a box between my feet so I could not run. I was also wrapped with a belly chain that connected to the leg chains. When the State came to get me they just handcuffed me in the front with handcuffs. The incongruity of these two different procedures used to make me shake my head in disbelief; the Fed's treated me like I was on a murder case when it was only a drug case. The State treated me like it was a simple drug case instead of a murder case. When the Fed's finally sentenced me, I was put in a cell next to my husband. He wanted me to take all the blame and state he had nothing to do with it. The attorney got them to offer me a plea bargain if I did not testify for my husband and take all the blame. It was not all my fault anyways because my husband was there when the deal was being made. My husband knew that the informant was dirty but did not tell me. He had heard through the street grapevine that the informant was busted by the Feds and was looking to some big time and needed to turn in a few of us in order to lessen his time. I almost did take the blame but my dope man said, Fuck that! don't take the blame. He is not a man if he is asking you to take the blame. So I was looking toward 4 years I was sentence to two years. Then I went back to the state and finished my trail with them. I got a bond with the Fed's but I was not able to pay for it because I had a detainer on me with the State for a murder case.

I accepted a plea bargain to a two year sentence as long as I did not have to testify in my husband's defense. The fed's knew I was taking all the blame and they wanted my husband too. So I was not allowed to testify for him and that was the plea bargain I took. The Feds at this time dropped the Flight to Avoid Prosecution.

When my husband and I was arrested earlier by the Fed's we were both put on bond. Thirty days later they took my husband to prison for a violation of that bond for having guns in the house. They revoked his bond. They kept me on bond and then dismissed my bond after a few months. I thought I was in the clear but they had me under investigation. But when I fell into this murder rap, the Fed's brought back my bond and re-instated the case they had with me and my husband.

Since my husband was on his third offense for drugs, it meant he was on a three year special, that's how the DEA set it up. The federal crimes are different than state. A third year special means he was busted before for drugs and this was his third offense. So a third year special meant he had to be on parole for three years instead of two years or one year. In this case, the main charge is the worse. I got the main charge that I was the dealer. He got the charge that he was around me and knew me, which was conspiracy. That is the lesser charge.

On the State's case, the other two men who were present at the scene also got charged with 1st Degree Murder but they plea bargained and turned me in to get a charge of Assault with Intent to Commit Armed Robbery with which they pleaded guilty to. This "Assault with Intent to Commit Armed Robbery" also showed up on my possible charges list. They had to place the same charge on my ballet that they gave them as a bargain. It is the law.

One event in the trial really stood out. The prosecutor had a witness stating that he had driven down the road that night of the shooting. This witness told the prosecutor he could identify me if he ever saw me again. So they put him on the stand.

I just knew he would point me out because I was the only defendant sitting right next to my attorney. How easy could it have been to pick me out of a crowd? But to my surprise, he stood up and picked out one of the jurists that did not look like me whatsoever.

This juror was larger in weight. I was maybe a size 5 and 112 lbs. She was maybe around a size 14 and possibly weighing in around 180. She had short hair that only went to her ears. I had hair down to the middle of my back. My hair was long and curly, blond. I was as skinny as a bean pole. I had just turned 23 years old two weeks before the case. That lady had to be at least 35 years old.

The courtroom went nuts when he picked her out, but regardless of this happening, the court overlooked it like it never happened. That part of my transcripts got lost and thrown out. My attorney came to me and told me before sentencing that they would be willing to give me 4 ½ to 15 if I would just tell on my connections, i.e., my husband and dope man.

Yet in court they kept stating my connections did not want anything to do with me, that was why I had to turn myself in. They also stated that I owed my dope man money and that is why I turned myself in. None of that was even close to being true, but I felt like I could not defend myself for fear they would use it against me.

They were not looking for truth as much as a conviction.

During the trail they found one of the co-defenders in 27 lies of stories that had changed from the time he got arrested. The other co-defender was found in 6 different lies.

The mainstay of the trial was a letter written to my husband. The letter was written in pencil. I wrote Vicenza Giuliano a letter and told him that it *didn't happen the way they said it did*.

Their whole case centered on this letter because their version of the letter had that I wrote instead: "*it did happen the way they said it did*". I wrote that **"it didn't"** and their version had **"it did"**.

Now the way I see it, my husband either erased the **(n't)** off the word **"didn't"** . . . . or the cops did. I will never know the truth. It would hurt me to my soul if Vicenza Giuliano did it but it would not surprise me. It would bother me more if our officers of the law did it, because we must believe in the law.

But I believe Vicenza did it to turn me in to the police to get back at me because he felt I had shot him that night. I also believe that is how he got off his sentence. Vicenza was supposed to get eight years for his part in the crime but he made a deal with them and received 4 years for his crime. I don't know what kind of deal he made, but he made some kind of deal to get from under an eight year sentence. The Fed's wanted Vicenza badly so he must have made some kind of deal. I got the main charge while he got the conspiracy which is the lesser charge.

The letter was written <u>in pencil</u> and I believe with all my heart, Vicenza Giuliano took an eraser taking the n't off the letter. So they used this letter stating: "It did (n't) happen the way they said it did." It was used during cross examination, which is never done. That was the only evidence they had toward me on this crime, besides two lying dope fiends that had been caught in several lies.

Since they charged me with robbery, I had the man from the party store that stated I pulled money out of my pocket and it had to be around 5,000.00 dollars. He stated I had a bunch of hundred dollar bills and then a few twenties. So I had that much money on me the night I caught the case. They did not allow him to testify.

The state authorities charged me with robbery but why rob for two hundred dollars when I had all the cash on me; this is nonsensical. It just goes to show that this was truly a kangaroo court.

During the trial, they only mentioned once how that man died on the case. The majority of the questions for the two week trial were about my drug activities.

Second of all, the cops believed the two co-defendants because they plea-bargained a deal with them and stated that they owed me money for drugs and were forced to set up their friend to rob him in order to pay me back. They told the cops that I robbed the guy because they did not know what they were doing.

After a long dragged out trial, the day of reckoning finally came. My life was going to be decided by a jury of twelve people.

I had five felonies on my jury ballot; First Degree murder, Second Degree murder, Attempted Armed Robbery, Assault with Intent to commit Armed Robbery, and the CCW charge, i.e. for having that concealed gun charge that I was given a pre-diversion charge if I stayed out of trouble for a year.

When the jury came back deadlocked after six hours, they only wanted to give me the gun charge, no other conviction! The judge sat there dumbfounded and told them the guidelines again and explained to them, "You cannot give her a gun charge without a felony charge."

Billy Joe

So he went back over the charges again. They did not feel I was guilty. The judge assured them not to worry about that, but to just come up with a charge to go with that firearm charge. (It's funny that so many of my transcripts came up missing when I sent away for them later on during my appeals.)

This time they did not stay in the deliberation room as long. The first time they deliberated, it was for six hours. On the second go-around, they went in there and gave me the last charge on the ballot which was 'Assault w/intent to commit armed robbery'.

The jury acquitted me of First Degree and Second Degree murder. They offered me the ability to cop to a lesser sentence if I gave my dope man and husband up. I would not do it.

The charge of 'Assault w/intent to commit armed robbery' was one of the elements executed on the two co-defendants. They were first charged with First Degree murder and were offered a lesser charge of 'Assault w/intent to commit armed robbery' if they turned state evidence on me which allowed them to receive 4 ½ to 15 years to testify in my case. Even though, each one was found in many lies during the trial, their lesser charge still stuck. It seemed to me that the authorities were comfortable in giving anyone a deal even if they have to lie to get one conviction. That is what they do to close a case. I was the chosen one because I was a known drug dealer.

Those two guys had set up that whole thing and pulled me into it. It was an accident how that man died. The courts and those two guys made it sound like I killed the man because the co-defendants owed me a couple hundred dollars. That was not true at all. Those two guys on my case were known for setting up dope houses and had done it before I came into the picture.

The courts knew I had big connections. They wanted me to give those connections up. If I would have snitched, I would not have seen much of prison. Just because of my loyalties and honor, I am considered as a dangerous murderer but if I would have given up my connections, I would've gotten a slap on the hands with small time and been back out on the streets in no time.

But I came to see that these bad turn of events was not the work of the court but of God protecting me from myself. I came to accept my predicament with calm detachment.

People do not understand the government and their system until they either are in the service of it or in prison. There are so many secrets that the norm of society doesn't even know about or understand. I am not saying I was not guilty of causing a situation that resulted in a death or that I should not have gone to prison, but what I am saying is, many times the law can be manipulated and abused by others.

The jury was not buying what the prosecutor wanted. They wanted to let me go with just the gun charge. They did not want to give me a crime to go with it. They understood the situation. On the other hand, the judge told them that they could not do that and they had to give me a crime to go with the gun charge. So that is how I received the last charge on my ballot. The judge could have ordered for non-voluntary manslaughter or voluntary manslaughter to be the charge and I would have accepted that gladly with no problem for that was the truth.

The next phase of a trial after the verdict is the sentencing. And just like all the previous events that got mangled, the sentencing part didn't go right either. The jury came back with the 'Assault w/intent to commit armed robbery' and was dismissed. Two weeks after that, the courts called me back and sentenced me to two years for the CCW charge, and 20-60 years for the 'Assault to commit armed robbery'. If they would have waited a little longer, new sentencing guidelines were going to come into effect which meant, the courts would not of been able to give me so much time. The new guidelines came down a couple of days later and I would have fallen under those guidelines which would have been 5-10 years. The co-defendants, the people that really caused this awful situation, got 4 1/2 years. As it happened, I received the full force of the government's ire.

These co-defendants were held up on sentencing because if they were sentenced within that same week in which I was sentenced, which is usually normal procedure, they would have had the same sentence I received. But because they turned state's evidence and made the State's case, they were given, I believe, a sweet deal. Before 1983, judges were able to give as much of a sentence as they chose; they had wide latitude and of course, some judges abused this power. This situation was just beginning to change but it was too late for me. The authorities waited to sentence the two co-defendants because they knew that a new law was coming down the pike in a couple weeks; they held their sentencing until they fell under the new law.

In the earlier system, judges would give who they wanted a bigger sentence and those they wanted a smaller sentence.

In my case we all received the same conviction for the same crime. In United States v. Coles, the ruling stated;

"If all offenders have the same charge they should receive the same sentence."

The two co-defendants were guiltier in this situation than me. They set their friend up of 12 years. They were trying to scam to get money for drugs. Since I was a woman, I was going to be easy-pickings.

I had been clean for two years and the judge used that against me in my sentencing. He stated in my transcripts that since I was sober, my actions of trying to rob them showed I was just greedy. If this accident was due to me being high or strung out on drugs or on withdrawal, he would been more understandable and lenient but as it was that I was clean—I was to have the book thrown at me.

This was totally unfair and showed where judges were abusing their authority. My crime only carried a sentence of 4 ½ years to 15 years just like what they gave the co-defendants. But they made sure to sentence me before the new guidelines came into effect.

The judge sentenced me 6 points over the old guidelines. This judge focused more on the fact of my drug dealing than he did on anything else . . . or like someone losing their life.

It was very strange to realize that my whole trial was only about the drug dealing I was involved with and that I was a federal inmate, sentenced by the fed's during the trial. The death of the man seemed to be of so little concern to them.

Weren't the two co-defendants on my case the major league players? Didn't they instigate this whole thing? Yet, I was the focus of the punishment. Even at my sentencing, the judge stated why he was giving me the time. He wanted me in long enough to lose all my connections . . . . which was 22 years to 60 years.

What about wanting me to pay for the life that was taken?

The trial court only mentioned one time about the **"seriousness of the crime."**

**I believe** when they are saying that, they meant the life of the man. Everything else was about my drug dealing. Now, call me stupid but wasn't that why I was serving a **federal conviction** for? **BEING A DRUG DEALER???** Nothing seemed right. It didn't make sense to me why I was given more time for the same conviction that I was already serving with the feds.

I couldn't understand why **this** judge had taken upon himself to give me more time for a conviction I was already serving. I appealed my case at least seven or eight times and never got anyone to agree with me in the court system.

If I had won any of my appeals, they would have brought me back to court and I would've fallen under the **Coles v. Supra Court** case:

"Where three defendants had the same case they had to give them all the same time of confinement."

The new tighter sentencing guidelines, I believe, was the reason I never won any of my appeals because they had certain cases they allowed to slip through the cracks and others did not due to political reasons. I will say it until the day I die: I was not sentenced for the assault case, I was re-sentenced for my drug business because the state was mad that the fed's did not give me enough time on those charges.

The shooting was an accident.

The fed's game was to give people like me short time so they could get you back on the streets and then arrest you in a bigger deal.

I received three sentences: 20-60 years for the Assault with Intent to Commit Armed Robbery; 2 years for the gun charge; and 2 years for the Possession and Distributing of Heroin.

I did not understand why things turned out the way they did for me at that time, but later on, I would realize that God was conditioning my life, and I did not even know it.

The man that was processing my paperwork for the state prison felt so bad for me, he sent me with a clean slate. He told me usually if you got into fights in the county those records would go with you.

He told me, "Man lady, you are going to be gone for a long time. I am not going to send your record from here and just send you with a clean record."

Then another officer came and took me in the elevator, when he shut the door he asked me if I wanted to screw (have sex) before I went for that long sentence.

I told him, "NO! I was just sentenced—I was not hard up."

He told me, "Yeah lady, you might talk that hard stuff now, but after a few years without a man, you'll wish that you had taken me up on my offer."

I just looked at him and felt very vulnerable. I told him I was not interested. I look back on all of this now wondering how many women he screwed with that same line.

Even though I went to prison with a clean record, it wasn't long before fights, trouble and arguments in prison followed me. I was always in trouble or getting into arguments with staff and prisoners.

Don't get me wrong, I deserved to go to prison. I am just stating my opinion.

So after sentencing I was taken to the Detroit Department of Corrections Facility with a population of about 280 women. They had one camp too. I am not going to speak on everything that occurred in prison because that is eighteen years of play by play activities but I will key into some of the things that stuck in my head.

# Chapter Six

## Life in the Joint

I was placed in a County van and sent out to the women's prison. It was the longest ride I ever went on. When we arrived there, it looked like a college campus with brick buildings or housing units, then one big brick building that they referred to as the control center.

As we pulled up, it was just like a Hollywood movie with barbed wire fence all around the brick buildings but there was a double wire on one building. There was a bunch of women standing in this little yard. They were hanging on the fence looking at me as if I was a piece of meat. They all gathered stating things like a man would, hootin' and a hollern' as if they were construction workers at a busy downtown are, but these were women. I rolled my eyes and knew I had more fights coming.

I started wondering if I was going to make it out alive or was it my destiny to die in prison.

I went into this door where they make you take off everything you are wearing. Then, they stick you in a shower with no curtain. Give you A2-100 shampoo to get rid of the bugs. After the shower, I was given a blue uniform to wear.

Every facility had a dress code. I was placed into a 8 x 12 room with white brick walls, a bed on the floor, and a toilet just like the one in Juvenile. For some odd reason, I had seen this in my future.

I laid there wondering how Sabrina was, and feeling how bad I let her down. I also felt bad for the man on my case for being at the wrong place at the wrong time. The first day went by as I lay on my bunk wondering if this was true or was I going to wake up.

It took three days for you to be medically cleared, sometimes a week. While I was lying there, I could not help but mull over in my mind about all those women and their behavior I saw when I was entering into the facility—Yelling like construction men hanging on that fence like they were hungry. I asked myself, what did I get myself into. This place was going to be a trip and I felt like this was going to be the end of my existence.

Three days of quarantine was over and during that time they test you, dip into your head and try to understand what makes you tick. They test to see where you are at academically and psychologically. They check you for all kind of diseases, if you need to be on medication or if you are half of a deck short.

I was finally given my blankets, sheets, pillow case, a change of blues, state shoes that looked like something a construction worker would wear. The shoes were black and hard, with a steel toe at the top. Trust me, after wearing these, you would need a foot doctor.

I was taken to close custody because of the length of sentence. That housing unit was the furthest on the property. It was kind of on a hill or hump. I walked in and it was shaped like two hallways, one on one side and the other on the other side. They were mirrored housing units with a long hallway to connect them together. Then, there was an officer's desk at the front by the outside door which was able to look down both hallways simultaneously. Then you walk down a hallway behind the officer's desk that was shaped like a tube . . . at the end of that tube, it was the same set up like the other side.

I was placed in a room and everyone was running around. I stayed in the room, until someone came to my door and stated, "You are new aren't you?"

I stated yeah, and they told me, you do not have to stay in your room. We are allowed out in the housing until count time. She explained to me what count time was and how much freedom we had to run around. We were not allowed that kind of freedom in the county jail. I was thankful to her, because no authority explained sh—to me coming in. They just dumped you in a housing unit.

Everyone looks at you when you first come in, if you are cute, they will express it to you. If you are ugly, they don't even talk to you sometimes instead they will dog you out and call you ugly. Giving you the flux (prison slang for aggravating and stressing you out; putting one on a mental and emotional rollercoaster).

I am not going to go through every single day while I was in prison, because most of the days consisted nothing but just trying to exist. Repeating the same thing daily for eighteen years and expecting different results would make one insane.

I sat in prison watching Mother Nature kiss my face daily in the mirror. Some days it felt like a slow death. Other days, it was just drama in the prison system. The only thing that kept me going was my daughter, just thoughts of her made me want to keep living. At the time, I was not aware that God was the lifeline that I was connected to.

I got into a lot of arguments and situations with officers and other convicts. I did my bit truly hard. I was not into getting high, so I stayed away from that crowd that participated in that.

But I did involve myself in the sales of drugs and ran "two for one" stores.

A "two for one" store is where one convict sells or barters convenience and toiletry items to other convicts. Usually, though, and this is the reason for the moniker, if you got one pack of cigarettes from me, you would pay me back with two packs. If you got toothpaste from me, you would pay me back with two tubes of toothpaste. That is how I made my money in there. The other convicts purchased food and personal hygiene items, or whatever from you just like a store.

Another gimmick that many of us women convicts would engage in, was what we called 'tricks'. A "trick" was getting men on the outside interested in us by teasing them through the mail, with letters and so forth, and getting them infatuated with us and then soliciting funds from them.

I did write one man before I was released that I really liked but was afraid to pursue it when I was released because I had so many head issues. Moreover, I wasn't able to transfer my parole like that or leave my daughter and grandchildren since he lived in another state.

I ran game (con games) a lot as well while I was incarcerated, but the great thing was, I never got caught running anything. I was only caught doing other things. They were dumb stuff, and I never seemed to get caught red-handed doing anything. In prison, the officers tried several times to catch me running a store. Because the officers could not catch me, they always had to write up the situation, as assumptions.

Let me give you a few examples of different situations that occurred with me.

One morning, I got up for breakfast as always, and walked into the kitchen. I was waiting in line and this girl who was half black and half white, named Nina started talking about how it stunk in the kitchen. She went on and on about how it smelt like wet dogs and baloney in there.

Of course, she was talking about "white" people. (It was funny to me, most of the women that were mixed always seem to have the majority of issues about white people). So she went on and on about this crap until I got sick of it.

So I told the girl in front of me in line, "Hey, do you hear that girl talking about us?"

She turned around with her coward ass and stated, "She is not talking about me, she did not say my name!"

I told that bitch, you are stupid if you don't know when you are being talked about indirectly.

So I asked the big fat mixed girl, "Hey, are you talking about me?"

She couldn't wait to feed into the situation, "Yeah, if the shoe fits, I am talking about you."

Then she asked me what I was going to do about it? I started pushing tables aside and going toward her. I picked up a chair and was getting ready to swing it and the officers came running into the kitchen. Of course, the big fat bitch that started it did not go to the hole, only I did.

Also a girl named Alicia, a Mexican girl, took a large metal can opener and tried to hit me from behind with it during the argument. I took it out of her hand. Well, I started to see from that day on, that things were a bit unbalanced in prison. Where it is unbalanced out here in society where the white dominate, inside the prison, the blacks dominate.

When I first got sentenced the majority of the staff was black. The majority of the prison population was black. Most of the products that were sold in the commissary store were geared for the black population. It was totally opposite from what it was out in society back in the 70's and 80's. I could totally understand because society had placed most of our black population in prison.

I met one black lady in there that was 78 years old that got caught trying to get some cat food and steal a pair of shoes to wear because her social security check was not enough to pay for rent, food, and clothing. She became desperate and took cans of cat food and a pair of shoes. The judge threw her in prison for her first offense.

I read her paperwork and found out that she had no other felonies nor been in trouble before. So our court system made a mockery out of the blacks in our country by placing them in prison so they did not have to deal with them in society. Many of them were there during their child bearing years both men and women. (Just my opinion).

So back to my story, I went to the hole and it was my first time. Of course since it was my first time, they only kept me there for three days and charged me with threatening behavior. I just did not know it at that time but my first time in was going to be a harbinger of things to come; "going to the hole" was going to turn into an everyday routine for me for the next six years of my life.

I came out and went about my business and then that same girl, Nina, wanted to be all right by me. Her woman and I were cool so she started to be cool with me too.

Everyone in prison was in a relationship with another woman. HIV was coming out in 1982-3; the people that I was cool with in the county jail had HIV. So even messing around in prison was a scary thing, because you did not know what anyone had.

I never thought I would mess around in prison but you will be surprised what you will do in a situation where it is socially accepted and everyone is doing it to pass their time. This girl took an interest in me and we started talking. She schooled me with everything in prison life.

They said she was one of the tough girls on the count (the prison yard). Her name was Peco. She was big, strong and built like a guy. Back in her prime, I am sure she was nothing to mess around with. Everyone in the prison was scared of Peco; she was no one to mess with.

One day, we were talking in the rec-room, a place where one was able to watch TV. She was watching me pack things for my daughter Sabrina. I talked to her several times concerning my daughter and how I felt coming to prison and leaving her with my sister.

I guess you could say, I learned a valuable lesson on that day.

Anyways, as I was putting a box together for Sabrina, Peco kept asking me why I was sending her this and that. Finally, I asked her what her problem was about me sending this box to my daughter.

She then started telling me about white people spoiling their kids and how blacks don't do that shit. She went on and on with it. I asked her politely not to continue to discuss this issue, because I did not like her opinion. She would not let the subject go.

She kept going on and on with it. I finally got pissed off and pushed her out of her chair. She was so outdone by my action, that she couldn't believe it.

We started arguing back and forth, and calling each other out on our races. She started calling me cracker etc., and yelling at each other at the top of our voices. She was about 180 lbs. and I was 115lbs.

We then started to roll around in the rec-room pulling on each other physically. Peco finally jumped up heading out the door, stating she was through with this. I told her she was not through until I said we were through.

We went out into the hallway, arguing and pulling at each other. She pulled on my hair so I grabbed hers. Then we would break away.

The officer's finally ran up to stop this and told Peco and I to exit to our rooms.

We were still yelling words at each other as the officers were yelling at us.

The officers repeated themselves.

Then Peco told the officer, "You better come and get this cracker."

I was totally outraged and leaped at Peco.

The male officer tried to stop me. Instead, I threw him over the desk and kept after Peco. She continually walked down the hallway trying to go the opposite way. While the officers kept trying to grab me, Peco was continuously crying out, "Ya all better come and get this cracker"

I was so mad, I could bite bullets. I was pushing the officers left and right trying to make my way to her. I busted the male officer in the nose as he went over the table. Finally headquarters sent in a goon squad.

They grabbed me and handcuffed my feet and hands behind my back. The one black officer stated, "Giuliano was doing everything. She started the fight."

She also stated that Peco did not do anything in the fight and argument. So they took me, but a little later, they brought Peco back there too. She kept crying about the only reason she was back there was because I was a white.

So finally, they let her out and kept me back there.

Deputies, officers and wardens came back to the hole just to look at me. They were wondering who this white girl was, who fought Peco. They all made a big deal out of it. It also created a name for me at that time. They just could not believe that someone white and thin as me went after Peco.

So here I sit again, in the hole. I did not realize that this was going to keep being my home for six years. I went to the hole so much that people would ask me when I came back on grounds, "Hey Giuliano, how long are you going to stay out this time?"

I got such an attitude that my personality began to build emotional and mental walls to protect myself. It slowly dawned on me that you never discuss and tell people inside how you feel about someone or something. When they become angry with you they will use it against you like Peco did me with my daughter.

Calling her spoilt and telling me that is how white people treat their children, offended me so, that I never spoke much on my daughter after that day. I learned to be very careful. I never discussed my case with people either, nor told people in there that I used to do drugs, or was a heroin addict. I really kept a lot of things to myself. I never would tell people what my real name was either.

Many would say to me, "Hey Giuliano, what is your first name or is Giuliano your first name, if so, what is your last name?"

I would let them know right away, "We are not that familiar with each other for me to give you an answer. Plus, I would never speak to you on the streets."

I was coldhearted with my words and did not care what others thought of me. No one liked me. They all disliked me from day one. Now, that I look back on it, it is funny because it seems I had this problem all my life.

They ended up moving Peco to camp before they would allow me out of the hole. They were so afraid about us fighting again since we tore up the housing unit. A couple officers thought it would be best to separate the both of us in the prison system there. They waivered Peco from a level V to a level I. They never did things like that—move a convict that many levels unless it was for a good reason. That was a big move for the facility to make a waiver like that.

So Peco went to camp. She even said good-bye to me by sneaking into the segregation area. She really liked me as a person. I thought well of her as well. She liked that I stood up for myself. She did teach me many things in there to stay away from. After she left, they let me out.

My custody level went up and I was pissed. Another year in close custody. Life in the big house so-to-speak.

Peco and I did become great friends, she drew a picture of my daughter for me, and it was beautiful to me. She went to camp and still stayed in contact. She would send me items from there when people came back to higher custody. When she went home, she even came and saw me when she was released. She came back to prison for another case eight years later.

I am not sure, but I heard later on in life she had a heart attack and ended up in a nursing home; my prayers are with her.

As time went on after I became clear conduct, I was able to apply for the factory. We made license plates and good money. I first worked on the silk screen and then inspection, and then the press. I learned to operate every machine in there.

We had a new deputy warden. His name was Robert.

He could not stomach me, though he did like some of the young black ladies at the Detroit facility. He would hide it well but you could tell that he was for the blacks and would dog out the whites. He hated me so much that every time my name was even attached to anything he would have me written up and sent to segregation, the hole. Robert was a joke. He was dirty in his approach and the way he did things. But being in the system for so long he was able to cover his tracks.

This of course is my personal opinion of Robert from the years of dealing with him in the system. I have to give him credit, because he succeed with only a GED.

One of the convicts I was associated with was having trouble with her girlfriend. One morning Sadie and l got up. We heard an associate named Donna arguing with her girlfriend Bonnie all night long. She went to her girlfriend's cell and took a pop can with her. She turned it into a weapon by bending it and tearing it in half thus creating a jagged edge. She jumped on top of her girlfriend while she was in bed cutting her face.

She came out of the room as nothing occurred but as always in prison, someone saw her coming out of the cell. That person reported it to the officer.

The person who saw it was one of the toughest girls on the count. She had a reputation of not involving the police, being a stand-up guy, so to speak.

When it came down to me, finding out later that she was the snitch on this situation, I was totally outdone.

This girls name was Denville. She was a stud on count, and she looked like a man and she acted like a man. She was always doing/saying things like a man would. It was very hard not to think of her as a man. She dressed like one, smelled like one, acted like one, and sometimes thought like one.

So when it was told that she was a snitch, it was very hard to accept this. The only reason I did find it out was because an officer told me.

They took Donna to the hole for disfiguring Bonnie's face. She sent a message to me, asking me to help her. I went out-of-bounds to the segregation area to talk with at her at her window. Sometimes if the person was in the right area, we were able to go late at night on our way to the administration center or the clinic for medication.

Prison life is a trip. The officers kept more crap going on than the convicts. They involved their selves in gossip, in affairs, eating inmate's food and passing bones of information. It would seem the officers enjoyed instigating sh—.

So I had to go to the admin center for some legal mail that evening. It was a great opportunity to run to Donna's window to talk with her face to face.

She was surprised by my visit and wanted me to make Bonnie come to P.C., which was "Protective Custody." Protective Custody is where convicts go when they are scared of someone on the grounds or scared of an officer.

It was dark and I had just a few seconds to make this move. We can only travel through the facility with a pass. A pass is a piece of paper that states the location we are going to and from. It will state what time we left one location and arrived at the other location. We have so many minutes to get from one location to the other or we will be considered "Out of Bounds." It is a misconduct if we are caught.

It can be turned into a major misconduct which can stop your date going home. Or it can be a minor misconduct that can go into your file and if you receive more than three of the same offence then they will turn it into a major. That kind of misconduct can stop you from going home.

When I say it can stop your date that is what I am referring to. When you enter the prison system, you receive a certain date to go home; it is a potential release date and it means you are released on that date to the parole board. It is calculated in your time sheet when you arrive. Every time you receive misconduct that date is moved up to make you stay longer.

So I took the chance and went to Donna's window to talk with her face to face. She was really upset telling me that Bonnie's family wanted to press charges on her. She told me that she was just angry. She did not mean to take it that far.

She begged me and told me, "Billy-Joe, only you can get her back here. I do not trust anyone else."

So I told her I would do what I could.

That night, I made it back in time because I ran the rest of the way so I would not be late. Plus, we had a cool officer, she did not trip on small issues like this.

I lay in my bed thinking how I would be able to help without getting myself involved. After thinking about it for a couple of days, knowing I would not be able to discuss this with anyone else. I came up with an idea.

For this plan, I needed gasoline and so I planned to meet this girl named Western. She worked on the maintenance crew. They cleaned the yard area. They ran the lawnmowers and did the trimming around the buildings. They had access to tools and whatnots.

So I went to recreation that night, which I hardly ever went to. It was a bunch of bull to me. I went to the recreation area to see Western because I knew she would be over there with her woman Maria.

I talked with her privately but one thing you start learning in there, is that nothing is private. We went off talking. I asked her if she could get me some gasoline.

She asked me . . . . "How am I going to do that?"

I asked her, "Don't you cut the lawn?"

She stated yeah! I told her, well, then just take it out of the lawnmower.

Then Western asked me how to do that. I just shook my head in disbelief trying to comprehend how some of these people did their crime to get in here.

I explained in detail with Western to lift up the lawn motor and turn it upside down to get the gasoline out of the tank, or take a hose and suck it up out of there.

She then asked me how I get a hose.

I shook my head thinking, "Are you kidding me? She must have missed the boat to the wizard to get a brain".

I took her to the window, and showed her the back part of the Unit, and told her, there is a garden back there, right?

She said, "Yeah."

I then went on to explain, you can take the hose they water the grass with and cut a piece of it. Make sure you cut at least about two feet and place it in the gas tank and suck really hard to bring the gas up, just like a straw. Once the gas starts to come up, lean the hose down and allow it to flow. Place it in a bowl from the kitchen or cup. Then take the gas and hide it somewhere behind this building or somewhere so I can get it.

I asked her, "Now, do you totally understand what I need you to do?"

Western stated; "Yeah."

Then she went off with her woman that night.

I had to stay over there, because once you go as a group, you must stay as a group until the recreation hour is over. I sat there bored out of my wits. We were a close custody unit, so we had to come over on a group pass. Other housing units were allowed to leave individually. I could not wait to get out of close custody.

Little did I know at that time, it would be a long time before the administration ever let me out of close custody!

I went back to my housing unit that night and laid in my bunk wondering if this plan was going to work. I also sat and thought about the Warden and the man she had as a Deputy.

The Warden's name was "Little" she was in charge of the whole facility. Everyone spoke about a book she wrote called *The Warden wore Blue*. My opinion of her is that she was the worst warden we ever had. Her and Deputy Robert, both of them to me, did not care about making things better. Warden Little had a lot of administrational problems in that facility. Some of the staff were prejudice toward prisoners. She had a lot of gay officers that were messing around with the prisoners. There was male and female officers having affairs with convicts. Only the men were blamed. Most of the drugs coming into the facility where through the officers. The convicts were giving them 500 dollars in cash money to bring it in. So many officers had a hard time refusing that cash on top of what they were getting paid they were making out good. On top of that, the administration was manipulating the numbers to gain more funds for security. The more confusion Deputy Robert could sow, the easier it would be to have stuff happen like fights between inmates. Deputy Robert was Warden Little's side kick. He liked to keep shit going on in the system, so he could fill up the segregation area to demand more security money. If the numbers showed that the convicts were violent and hard to control then they could pull more funds for security.

Warden Little just wanted to be known as the hardest woman warden that took no shit and got her name in fame. Warden Little replaced Warden Quarrelers who was a good warden; she was only there for a year or less when I first got there. She went to work up in Michigan in Lansing now. That is how Warden Little took over; she was the deputy warden at that time. When Warden Little left, she left a web of bullshit for the next Warden to clean up. Knowing this information, I knew I had to play this cool so I did not get caught up into that number game that the administration was playing with Lansing. I knew they would really go crazy about some gasoline. Having gasoline in prison was like having a loaded gun. We were not trying to hurt anyone, just scare them so they would go to PC (Protected Security).

My brain was thinking too much, I needed to lay down and get some sleep. Whatever was going to happy would be. I made my choice and now it is hard to stop the wheels.

So, Western went and got the gasoline for me and placed it in front of the housing unit right by a tree which is right before you walk into the unit. When she ran the buzzer to get in the door, because the close custody unit doors were always locked, the officer smelt the gasoline on her person when she let her in.

She called the control center to tell them what she smelt. Then she walked outside the housing unit where she saw Western lay down a pop can.

That pop can was half full of gasoline. She took it back to the housing unit for evidence. I guess I picked the wrong person to do something for me.

My plan was to, take the gasoline sneak it into Bonnie's cell pouring it all over the room, leave while setting a match to it, burning her room up. I could get in her cell with my prison ID card by using it to click open the latch to Bonnie's door which her cell was easy to do that with.

She would become scared to death thinking someone wanted to hurt her badly. This would make her seek P.C. "protective custody" arrangements. My mistake was telling Western what I wanted the gasoline for. I did not tell her my plan or what I was going to do with it, just that I wanted it for Bonnie.

Well, when Western got taken to segregation, "the hole", I did not find out until I got out of the factory. Everyone was talking about a girl who was going to blow up the prison and catch everything on fire, so she could escape. I was hearing this no matter what room I went to in the housing unit.

Then I heard it at dinnertime. I asked someone in the chow hall who is everyone talking about?

The girl leaned over and told me some girl named Western got caught with some gasoline and went to segregation. They said she was going to blow up the prison so she could escape.

I just leaned back in my chair and was tripped out totally. I could not believe the dumb bitch got herself caught. But then again, I should have known. She was not the brightest apple in the bunch.

I had to help her, she was there because of me. I called home asking my brother to send her $150.00 dollars to take care of her for the month. We were allowed to spend $75.00 dollars every two weeks. One hundred and fifty dollars a month would take care of any needs we had in prison.

So being from the old school, the way I learned it in the streets, it was my duty to care for her needs and help her to come out of this. I had a paralegal degree and found myself being pretty good at administration law. Sometimes, I needed help from some of the old timers, but as a rule, I was able to look up policies and procedures and get misconducts dismissed.

So I had her send me all her paper work. I went out-of-bounds to talk with Western about the situation to see what actually occurred concerning her confinement.

She told me what the deal was, but something was missing. So I had her send me all her paper work so I could do her appeal. Her statement was missing, I could not get it. She had made a confidential statement no matter how hard I tried no one would let me near it.

Western was in the hole for about one month; I was getting ready to call my brother to place another 150 in her account for shopping. I was sitting at work, laid back in a chair with my legs lying up on the desk, kicked back, being comfortable.

Deputy Robert had everyone in that prison scared of him, but he knew he did not scare me one bit. He had convicts bow down to him for his strong steal hand of discipline.

At that time I did not scare easy. I was still too strong with callous feelings. When Robert walked in the room, everyone booked and ran to their location.

Robert walked in with Deputy Dyer, his guppy. Wherever Robert went, Deputy Dyer was with him. He did whatever Robert told him too. He would even take the fall when it came to things. So when Robert walked into the room everyone else took their punk ass up out of there out of fear.

He walked up to me with my feet leaned back on the desk. It was only me and one other inmate that was in the room. She was like me, she did not scare easily.

I greeted him, "Hey, Robert, what do we owe this privilege?"

Robert stated, "You don't get scared of me do you Giuliano?"

I told him no, should I?

He told me in a very low voice, let's see how you feel in a couple hours.

Then he walked out of the office. I kept wondering what he meant by that. I looked at my friend Adeline and told her, "What did Robert mean by that Adeline?"

Then I told her, "If anything happens to me, please stay in contact."

She told me not to worry she would be there for me. Adeline was a solid person. She was no one to play with, she never got off into prison bull crap.

I grabbed a couple packs of cigarettes. Adeline gave me her half of a pack, just in case. I did not smoke non-menthol, but beggars cannot be choosy. I went up to the control center knowing there was going to be trouble. I could tell by Robert's face. I convinced myself, not to go off, they did not have anything on me.

I ran over to the segregation area knocked on Western's window, making sure they did not have anything on me. She assured me, that she had not said anything. So I walked up to the control center and sat in the hallway waiting for someone to tell me why I was there.

After waiting for about twenty minutes, finally someone came and took me into the seating room and placed handcuffs on me. I did not get mad or try to argue with them, I did ask, what was the deal?

They responded that I would be given the misconduct in twenty-four hours.

**(This is not the actual photo; only a photo to give a mental visual of the area.)**

They took me to segregation (the hole) to place me in a cell.

It was a dark long hallway the doors were made of steel, with dark deep blue painted walls. It was separated from the population with a thick bullet proof looking glass, sliding door that had to be opened through a control panel in the officer's bullpen. The door looked over the hallway and our activities.

When they opened the sliding door, you could smell the piss and funk of everyone's body odor. The ladies were only given a shower every three days and one hour out of their cells. Plus many of the women would throw piss on the officers when they did not like things that were said to them.

The women back there would talk back and forth with each other at the same time. Noise, is all you ever heard while back there. They would stay up all night long talking, cussing each other out, for no reason, and talking about nothing. The hole was set up like one long hallway, which consists of rooms, on both side of the building. There might have been at least fifteen rooms back there. Each one had a door that was thick and hard. There was a slot in each door that opened just enough to slide in a tray of food, or small items.

There was double paned glass on each door, where an officer men or women could walk by and see what you were doing at all times. Some people had metal guard racks on their windows because they threw things out their window.

Back in segregation, it was cold and clammy and the rooms were not very clean, you could smell piss throughout the hallway.

Everyone yelled out, "Giuliano is back here."

They were all surprised because I was able to stay out for a year. I had gotten into the factory. To get into the factory, you had to have at least one year of clear conduct. If I lost the factory job, I lost a lot of income. I made good money there. Sometimes even a 1000.00 dollar check a month with bonus from the sales of license plates. I put all of my bonuses in saving bonds.

I laid back on my bunk, no sheets, and the smell of the toilet right there in the cell.

Things looking so filthy, you were afraid to touch anything. I would always wait a minute and ask the officers for cleaners, so I could sanitize my area. I lay back wondering how I was going to play this hand out.

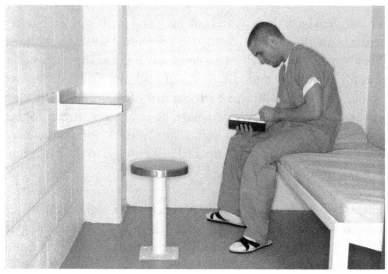

*(This is not actual room but a photo to give a close mental visual)*

Western called out to me, but at that moment, I did not feel right about her. Some inner feeling, kept telling me, she was lying, and sold me out. I did not know what they had on me. I wanted to be quiet until I knew. So I did not answer her. She was at the end of the hallway.

I laid there on my bunk concentrating on what my next move was going to be. I knew I was busted. I just wanted to find a way to beat the charges that were going to be applied against me. I laid there just looking up at the ceiling thinking, trying to figure a way out of this.

The room was empty, just four cement walls and a toilet/sink combination. I was in segregation for at least 72 hours before charges were even brought against me.

Finally a staff member came back there to read me the misconduct that was written against me. As the officers stood outside my door reading to me through the slot, I realized that they had nothing on me except for what Western had told them. I refused to sign the misconduct and took my copy and went back to my bunk to lie down.

I could hear Western in the background calling my name, "Giuliano, Giuliano what did they say, what did they say!"

I cannot believe that she was sitting there talking to me knowing that she snitched me out on this gasoline even after I looked out for her and did her appeal.

I lay in the cold room, with nothing but cement walls and a steel toilet with the sink above it.

I had not had a shower for three days, and then finally an officer came to my door, knocked on the door stating, "Hey you, Giuliano get up and get ready. They're coming to hear you on the misconduct."

I could hear the officer walking down the hallway, and his keys were hitting against his pants. I wiped Vaseline in the middle of the palm of my hand. I wanted to make sure I was able to pull my hands out of the handcuffs.

As I walked down the hall I spread the Vaseline on my hands making my hands slippery. All the ladies stood at their doors yelling out to me. I did not look at them or answer.

I walked with my head high and my hands cuffed behind my back. I approached the office.

I looked in and saw the bald headed man sitting behind the desk, with his typewriter on the side. He had a lot of papers on the desk, as he shuffled through them. I walked in and there was nothing but silence in the room.

I sat in the chair, looking around at the empty walls. There was only an old wooden desk and a metal rollaway table that the typewriter was sitting on.

Finally after five minutes of silence, he looked at me and said, what is your name?

I told him, "Giuliano."

Then he asked me for my prison number.

I stated my prison number.

Then he read the charges to me, "Giuliano was getting gasoline at some time around this time. Those were the charges."

He asked how did I plead?"

I told him, "Not guilty."

He sat there typing for a long period of time, as I sat looking round the room. I was working my hands out to the handcuffs because I knew he was going to find me guilty.

He then asked me did I have anything to add before he delivered the sanction.

I told him yes, "I told him I had evidence that I was at work at the time the incident occurred and my time card would prove that."

I also told him that I had not had any contact with Western for three days before the incident took place. I also told him that the Deputy was writing misconduct on someone's word and that is hearsay. I told him that there is nothing to tie me to the following allegations.

Then I became silent. He asked me if I was through?

I stated yes.

He begin to type some more. I had finally pulled my hands out of the cuffs. I sat there as if I was still cuffed. He finished typing and then looked up at me stating, "I found you guilty of the following charges."

Before he could get it all out of his mouth, I jumped up from the chair and ran around the corner of the desk. I kicked his typewriter stating, this was a kangaroo court hearing.

He went under the desk staying under there, scared to death.

I went out of the office told the officers standing behind the glass to kiss my a—.

Then I went and opened up everyone's slot to their door. I started to pass items and running back and forth yelling, telling the officers I was not going to accept this crap lightly.

Officer Puba and another officer opened the sliding glass doors trying to go on each side of the hallway to corner me. As they came into the hallway, I backed up from them. Telling them to stay away from me or I would have to do something I did not want to do. I stood in a karate stance to let them know, I was ready to fight as they came closer.

I backed up and saw Lehelma's door. (A convict behind the door) She was standing there looking out her glass window.

I took my fist and hit the window as hard as I could to break the glass. I took a piece of glass and waived it at the officers to show them I meant business.

They backed up and did not come toward me anymore. I kept shoving the glass piece at them yelling out, "Get back, I don't want to hurt you but I will."

So Officer Puba went back and called the other officer to come back behind the glass. Then they got on the phone and called the Warden to get permission to gas me.

I knew what they were doing, it was the regular routine.

I kept telling everyone in the rooms, that I was going to run in my room before they gassed me. That gas burns and it takes a long time to get the sting out. You have to bathe in a special solution or tomato juice. The officers were gearing up and placing their suits on and grabbing their helmets, and shields. They opened the door and told me, they were giving me one last order to return to my room.

I backed up and threw up my one leg behind me and said, "Thaaat's all folks" and went into my cell.

I played with them for a moment before I went into my cell. I did it long enough before they gassed me.

Because of my behavior they wrote me up for misconduct, for getting out of the handcuffs, for breaking the window and they charged me for the window. They did not charge me for trying to use the piece of glass as a weapon. They knew they did not have charges on me for that gasoline. But my misconduct stood as is.

They turned off my water in my cell for seven days. They kept my ankles and hands in handcuffs. My hands were cuffed behind my back. I had to stay like that for over 24 hours. I slept like that.

I had no water whatsoever so I could not wipe myself to use the bathroom with the cuffs. When my brother tried to come see me they refused the visit. They told him I was causing trouble. I could not call him or anyone else. I lost my phone privileges, yard and everything else.

The days went by, but it felt like a lifetime. I finally got a shower. I was able to get my water turned back on in the cell. I did almost a year back there in the hole. Every time I would meet the committee to release me they would deny me. I sent Adeline, a message to help me. She knew the administration law well. I knew she would help me.

So I sent her a note the next thing I know. I was looking out the window and saw Adeline walking up the sidewalk.

The officer came to my door stating I had company. I do not know how she did it because I have never known an inmate to be able to do that before. I have never saw an inmate do it afterwards.

She was not able to see me, but she was able to get all my paper work. I was able to tell her what was going on with my situation. Adeline charged me 400.00 dollars to do the appeal. It was worth it, because she got me out of there.

It might have taken almost a year, but they released me around 12:00 midnight and placed me in Unit 3 which is the unit for those who need special care. (It was for special needs and mental health prisoners).

It was ordered by the Ombudsman for my misconduct to be expunged from my file but Robert did not want it out. He had to do as Ombudsman stated, but he placed a note in my file that stayed in. He kept notes in my file even though nothing should have been in there. I was granted complete expungement of the misconduct.

Robert was so dirty, that he started a rumor with the population about me. He wanted everyone to think I hated blacks. So he called many of the prisoners up to the front office and interviewed them. During the interview he would ask them what they thought Giuliano was going to do with that gasoline.

Then he would plant ideas in their heads by saying, "Have you ever heard Giuliano say the "N" word?"

Have you ever seen Giuliano argue with any whites? She only seems to argues with the Blacks doesn't she?

Then he told them that the person the gasoline was meant for, was a Black girl named Bonnie. He told them many other things to plant a seed in their heads. He told them that I was trying to create a riot with all the black people on grounds. That I was going to take that gasoline and burn up all the blacks on the count. Many of the convicts believed him, because he called the ones up there he knew that were shit starters.

He had the whole grounds believing this was a racial issue. I had people sending me notes with a cross on it, telling me they were going to beat me up or burn me to the cross when I was released.

I had people who would ask me if I was going to burn up all the black people on the count (a 'count' being the prison yard).

Robert hated me so badly that he could not stand that I was a stand-up person, that I did not need anyone; I stood by myself.

Before I left segregation, Robert came to me and said, "You really think you're tough don't you?"

I told Robert, "No, but you must think I am because you are always trying to sabotage me." I walked out and packed my items.

While I was back there I had someone send me the policy and procedure of the facility. I got the one on segregation. I wrote grievances on everything that they did wrong while I was back there. I was a thorn in their side.

The Warden got so angry, that she came back there in my cell and cussed me out. She had never had Lansing get on her so tough about what was going on in her prison. In a way, they were glad I was leaving back there but Robert made sure he placed me in a situation to return to.

I was out on the grounds (prison yard) again. I walked with my head high regardless of the physical threats I received back there. I was not going to let anyone think I was scared. I was at the point of being angry. The threats, a picture of me burning on a cross was to the point. I had an attitude and was willing to die for it if needed.

Everyone felt I was now prejudiced. My days were going to be a challenge now, associated with many fights thanks to Robert.

Robert moved me right down the same hallway Western lived down. He moved me right across the hall. Wow! Wasn't that a shocker? They even moved a girl out of the room to move me in. If that is not a set up . . . . I do not know how plainer it can get. I asked them why they were doing that. I felt like that this was a set up. They told me those orders came from Robert they could not overturn them.

So I figured since Robert wanted to set me up. I would feed into his madness and go with the flow. But I did things a bit differently. I made Western my best friend. I ate with her, cooked items at night with her, did her laundry, of course she paid me for doing her laundry. We did everything together. Because of the gasoline incident, I had lost my job at the factory making license plates. I started working in the laundry department. I sorely missed working in the factory and its bonuses.

So I got the laundry job. I charged 5.00 dollars for washing out the laundry bag and 10.00 dollars to fold them and place Downey in the laundry. It was a good hustle. I went back to running a two for one store.

To make a long story short I made Western my best friend for a whole year. Each day I thought about getting her back and showing her that she messed with the wrong person. I was a very angry person inside.

One year later I was in the rec-room where the convicts play cards. There was a card game going on. I was sitting down watching out the window. Western came in stating to me she did not have my five dollars for the laundry.

I usually sat there on token day to collect my money owed for laundry.

She just stood there saying, "Because I just don't have it."

She had a smart attitude. I was so mad, I could see red. I stood up and leaning against a table with both elbows on it.

Western was leaning the same way to the right of me.

I just leaned there for a moment then my temper went from 0-100 within seconds. I stood up taking my right fist, balling it up and pulled back my hand and hit her as hard as I could on the temple of her head.

She flew up as if she was going to hit me back.

I just punched her in her face.

She flew back against the wall then I kicked up my one leg karate chopped her in the chest as she landed against the wall.

I watched her slide down. I just started to kick her in the guts.

There was a table of four women playing cards. No one in that room moved. Once Western was down on the ground I knew she was through. I walked out of the room.

There were no officers around. I walked to my room and got my shoes on walked out on the yard looking for Cadillac.

Officer Shawn came up to me asking, "Giuliano, can I see your hands?"

I told him, "Yea, why, what's up?"

He told me that Western was just sent to the hospital.

He asked me did I do it.

I told him, "No Mr. Shawn!"

He looked at me funny and stated, "I hope not Giuliano because you have been doing really well."

I hated to lie to Officer Shawn he was one of the best officers to me. He did his job and would write you up but he was fair. I talked with Seda for a few minutes told her what to do with some of my stuff. I went back to the housing unit because I knew it would not be long before the women started snitching.

That is the way things went in prison.

Officers never had to do their job, the women or convicts would. I went back and packed up my room. I put everything in my footlocker box and the rest in a duffle bag.

I was sitting on the foot locker when Officer Shawn came to the door shaking his head. As he opened the door, I told him I was sorry I lied to him. He asked me why I did it. I told him she owed me 5.00 dollars.

Mr. Shawn looked at me stating, "Come on Giuliano, I know you, 5.00 dollars is not a motive for you. Why did you do it?"

I looked at Mr. Shawn and said, "I hated that she lied on me about that gasoline. I did a year in the hole over that crap."

"Did you ask her to get the gasoline?" Mr. Shawn asked.

"Yeah," I retorted, "but all the racial crap was not true. She sat with Robert making up crap about me to get that rap on me. None of that crap was true. I did not pay her to get the gas either. She agreed to do it."

I continued, "Officer Shawn, do you know I get into arguments every day about that racial crap?"

He shook his head stating he understood, handcuffed me and took me to segregation.

"Well, was it worth it Giuliano? Now you are going to lose more good time and go back in the hole they will keep you there for a while. They are already pissed at you for getting out of that gasoline charge."

I just looked at Mr. Shawn said, "Right now Mr. Shawn, it was worth it to me."

Officer Shawn said, "Giuliano, they say you really hurt that girl, she has a small concussion, and bruised ribs, they are also saying that you also took a broom stick shoving it up inside of her."

I hurried up told Officer Shawn that was not true. I did not do that. There was a room of people in there they can tell you that is not true.

Officer Shawn took me to the hole and dropped me off.

While I was back there, Officer Oz was going to the hospital to sit with Western. I asked her to please have them check up inside of her to see if there were any bruises up in her walls. I told the officer that I was being framed that I beat her butt but I did not shove a broom up in her. I said that she is lying, so I asked Officer Oz to promise me that she would do that. I asked her if she wanted to see me go down like that if I was innocent.

This was a scary situation. An assault like that would be another charge and run consecutive to my 20-60 years plus the two years for the gun. I would have to complete that case then do whatever time they gave me on a sexual assault.

I sent a message out for Western, if they find me guilty for a sexual assault, they better take you or me to the federal joint because I will beat your ass every time I see you.

Later, they woke me up stating, "Giuliano, we are here to hear you on your misconducts."

When I heard the charges of sexual assault, I was pissed. I could have ripped right through Western if she was in front of me. I was so angry.

I refused to sign it and took my copy and laid back down. They let me know the police department would be by later to bring the charges. I was just hoping and praying that Officer Oz did what I asked her.

Well, here I am again in the hole, but this time I felt better. I was not losing a good job, I kicked Western's butt. I have wanted to get her for a year. I felt very satisfied. I did not want to be in the hole again, but I was glad that she got what was coming to her.

I went through the hearing and was found guilty for the assault but not for the sexual assault. They found me not guilty of that charge. The evidence proved she did not have bruises inside her walls but bruises on the outside of her thighs. Her woman Bonnie sucked them on her legs to make hickies as if they were bruises. Those hickies is what they showed the authorities to write the misconducts as a sexual assault.

I thought to myself, "Really." You and your woman had time to place hickies on your leg before going to the hospital? Or were those things there before I kicked your ass? I was surprised that the administration did not write her up for those hickies. Shoot, we get written up if we get sunburn for damage to ourselves. Everyone knows if you catch a misconduct charge for sexual assault you could get up to 5-10 years added to your time. That you will do that time consecutively. Good thing that did not happen, because they would have had to carry me out of there or Western. I would've hurt her good in there if something like that had happened.

Time went on, every day was a different story, I never did live down that gasoline crap. Officers and convicts would ask me about it unremittingly.

Some people were afraid to ask me, others would state, "They say you are prejudiced, but I don't see it."

A lot of times I would not even respond to issues like that. Sometimes it would depend what kind of mood I was in.

A bunch of people I jailed with, Cadillac, Cheery, and Florida, came to me after they were released from the hole (segregation). They stated that Robert came back there to the hole with some roll of toilet paper. They said he told them that Giuliano thinks of blacks as a piece of toilet paper and balled up a piece of toilet paper and threw it on the ground. He told them to stop me from being disrespectful to the black women.

Now, all of these people could not be lying on him. If he did that, it was unprofessional and could have caused me fights. This is just some of the crap I had to deal with inside because of those accusations he placed on me.

I remember once I was going to eat in the kitchen. I usually went by myself everywhere. I sat down at a table and all the ladies were sitting there asking questions about the gasoline caper.

So I grabbed a napkin off the table and started making little holes for eyes. Then I made the napkin look like a sheet. I hung it over the salt shaker making it look like a Klu-Klux-Clan costume. When the girls saw it, they moved to another table.

343

Sometimes my life was so lonely.

No one really liked me because of the way I carried myself, then the gasoline incident didn't help.

I sold dope, ran a "two for one" store. I survived while I was in there and thought about my daughter. I saved money up and sent it home so if I died in there my daughter would have something to remember me by.

It took me over ten years to get my security down to leave close custody. I watched people leave and come back to the facility. It made me wonder why they were not able to stay out there in the world.

Years later, I would find the answer to this question. But for right now, I could not help but think they were stupid for not staying out there. I would sit back and think, if I could only have freedom, I would never do anything to destroy it.

No one would really deal with me. They all felt like I was biased. As if I was a bit crazy.

There was a girl that kind of liked me, and I would talk to her. Many people would tell her she should not talk with me because I was prejudiced.

We hung around each other and got into a lot of trouble here and there. We ended up going to segregation many times together.

The relationship was dysfunctional and after dealing with each other for a long period of time. I realized the relationship was not good. I needed to step back from her. I told her one day in the yard and walked away. She was so angry with me, she ran after me and grabbed me from behind. She turned me around throwing me to the ground. She could not deal with rejection.

She got on top of me and hit me in my lip. That was the first and last time anyone did any damage to me like that.

Because I had such a big reputation, she really felt good about herself giving me a split lip.

I did not want to go back to the hole. I was about to move out of close custody that week. I was waiting on my federal papers. I had been working hard to get my custody lowered when this happened. I refused to allow myself to get caught up. Lose the low security level I just received a couple weeks ago.

I did not tell anyone I had gotten it. Like I said, out of eighteen years in there, it was the only time anyone was able to cut my lip.

They sent Linda and me to segregation. We both stuck to our story that we were horse playing. I had to take kotex and stuff my lip to heal it before they saw us.

They heard us on the misconduct breaking it down to a minor misconduct. They let us go back to the prison grounds. I never dealt with Linda again.

I had a federal case for narcotics. I knew if I ever got out on appeal or lived long enough to get out, I had to get rid of that federal case because they were running it consecutive to the time I was doing for the state. I was with the state first, then the fed's picked me up. I had my attorney fight to get me back down to 1300 Beaubieu Street. So I started looking into different avenues to appeal it.

I talked to this one girl in legal service named Tina asking her for assistance. She worked for legal services in the prison. She was a smart lady. She was very knowledgeable. She told me to F.O.I.A. my husband's federal file.

My husband passed away in1989. He got out of prison and did not really do anything with his life. He did send a lawyer up to talk to me, but nothing ever came of it because Vicenza Giuliano died before the attorney could ever assist me.

So I sent away for his file and sent them a copy of his death certificate. They sent me the file and that was the day my life started to change.

I could not read much out of his file because a lot of it was blacked out. I did find out he was associated with the Mafia in Detroit, he was a shylock for them in 1974. He was not one of them he only did work for them, something like a subcontractor.

As I was reading what I could, I realized that the police talked to Vicenza Giuliano many times. He **never** told on the big boys he messed with but he sure did tell on the other's that meant nothing to him. He also told on me that really got to me.

I started to cry. I thought about everything that happened in our home.

The time the fed's came up to our house up north wanting to talk to Vicenza Giuliano about a jewelry heist that occurred in Detroit. I was wondering why they made Vicenza Giuliano stand against the wall, as if he was a suspect then took him outside to talk to them. They were out there for a long time.

Then another time, Vicenza Giuliano told me to never say anything to anyone that he did heroin. That if anyone ever called the house asking about it. I was not to say anything. I could never understand why he told me that. Why would I ever discuss him doing heroin with someone I did not know on the phone? I listened and agreed.

My whole life flashed before my eyes and I realized that I had been living a lie.

That the streets were a lie. I did not believe in anything or anyone any more.

I was crushed. I could not believe that I lay next to this man for three years and did not know anything about him.

I cried and cried when I realized that he had given the feds photos of me.

That he had talked to them about me, it was all blacked out.

What a dirty rat he turned out to be. He should have gotten eight years for his crime and finish the three year special he was on. He turned me in on bullshit to save his own ass. He was snitching and it was all in the file, telling the fed's how others people are dirty rats, he was one himself.

I was so disappointed that Vicenza Giuliano turned out to be everything he stated he was not. He was an undercover informant for them. He did not tell on the Mob but he told on everyone else.

I wonder how many other street, tough street thugs where telling. May be there is not honor on the street. That is a bunch of crap, everyone was out for their self. I saw the streets for what it really was. I really did not realize the change that was taking place inside of me, but there was defiantly one occurring.

My whole world and dreams were all a lie. Who I thought I was. The life I believed in was all a lie.

Billy Joe

I thought of myself as a real one, a stand-up person. I came to realize that I was nothing but a fool. I was caught in a lifestyle that I thought existed, but it was all a lie.

I felt like crime was a suicide. It finally dawned on me, that life out in the streets was controlled by an evil spirit. It was the master manipulator of destructions.

That's why you lie, sneak, cheat and hide your deeds because you have to be just as deceitful to survive in that lifestyle. It entices you. You hear it calling, things you thought and stated you would never do, now you are doing them, lying and hiding your deeds. It will pull you in, get inside of you, where you will forsake your children, family and loved ones.

It is jealous and only wants you to itself.

It is truly evil and will not stop until you are dead, in jail or prison. It will push everything, even humanly-love, out of your existence.

You are in a domestic violent relationship with it. You will feel the honeymoon of having fun and enjoying the good times. Then the other part of your personality will surface. You will hide who you are becoming to others. You will push others out of your life. It will not stop until your soul is destroyed and there is nothing left of your life.

Vicenza Giuliano was not my knight in shining armor, he was my nightmare.

I appealed my case to United States Federal Court in Ohio. They granted me my appeal after going back and forth with them.

I stated I have done everything they had asked of me. They wanted me to participate in a drug treatment program, I did.

They wanted me to continue my education, I did.

They wanted me to be evaluated by a psychologist, I did.

So when I appealed the case, I sent them papers of everything I accomplished in the state joint. I even sent them transcripts where my judge talked about my drug dealing more than he did someone dying. I showed the fed's that I was sentenced under a drug law more than the assault law.

They ran my federal time concurrent. I was so happy now. I just had to live to get out of prison. I was finally able to get out of close custody.

That detainer from the federal case was keeping me in close custody too besides my conduct. I could see the light of getting out. I felt freedom, seeing my daughter and making up to society what I took.

I moved down to Unit 9 which was in the back part of the prison. The prison was located in the suburban area of Detroit.

At this time, Warden Little finally left and Warden China became our warden. I really liked her a lot. She was the best warden I ran across besides Bolts and Deputy Premont in Camp State Prison. They treated you as if you were human. They disciplined but they were not malicious.

When I graduated from the Paralegal program we had a graduation party for our families to come to. Warden China told my brother Rip that when she became the warden she asked the staffs who were the shakers and the rollers of the institution. They told her Cadillac and Giuliano. My brother just shook his head.

I told him, "I did not know they classified me as that."

My brother stated, "Damn it Billy Joe, stop playing this role or you'll never get out. You are playing the same role you did on the streets."

So I moved down to Unit 9. The girl that was my Bunkie had long blond hair and she was kind of a cute girl but I found out, she was a sneaky girl.

I was on the bottom bunk, she was on the top. We bumped heads here and there but nothing to worry about. One day, she asked me several times did I see her earrings? I kept telling her no. She went through the room looking for it and did not find them.

Then one day, when I was cleaning, I was straightening out my footlocker. As I was doing that, I saw her earring **inside** my footlocker. I was burning mad. I knew she had been sneaking in my locker reading my case and my paper work.

I got so mad, that I took my whole footlocker and dumped the whole thing in the dumpster.

Later that evening, I waited for my Bunkie to come back to the cell and shut the door. I placed a cardboard cover on the door that we used while getting dressed. I asked her if she had been in my foot locker. She denied it.

I told her, that I had evidence that she had been in there, then I showed her the earring she lost at the bottom of my foot locker. She tried to tell me a lame story. I told her I wanted her out of this room or I would kick her butt every day.

She ended up leaving and going to camp two days later.

I was so glad and every minute that she was in that cell with me, I made her miserable. She was trying her hardest to get out of there.

Living in Unit 9 was okay, but there was drama wherever you went. I knew that my friend Cadillac's woman was cheating on her with another person. She came to me and asked if I had information on it. I refused to say or get involved. Cadillac knew I was hiding it because the girl she was cheating with was cool with me too.

Because Cadillac had so much influence with the black women on the count, she was able to persuade them to believe as she did. I stuck up for the girl that was having the affair and Cadillac and I did not see eye to eye with the situation. I felt that if she had a beef with her girl, she should've taken it up with her. She had to keep her woman in check, not me. We have had our ups and downs before but we were also very strong together at times.

When I lived in close custody, our token draw was on one week and the medium custody units were the opposite week. They drew tokens one week and then we drew tokens the next week. Everyone drew every two weeks. Tokens were like money. You could draw them from your account if you had money in your account to purchase items like pop, food or personal hygiene products.

They even sold ice cream at the store. You could get ice cream. That was back in a time, where doing time was not that bad. Trust me, in time, everything changes and everything goes in a cycle, and within a few years that cycle would occur.

Time was going to result back to the olden days, where it was steel beds and uniforms. So Cadillac lived in medium-low custody and I lived in close custody. We would exchange tokens with each other to run our stores.

She would get tokens from me and bring them back when she got paid. Reverse the situation each token draw. I did the same thing, I got tokens from her to run my store.

By doing this, we cornered the market on the "two for one" stores. We multiplied the market in close custody and lower. It was sweet while it lasted.

I used to work on the Warden's forum. I was the head of it a couple of times. I introduced Cadillac to the warden and placed Cadillac on the committees. When we worked together, we did well, but Cadillac was always crossing me here and there. So when we did not agree with this incident, we fell out big time.

The funny part of the whole thing was, Cadillac's woman Lena was cheating on her, but Cadillac was cheating on her with another woman as well. She ended up going home to that woman.

So I was in the rec-room one night which I never go in there, because of the drama. Cadillac threw some lugs (a lug is hinting around to something someone else did) to me across the room about sticking up for that girl that was cheating on her.

So I could not take it anymore. I told Cadillac to place a label on that lug meaning telling the person face to face and saying their name, so they know you are talking about them. (I have come to learn that this is passive, aggressive behavior.)

So Cadillac stated if the shoe fits then wear it. But she would never come out saying my name. So I helped her out and stated I knew she was talking about me. So she threw out the charge about me and that gasoline, stating I was biased.

I was really mad that she bent so low to attack me because I did not agree with her.

So I said, "Well at least I don't have HIV and claiming that it is cancer, with your HIV infested self." I felt immediately bad when I stated it because no one should ever hurt someone about their medical condition plus I did not mean that.

Cadillac was more hurt from what I said to her than what she said about me. Cadillac hid it from everyone that she had it.

I even sealed the hurt by yelling out, "I will be at your funeral bitch."

I walked out of the rec-room.

(I was angry and felt bad for saying that to her. I have advocated for many with HIV while incarcerated. I have assisted many people to get medication, etc., so this was totally out of character for me. Anyone with this disease, please understand, I do not feel this way and I was foolishly lashing out.)

I remember when she was first diagnosed with it in 1983. I was sitting in the gym working out, when I first got locked up. Cadillac was one of the so-called boys on the count. We called these types "studs" because they acted like a man. In prison, they would create families in there. Us prisoners would call certain people mom, or sistas, or bro (brother) and Cadillac was all the stud's so-called Daddy in prison. I referred to Cadillac as my brother.

I was over there working out and she came in just sitting there. I asked Cadillac what was wrong. She was crying and I sat on the bench with her. She told me that they found some lumps in her throat. They had to operate on them. I asked what the lumps were.

She told me that they took a biopsy of it and it was HIV associated. She just started to cry. I was afraid to touch her, but I did not want her to know that. (We did not have a lot of knowledge of the disease back then.)

So I put my arms around her telling her stating it would be alright. That incident happened in 1983. Then I leaned over and kissed her on the side of her cheek.

I wanted her to feel that I believed in her. After that, a few weeks went by and Cadillac flagged me down on the yard.

"Hey Giuliano, guess what?"

"What's up Daddy Dee?" I stated.

"They were wrong, I don't have HIV, it is cancer."

I just knew by her face she was deceitful. I let her tell me about the mistake and how she was going to sue them for misleading her.

I could tell by the way she was telling the story. One thing the street does teach you, how to read people quickly. Reading someone might save your life. It will allow you to know who you are dealing with within five minutes. And let you know if you will make it out of that establishment in time to save your life.

She would not look me in the eye or the face while she was talking. But what hurt me most, is that she did not trust me. Maybe she had good reason because I just sold her out during an argument in the rec-room.

Now that I look back on the situation, I can understand her not having the complete trust. I just broke that trust, during our words with each other. You could see it on Cadillac's face, almost like she thought I would never stoop that low.

That gasoline comment threw me there, but I should have been the bigger person. That is why, it is hard to totally trust a human being. They will always disappoint you.

Sometimes it is best to keep things to yourself, or go to that secret spot in your heart. Talk to your higher power that you believe in. That way, no human being can hurt you or use things against you. They can't throw things in your face. They won't have any knowledge of your personal business.

So Cadillac and I were at war, when I tried to get a job in the Food Service Department, they denied me because Cadillac told them I was prejudiced and let them know of that gasoline caper. She even told them about the Deputy Warden going back in segregation and throwing the toilet paper. She stated I was calling people the "N" word as they went through the line.

I told the supervisor that was not true but they did not want to take any chances. So they fired me. Who gets fired in a prison job? "Me"

So I went over to the school and tried to get into Food Service Vocational Training. Even the teacher there did not want me in her class because of the gasoline charge.

I fought it this time. I grieved the denial. My grievance went through. They called me in the office to talk to me about it. I talked my way into the class. She decided to give me a chance. She ended up liking me a whole lot.

Later on, I became her teacher's aide. I was good at cooking and working in food service. We would have dinners for the staff. I cooked the meal and waited on the tables. I was able to socialize with staff on a different level. Instead of being a trouble maker, I started learning to work with the system and not against it.

At this time, I was caught up in a general lawsuit about demanding the same equal educational opportunities that were available to men; the men got college classes and we didn't. They needed people to testify and I was one of the people who were pulled into court to testify what kind of schooling was really given to us.

I used to take a construction/maintenance course taught by Mr. Folly. Mr. Folly's class, where you worked with lawn mowers, tools, piping, basic wiring, and welding, was a joke. I went through his class when I left segregation after the gasoline write-up. That's when I lost my factory job, too. I was in the hole for a year until I won my appeal. It was not a pleasant experience. I was there a whole year, only allowed out of my cell one hour a day and only allowed to take a shower twice a week. There were no showers on weekends. If your mind was weak, you would surely break.

I then became his teacher's aide. He was disgusting. He knew I was trying to move from close custody, and needed good work reports. Plus housing reports were done on me for my file. He took me in a room and asked me how bad I wanted that report. I knew what he was trying to get at. I just let him know, I did not need it that bad and walked out of the office. I never worked with him again.

I also testified on another class action prisoner case which was about how our legal property and personal property were handled.

During this case, (it was funny), I ran into the man that was in prison for shooting our friend Doodle and Carney; it was Pep. He and I talked for a few minutes during the break of the case. He kept stating I looked familiar and then he found out who I was.

I expressed to him, thank God I got sick that night from free basing that cocaine because we left Doodle's house because of that or Vicenza Giuliano and I would've been shot too.

I will never forget that night. Carney and Doodle were both such a nice loving couple (Yeah, I know, they were drug dealers and how nice are drug dealers for real. Now that I think back on this. I realized that God was getting me out of there because it was not my time.)

So once Pep found out who I was he asked them to take me off the list and not allow me back into court. Tina and Sara came to me and apologized that I would not be able to go to court anymore because Pep did not want me there. They asked what I did to him, to make him have this attitude. So I told them the story. (Tina and Sara worked for Prison Legal Service in prison. They were prisoners that got their paralegal degree on the inside. They were good and everyone came to them for help. When the law suit started they were asked to work on it. The case was named after Tina.)

Due to the lawsuit, they shut down Mr. Folly's class. I of course moved out of close custody without his report. I and the cooking teacher became close and I trusted her to tell her the story about Mr. Folly. She used to like him but after what I told her, she never talked to him again.

Each season passed and time kept going on.

Soon the administration came to the conclusion that the women needed to be moved to another location. When I first started doing time there, there was 200-300 women. Now we were at a 1,000 women. They stated that the ground was not safe and they were getting another facility from the Department of Corrections for the women. It was a rumor for a long time before it became a reality.

Everyone that attended college went last. Inmates that were not in college went first to the new prison. They were shipping the women out by the bus load. This new facility once housed male prisoners. They shipped many of the men out to many other different prisons. Rumor had it that many of them died or committed suicide after being shipped out because that was a more protected facility.

I was shipped out on the second bus after my classes ended. I was not accepted at all by the new facility. They had heard about the gasoline situation way before I ever got there.

The majority of the staff was men. Most of them were African American men.

They were polite but you could tell they were Leary of me.

Finally, one of the officers asked me about the gasoline. It was Deputy Sales. He was a good deputy. I liked him a lot. He helped me out in many ways.

As time went on, he was someone I was able to trust. I explained the situation to him. I told him I was not prejudiced. He let me know he was worried about his staff. He did not want any crap in his prison. I told him the truth about the whole incident. I told him to give me a chance and see me for what I am, not what they told him about me.

I also told him, nothing should be in my file about that. He told me there was a note. There wasn't any misconduct, just a note. Deputy Robert should not have had a note in there. He was dirty.

The new place was pretty cool. This new atmosphere where the officers were not petty was great. They were used to dealing with men and did not press small things like the officers at the Valley. I felt like I was in heaven in this prison. They had a big yard. A track to walk and run on. The rooms were set up pretty cool. The kitchen was better and bigger. Everything including the gym was great. I felt like doing time would be okay over here. I was not stressed out.

I was on the warden's forum there too. The staff was getting to know me better. They started to realize that the Valley staff just placed a bad rap (characterization) on me.

Soon the Valley shut down. Everyone was transferred to this new prison.

With the women came the drama. There was this girl that worked in the gym; she had an instant attitude with me. I am not sure but I believed they called her Wig and her girlfriend Jill. They tried to attack me in the gym because she did not like the way I was bouncing the ball.

Give me a break!

Both her and her woman jumped on me. I was trying to fight both of them off me. They both ganged up on me at the same time. I was holding my own but I was glad that this girlfriend of mine saw the fight.

Her named was Silvia. Silvia knew my husband from Detroit and we bonded because of that. She pulled the one girl off me. That allowed me to fight one on one so I could blacken Wig's eye. Her woman was on my back pulling my hair.

The next day, Jill, Wig's girlfriend, came to me and apologized for doing what she did. She told me Wig just didn't like the way I carried myself and hated the way I talked to other people. Oh well, I was not in there to please everyone.

We did not get busted or go to the hole. Right after I busted Wig's eye, another girl busted her eye a week later. Boy, it sucked to be Wig that month.

We were able to pick our Bunkie's so Lina a Hispanic woman that was cool with me asked if I would bunk with her. I picked up a few Spanish words from being around her. I knew her from the start of me serving time, so I felt like I could get along with her.

We did well together for a while, but we had a few little mishaps. She ended up moving to another friend that she also knew for many years. They knew each other's families and lived in the same area. I was a little pissed because it left me open for anyone to come in my cell.

Sometimes she and I argued because she was doing 20 years for drugs and I was doing 20 for a lower charge from a murder case. She felt like she should not have to do the same time as me that I should be doing L.I.F.E.

I got another Bunkie from hell it was not long before I got rid of her. She was an African American woman and you could tell she was a little special, meaning she was a few cards short of a full deck; the elevator did not go all the way up to the top floor so to speak.

I worked in the kitchen which meant I had to be up at 4:00 am every morning. So I would go to sleep early. She would keep the light on until 12:00 midnight reading. I asked her politely several times to turn off that light so I could sleep.

Her smart ass told me, she was allowed to keep her half of the light on until 12 midnight. So I got mad and said fine . . . . I will make sure your half stays on and got up out of the bed.

I jumped on the table and snatched the light bulb out of the socket. I took the light bulb and smashed it into a million pieces on the floor and got back into bed and said, "There, my half of the light is out."

The lights were long fluorescent and once you pulled one out, the other one would go out automatically.

That girl sat up on the bed in the dark for a few minutes. Then she flew off the bed and out the door. She ran to the officer's desk to tell the authorities what I had done. She was scared to come back into the room.

The officer wrote me up for destroying property of the institution but I did not care about paying for that twenty dollar light. It was worth it to me to have some sleep with the lights off in the dark.

The next day, Deputy Sales came to my room shaking his head saying, "Giuliano, what are you doing to my residents."

I told him about the kitchen and what time I had to get up. How she was leaving the light on until 12:00am. I told him I could not do it any longer, that light had to go. He just laughed. He said he would move her. So he did.

They allowed me to pick someone else for a Bunkie. It was Jenny, a girl I knew and thought I would get along with. We did for the most part. We lived together for a while. I was selling drugs and running a "two for one" store as always. That gave me money to purchase perfumes and special soaps and send money home.

I had some perfume hidden away. Jenny and I got into it because I believed she touched it and used some of it. She denied it, but I really felt she did. The room smelled of it.

Deputy Sales was going on vacation. He did one last run through all the housing units. He always looked out for the prisoners.

I went to him asking, "I am not going to get shipped out while you are on vacation, am I?"

He told me no that I was in school and they are not going to be shipping anyone enrolled in school.

He was not gone more than three days when the staff came to my door and told me to pack up. I was going to Camp Stand.

Camp Stand would never accept me before, because of that gasoline situation and that federal detainer. They denied me several times, because I tried to go a few times. I was really pissed because I always believed that this bitch I knew had me shipped out. She owed me 200.00 dollars for drugs. She had not paid me and kept giving me excuses. I believe she faked a letter saying you wanted to be shipped out because she owed me money. It was nothing to drop a kite (prison slang for a note) to the administration stating you wanted to be shipped out. That was a dope fiend move that she did.

I fussed packing my clothes stating, "I'm going to find some way to come back."

Before I got on the bus, I put an X on my forehead telling everyone I was Malcolm X. I had this gigantic rubber band around my hands. I kept rolling it back and forth, staring off into space as if I was crazy. They told me to grab my bags. I refused.

I got on the bus telling them, "Malcolm X does not pick up no bags."

They gave me direct orders to take the X off, but I acted like I did not hear them.

They took me out to Camp Stand telling them I might have gone crazy or was acting crazy. Deputy Faults came up to me trying to talk me. He threatened to put me in segregation until I would tell him what was going on with me. I still refused to talk and went to the hole, which was no big deal to me.

I did six years of segregation time during the beginning of my bit. I was considered the queen of segregation. So I went to the hole and they called Tina to come talk to me. They knew she was my friend. She could get close to me. So she came up to talk with me. She told me to be careful because the hole had microphones everywhere and they could hear every word.

So I was very careful in what I said. Tina brought candy bars for me to eat because she heard I was not eating and they were concerned with that. She had been shipped out here to this medium prison a few years ago when all of us got shipped out to the other prison.

I told Tina I had to go back to Yippy Prison and asked her if she would please help me. She told me I would have to go through the crazy unit in order for them to send me back.

Tina went out there and told the Deputy that I needed to be sent off to the nut house. Deputy Bolts told Tina, he was not going for it.

He stated, "If she was crazy, she would pee on herself."

That is all he had to say. I stood up and peed down my pants. It flowed down onto his administration floor. He wrote the order and had them send me to the crazy hospital.

They took me to Valley, on the men's division. They had men that were trustees working and cleaning up the floors. There was this African American man that would clean the floors. He was dark complexioned and tried to leave cigarettes around if you needed some.

I did not give him the time of day. He would stare from the glass into the rooms as if he was going to get a peek at some skin.

I went without eating for seven days. After that, I could not hold it any longer.

On the seventh day, at lunch time they threw a baloney sandwich into my cell as usual. That baloney sandwich in that brown paper bag looked pretty good. I could see the oil coming through the bag. The smell of it was in the hairs of my nostrils.

I looked down at that brown bag. I wanted to just smell it. Then a few minutes later. I said to myself, I will just take one bite. Then a few minutes later. I could not stop myself—I tore into that baloney as if it was a prime rib steak. That was the first time I ever thought a prison baloney sandwich tasted so great.

That man who was the trustee came over to my cell. They took me out of that bam-bam dress. It was suicide clothing they place you in. Now, I was wearing regular pants and a shirt.

He came up to my cell. Opening the slot of my door where my food goes and placed his dick in the slot. I got up from my bed yelling at him. If you don't get your dick out of my slot, I am going to shut the door on it.

He said, "Come on, I know you want some. I saw your prison number so I know you have been in here for a while."

I looked at that man and said, "I might be locked up, but I am not hard up. Now, get your dick out of my slot before I scream."

So he did and he went away. The next day they shipped me out. They did not send me back to Yippy. They sent me back to Camp Stand, so much for playing the crazy role.

I was upset, I did not want to be there. All of that for nothing! My brother was talking with me on the phone and told me . . . .

to stop the madness. He stated that all I was doing was making things worse for me. So I complied with Camp Stand's rules.

I asked Sena to get me moved somewhere. She was at the camp too. So she went and asked Deputy Bolts. He told Sena to have me to come to his office and ask myself. So I sent him a kite, which is a piece of paper requesting to be seen.

He called me up the next day. I went up there. He granted me everything I asked for. He told me I was different than what they were told. He then asked me about that gasoline charge. I told him that was expunged from my file. He told me that there were notes in my jacket. (Jacket means my institutional file).

I asked him how I could get that out, because I do not want it in there if I ever see the parole board. He told me they were notes and the parole board would not get that. He explained the information was in the institutional file, not at the file in Lansing. We talked for a while then before I left his office. He started laughing. He told me not to pee in his administration building anymore. We both laughed and I went back to my housing unit.

They moved me in a housing unit where we had dividers to separate our areas instead of cells. I was not used to living like that, in an open dormitory.

One night I was watching my TV and a bat flew into the housing unit. Everyone started running down the hallway of the housing unit. They were screaming like it was the end of the world. I looked to see what everyone was yelling about.

Then out of nowhere a bat landed on the curtains in my area. Out of all the dorm area's to land, he had to pick mine. Now I knew what everyone was yelling about. I covered up my head with a towel and continued to watch TV. I knew after all that screaming, he was more scared than me.

Every day was the same thing. The place looked like a dump to me. I started talking to this white girl; she was a so-called stud. I had known her throughout my whole bit but we never really talked before.

She was always with this pretty African American girl who was down with the law (a jailhouse lawyer). When she came to prison she was about her business, i.e. working on her appeals. She had a history with this particular stud. They were together in the streets too. They never really talked to anyone else.

Well, the stud's name was Jimmy and she lived in my housing unit so we were able to talk. I found out a lot about Jimmy and realized she did have a brain. I always thought it was her African-American girlfriend that had the brains. She was not just the guppy I thought she was.

We ended up becoming cool. Her girlfriend would get mad because we were hanging out together. We were not doing anything just talking. Her girlfriend came over one time, trying to check me and I set her straight.

I let her know that she needed to talk with Jimmy not me. I don't take kindly to someone telling me who to talk to. I told her that if you don't want her talking to me, you need to check her, not me. I am not the one.

So she checked Jimmy but she would not stay away from me.

Then one day, Jimmy wanted to get high and knew she had to slip away from me. I told her I was not into getting high. She kept lying to me telling me she was not getting high. I found out that she was as high as a kite.

I confronted her about it and she lied again to me. I got angry at her for her lying to me and knocked her in the back of her head. My diamond ring went into her head and left a big hole. There was blood everywhere.

I went to give her my bandana to place on her head and she ran out the door before I could give it to her. She ran to the control center to turn me in.

I went to the library to see Sadie who got shipped to Camp Stand too. (She was an acquaintance while incarcerated). I told her what was going on. I asked her to hold onto my ring until I knew they were not going to write me up for hitting Jimmy.

I looked at my hand to make sure no markings were on it. They never came and got me, so after a few days, I got my ring back.

Jimmy and I went our separate ways. That was a pet peeve with me: I was not into getting high and did not want to be associated with that crowd.

A cold day hit the facility and I am not speaking on the weather.

Deputy Bolts died; he had a heart attack. That was a sad day for everyone at Camp Stand. He was such a great deputy. They should have made him Warden. They were so dirty to him. They made him Warden after he died. Or they had made that decision and did not tell him. It was a very sad day.

The place was not the same after Bolts died. I went to Deputy Premont and asked him if he would ship me back to the Detroit area. I asked him to let me go to school out there and finish my degree with Detroit University. They had a psychology degree I wanted. I told him I did not want to be in Camp Stand any longer. He told me that Deputy Bolts was going to ship me back anyways so he would do it now. Deputy Bolts saw I was not as bad as they claimed. He had respect for me. He knew I wanted to be closer to home and get that degree in psychology.

Deputy Bolts and Deputy Premont were the best of friends. Deputy Premont was in a daze and just sat there without emotions. I felt for him.

I got myself ready and they shipped me out. I was going back to Detroit. I did not want anyone to know. Sadie got sent back almost a year ago, and she was the only one I let know I was coming.

I had been gone two years. I wanted her to help me collect the two hundred that was owed me when I got shipped out.

I arrived at Detroit and everyone wanted to say hello. I did not want to speak to anyone except Sadie. I went looking for her asking her to help me collect this money from this girl. I told Sadie that I did not trust this gal; I did not want her to set me up. Sadie agreed to take the money for me in case it was marked.

I went to the chow hall (Dinning area) and sat with the girl. She was a bit surprised to see me, but was prepared to get me straight with what she owed me. I told her to pass the money under the table. Sadie was sitting next to me. She placed her hand under the table to grab the money. I acted like I did.

After we got it, I told her, I wish I could sit and socialize but I have other things I must do and got up and left. I took the money from Sadie and sent it out in an envelope to an address I always sent money to.

I had Dee (from home) send me in packages of cannabis and pills. He was out of prison now. I would have him send me some weed and valiums and I would sell them on the prison count. I was making money on that and then I opened up another "two for one" store. I placed a few ads in the paper, in the singles department, looking for lonely men.

I had lots of responses. You would be surprised how many men will write women in prison and send clothes and money.

Then Dee died. One year later, so did my father and also Acacius.

I felt like my whole world fell in when my father died.

Acacius would come to visit me bringing clothes and money. He would sneak in with fake I.D. He visited me about seven times until cancer got him.

One year after Acacius's death, his mother died. I had given her my jewelry when I went to prison; there was a full Karat diamond piece, rose/gold/ white gold bracelets and my necklace.

I really started to realize how important my life was and living life.

Mrs. Purple, who was our Resident Unit Manager (RUM) and counselor of our housing unit, called me down to her office telling me my father died. I asked if I could go to the funeral. They monkeyed around with my paperwork so much so I was not able to go. Then, they stated I was a security risk. I was so angry. I just wanted to see my dad one more time.

With my father's death I did not want to call my mother. I felt she was going to say something bad about my dad. I did not have a good relationship with my mother even after all these years.

I was really surprised that she was really sympathetic to my father's death. My brothers kept bugging me to call her. I talked with her for a moment and it started a new relationship with us. I wondered at times, if my father's death was going to bring us back together. Sadly, later I would find out NO. I took it day by day with us getting along.

My attitude was very shitty. I really did not care after losing my father.

I saw Peco in the hallway going up the steps. She had come back to prison to do a small bit. She got smart with me. I was not in the mood after the news of my father.

So I said a smart comment back. She called me pink bitch.

That is all it took.

I pulled down my pants and told Peco to kiss any place that was pink because as far as I know, it was brown from all the shit coming out.

Peco and a few ladies tried to get the officer to send me to segregation but she was not going for it.

Then this tall old timer Polly got into my face a few days later and pushed me, so I pushed her back. She did not like it that my tough attitude, personality or the way I carried myself.

Polly was about 6'1 tall and was a big person. Everyone was afraid of her. She had been there a long time and was miserable. She was so shocked by me pushing her that she also went to the officer to get her to send me to segregation but the officer stated she saw Polly push me first.

The staff stated, "You are just mad that Giuliano just pushed harder."

I knew by my attitude it would not be long before I went back. I could feel the pain of losing my father haunting my soul. Now, I would never be able to apologize for my actions. He would never see me straightening my life out.

I was sitting in my cell hurt and angry at myself. I went downstairs. I was getting some water and the officer started yelling at me to get off the floor.

I looked at her as if she was crazy. I continued to get my ice and water. She repeated it and I told her I was leaving, I just wanted to finish and get my water and ice.

She told me she was going to write me up and I got mad. It had been almost a few years since I had misconduct for anything.

I told the officer if she wanted something to write up, I would give her something to write up about. So I told her to go F—her-self and leave me the F—alone.

She kept repeating her command for me to leave the area and told me to watch my month. I then told her she was lucky she had the upper hand, because on the street she would not talk to me like that.

She wrote me up for Threatening Behavior, which is automatically a segregation sentence. So they handcuffed me and took me to the hole that night.

I did not care. I wanted to grieve my father's death in private. I had not been to the hole in almost ten years. I went to the hole the week I heard my father died.

In the morning, Warden China looked at the housing numbers and saw that I was sent to segregation. She came to the hole to talk with me about it to see what happened because I had so many years of clear conduct. I told her that my father died she already had that information too.

She told me she was going to let me out on the grounds, but she would not dismiss the findings of the misconduct. She was a little disappointed with me, but she still liked me a lot.

I was found guilty and they gave me three days, I did them in the housing unit and went right back to my room on the grounds.

I did apologize to the officer. She and I used to get along, but after that she really stayed clear of me.

It took me a long time to get over the death of my father. I had got a phone number for Billy (He was the roommate of Dee a long time ago). I asked him did he have anything to do with Dee's death. Dee was murdered. Someone snuck through his basement window and came upstairs while he was laying on the couch sleeping and shot him in the head with one shot. He was murdered.

My attitude was resulting back to street mentality. I was relapsing as they call it. I could not help but think it was him. It was like Billy's work, sneaking in the house shooting the person in the head with one bullet while they were asleep.

Billy told me he was doing well and he was not into that stuff. I knew that Henze did not care for Dee or me. He felt like we had something to do with the shooting of Vicenza Giuliano. So I knew that Billy was Henze's right hand man and that he really admired Henze and would do anything he asked of him.

Dee was accused of shooting Vicenza Giuliano. I figured that Henze had Billy take care of Dee once he got out of prison. Billy knew that Dee did not shoot Vicenza Giuliano, but he would not tell Henze how he knew. I told Billy on the phone that I'd better not find out that he had anything to do with the death of Dee.

Billy told me that he liked Dee that he had been living in Waterford. He was not off into any of that stuff anymore. He was living a straight life now after 15 years in prison.

When I talk to Dee's mother, she told me that Dee was about to get married. They believed a man named Billy shot him. That is why I thought it was Billy. I never did find out. Nor did the police ever find the shooter.

I felt like I was losing everyone. Later I heard that Nick (the boy I liked when I was younger and owed me money) had also died.

I am not sure if I believed that one. I think he knew I was getting out of prison he just did not want to see me. So he told this girl that knew me in prison to say he was dead. Maybe he is, maybe he wasn't. He was probably afraid of me coming home. He did not want to see me. He owed me a thousand or so when I went in.

Everyone I knew from my past was dying. The ones that were alive, I did not know how to get a hold of them. Some found me after I was released; others I did not care to find.

Then Lori came into the prison system. She was the one who hired two gun men to shoot me and my husband going down the 75 Freeway. She was scared and told the control center that she was afraid of me. She should have told them because she tried to kill me. She had lost a lot of weight and stayed clear of me.

I was not thinking of Lori and that phony life style out there. I knew that Lori would get hers one day. I did tell many on the prison ground not to trust her. She was shipped out of the camp within two weeks making it sound as if her life was in danger. Wow, what a guilty conscious will do to some people. Everyone was dead and I had found out who my husband really was. But as far as I was concerned the fight was over. There was no reason to get back at her or take revenge because as far as I was concerned . . . that street life was over for me. I did not care about what she did or where she went. I was no longer fighting a fight that was in the streets in our gangster days. Those days were dead to me.

Time kept passing and Celeste F. came into the prison again.

She had been in and out many times. When she came in, Sadie kept hinting to me that she felt like Celeste liked me. I told Sadie that Celeste was used to those women that took care of her. Every time she came to prison, because she looked like a man, the women prisoners would pay her to be with them. They would buy her clothes, food, whatever she wanted and whatever could be bought in prison they would buy it for her.

I would not take care of her. Sadie said, "Teach her how to hustle."

So Celeste and I talked with each other. She had a great personality. Everyone liked her. Everyone disliked me. Maybe I needed to get my mind off the streets and all the loss of loved ones. She was living with this girl, Betty who was abusing her. She was not happy. She would call Sadie 'Puddle' as a nickname.

She cried to 'Puddle' and me about wanting to get out of that situation. I told her, "I could get you moved but you better be serious."

Then Sadie said, "Move her in as your Bunkie."

Celeste said, "Yeah, I will be your Bunkie."

I was a little nervous about her being my Bunkie, but I said okay.

"I will ask for you as a Bunkie."

I wrote Warden China. I asked her if Celeste could be my Bunkie. I explained to her, that everyone picked a Bunkie but I never did. She looked on the records and saw that this was true. I never chose a Bunkie. When we first moved from Detroit, everyone got to choose our own Bunkie's. Lina chose me but I did not choose her.

The facility felt this would keep friction down if everyone liked their bunk mate that they were forced to live with. It was a onetime pick, you were able to pick one time. I never did pick my Bunkie . . . .

So Celeste became my Bunkie. We did well together. I showed her how to write letters for herself, turning tricks, getting men who were not incarcerated. We took her picture and sent them off for copies to send to the men. When Celeste dressed up as a woman, she was nice looking.

When she dressed up as a man, she was nice looking. She could go either way. She started getting answers from guys. She found a few guys that really liked her. They were sending her money and she was putting it away. I taught her how to save her funds for when she got out.

I ran my "two for one" store. I was able to bring in more funds that way.

Here and there I would get packages of weed or pills. Often I would have Lina who worked in Hobby Crafts sneak packages in for me containing perfumes.

Lina also had a friend in Franklin Camp who came to the law library where she worked every week.

I had people drop off packages at the control center in the waste basket. Lina's friend would pick it up and bring it over to the library. It would be a twenty dollar bill for the package and a twenty dollar bill to Lina for bringing it in. I would have to give Lina so much for doing it. Once, I felt like she cheated me, and we kind of fell out.

Celeste was there in prison for a year or so. She was getting close to going home. She kept sneaking around getting high. I did not condemn getting high whatsoever.

I told Celeste from Jump Street. I did not want any drug use in the cell. I was raised by ol'school ways; for one (1) you don't do your own product and two (2) you need to be aware of your surroundings at all time. Getting high was stupid to me now. Being a drug dealer, I realized the evils of it that would bring you down.

I came in the room one day. I knew this girl sold her some drugs. Celeste kept telling me it was my imagination. I was lying on the bunk, watching Celeste sitting at the desk. She was doing something like writing or something. She kept hanging her head down. I was watching her nod out while saliva was drooling onto the desk.

I jumped off the bottom bunk. I reached all the way down toward the floor and brought my fist up hitting Celeste as hard as I could in the back of her head.

We started fighting in the room. You could hear us banging against the walls and lockers. It was making a lot of noise. Sadie heard us and came to break it up.

I was so mad at Celeste for getting high. I even went out of the cell and cussed this girl Deb out for selling her the crap.

I blacked Celeste's eye and many people kept teasing her about it. She was embarrassed by it but would not let them know it.

Celeste finally went home. I did not hear anything from her, she never kept in contact or bothered to tell anyone to say hi to me. I taught Celeste how to save money. She put away a little over 5,000.00 dollars to take home.

I was getting closer to my out date. I finally got a response from the U. S. Federal Court and this time they sent the information to the facility. They dropped my detainer and ran my case concurrent earlier in my bit. The paperwork was never given to the facility. The state authorities can't accept the paperwork from me; it had to go to Lansing first and then to the facility holding me so my time can be calculated correctly.

Now I was able to go to camp, my original prison, if I wanted too. This was a low security prison where I could work outside the prison and be assigned to work crews cleaning buildings, streets, parks, graveyards, and expressways picking up litter and such. Just knowing that made me feel good, but I was in college with Spring Arbor University. So I was not eligible unless I dropped out of school. I stayed to complete my degree, graduating with my Paralegal Certification in 1998 and my Bachelor's Degree in 1999. It was June 1999 and I no longer had the detainer on me from the fed's so I was able to transfer to camp

What a day that was. Then we took our certification for Substance Abuse, the fundamentals test and the S.P.E.C. test dealing with diversity.

As the date got closer, I had some money put a way to go home with. I sent away for my birth certificate. It cost me 10.00 dollars and my social security card, which was another 10.00 dollars. They kept them in the safe until I was ready to go.

I had not seen the parole board yet, but I was scheduled to see them in August of 1999.

Just as everything was going well for me, Sadie met me on the yard and told me she had something to tell me.

I went out there. She told me that Celeste was back. I told Sadie that she did not even write me or bother to even send word to me when she went home. Sadie told me it was up to me, but she heard that another girl we knew, Tecie (one of Cadillac's women), was trying to holler at her while she was in orientation.

I acted like I did not care, but inside, I was wondering how I was going to act when I saw her. I was trying to change my life. I was not into the homosexual scene any longer. I knew changes were taking place with me, but I really did not quite understand what kind of changes I was going through. I kept having dreams that did not make sense to me.

One time I dreamt that I was standing at an elevator and when the door opened Cadillac was standing there.

I could see a man with a long white robe and long hair.

When the door opened on the elevator he kind of melted out the door.

I looked at Cadillac and said, "Who was that?"

I could not see his face. I could only detect his image as a man.

Cadillac looked at me and said, "Man, you don't know Christ when you see him?"

Then I wake up. That was strange to me. I kept having weird things like that happening to me.

I quit smoking cigarettes. I used to smoke two packs of Newport's a day. I got my degree, quit drinking, getting high on anything and was totally against drugs. I was wondering about God and reading books on him.

The small stuff did not matter anymore. What used to make me mad no longer phases me. I did not want to get into trouble and tried to stay away from it. My life was changing. I really was becoming another person.

I did have this one Officer Pier who kept writing me up as much as he could. He did not like me from the very beginning and he took things personal when it came to me. Every time I did the smallest thing he wrote major misconducts on me.

Pier wrote three (3) misconduct on me within two days. That could stop my date and Pier knew that. Some officers were dirty like that. They would take your date because they had the authority.

I finally went to Deputy Ward telling him this man was after me. Deputy Ward looked into it. He told me he would not pull my misconducts but he would make sure I had a fair hearing. He did just that.

I beat all three misconducts which would have stopped me from going home. Deputy Ward knew I was getting ready to leave after 18 years and the change. He had personally witnessed my change for the better.

After I beat those misconducts, I had to go to Ms. Purple (my counselor's) office and answer a bunch of questions.

Officer Pier accused Deputy Ward of having an overly familiar relationship with me because I beat the misconducts.

That was a laugh.

Deputy Ward never, out of all those years I was in prison disrespected me. He had never done anything inappropriate. He was one of the best guys there. He would not pull my misconducts. He refused and told me I had to go on the evidence. What a joke Pier's accusations were. Was Pier serious?? What is really going on? The devil was trying to throw me off my square for real.

There was so much scandal going on with sexual crap in the facility. Every man had to protect themselves. Most of those women would dress sexy. Stay up in the officer's face. Offer to suck their penises. The women would rub on them under the table. It was a trip.

I realized that the officers were not able by law to agree or have the right to have sex with these women. But there was more to this story that I will not even going into in this book about. I have my own opinion of this situation.

Anyways, I was not into exchanging sex for favors. So Pier was really wrong about the Deputy being over familiar with me. I beat the misconducts because of the evidence. Point blank.

***This is not Detroit just what it looks like.***

Celeste came on the count, the prison grounds. The administration shipped her to Franklin camp part of the Detroit prison. She asked me to follow her and I did.

I asked Warden China to sign my papers sending me. I had graduated and only had a few months left before I saw the parole board so I was free.

Celeste and I were not intimate at this time. We were only good close friends.

I followed her to Franklin, then they sent her to Camp Stand.

I went with her, I did not want to go, but I did. When I arrived, I was surprised that the same Deputy was in charge.

I was so happy to see him again. His wife worked in the administration department too. They were a great couple and Deputy Premont was easy to deal with.

I asked to see him. I asked him to move me over where Celeste was. I also asked to be placed on PW, which was public works. I had not been out in the world for 17 years. I wanted to make sure that I surrounded myself with the outside.

Things were going good. I loved working out in the world.

Officer Abe was our supervisor and he was great. He was strict about the rules but easy to work with. I cleaned up cemeteries, parks, roads and whatever was asked of me.

Then a job came available for the Robert Colon Police Department. They asked me if I wanted to take it. I thought this was their way of keeping an eye on me. I took the position. At first it was a little odd. I just never thought I would work inside a police department.

I cleaned their building from head to toe. I worked really hard trying to do the best job I could do. I striped their floors, painted their ceiling because of the smoke in there. They really liked me a lot.

I found a bag of weed one time in the holding tank and gave it back to them. They liked me so much and the work I was doing.

I saw the parole board and my brother showed up for my hearing. The parole board asked him if he would see to my needs until I was able to do for myself.

Of course my brother said YES.

The parole board told me, if I ever come back in front of them, they would keep flopping me until they could not flop me anymore. (Flopping is where you go in front of the parole board and they continue you. So your sentence may only be 5-10, they can flop you up to 10 years.) I understood that message. They gave me an undercover flop.(Which means they gave me a fixed date to go home which was one year away). So I had to do another year, but if I got any tickets I would lose my date.

I did not tell anyone. People like to pull you off your square and make you lose your date. When the inmates know you have a chance to go home they will mess with you out of revenge or jealousy.

I was still running my "two for one" store. I really needed to give it up because it could have stopped me from going home. I ran that until I went home. I gave it to Celeste when I left. I had hundreds of dollars in merchandise when I left for home.

The last year at the Robert Colon Police Department was great. I got to know them better, even the Chief of Police. He had a different opinion of criminals after meeting me. Many of them felt the real test would be when I was released.

It was getting closer to my date to go home. I was so excited. Many things were going through my head. I had saved up a thousand dollars to go home with from jobs and other things. I was in pretty good shape.

I had boxes going up to the ceiling at my mom's house. I had towels, sheets, pots and pans, etc.

I was so surprised when all the girls that I had been jailed with, gave me a picnic party. At the party on the prison yard they asked me to make a toast. I stood up and looked around the table. I realized I had an argument with everyone sitting at that table, but it did not even matter anymore. I was going home for the first time in 18 years. I said my little good byes. I told everyone, even though we did not see eye to eye something good.

We had all grown over the years. We grew up with each other. I was 23 years old when I became incarcerated in the county jail. Now I was leaving as a 43 year old lady in menopause.

The night before I was leaving this one girl in my area kept giving me trouble. She kept messing with me stating I was doing LIFE and was never going home.

I really did not feed into her negative spirit but she just kept it up. My old personality kicked in.

I jumped off my bed to pull her out of her bed and Celeste jumped in saying, "If anyone fights here, it will be with me. Giuliano has been down a long time and needs to go home. So let's end it here, or I will be the one who is fighting."

Celeste yelled out again "Because Giuliano is going home tomorrow!!"

I was so proud of Celeste, because she was never a fighter, but that day, she stepped up to the plate.

"U go girl" (I thought to myself).

# CHAPTER SEVEN

## HOME COMING

That day finally came and I was released.

My brother was late picking me up, he had my mother with him.

She was happy to see me and was smiling. My step father Tom just died two years before my return. My mother moved back to the Detroit area. (She was living in Alabama.)

I was glad she was up here, because no one wanted me to do parole at home with them. They were all scared because before I went to prison, I had a 10,000.00 dollar hit on my head. They said that Henze H. had that hit on me. Everyone in my family was afraid to let me stay with them. Everyone in my past was either drug dealers or hit men.

My mom said, I could come live with her. She felt she lived her life and was not afraid. My mother was trying to show me she was a solider. She was trying to make up for the past. I was glad I had someone to parole home to.

When I came home, it was so beautiful to look at the world without a fence and gun towers.

I went to the park to stare at the waterfall and prayed with warmth of a bleeding heart for freedom. I saw beauty where the average person missed for being around it all their life.

I made an appointment to get my nails done and a pedicure. It felt like heaven to have someone pamper me, relaxing back in the vibrating chair while the Asian women massaged my legs. She placed gels, sea salt and then hot stones. Cleaning my toe nails and scraping my feet to make them look perfect. I felt like those prison walls were disappearing and I was a million bucks.

I went back to my mother's place. It was great to eat whatever I wanted to. Just getting up to use the bathroom without getting permission was a blessing.

My mother and I rode over to Robert Colon Police department. They gave me a coming home party. It was so beautiful. I felt so loved and welcomed by them.

Robert Colon was a laid back town and it seemed to me a great place to start off the slow reintegrating back into society. I looked out their window many times to imagine what freedom would feel like. So I looked for employment close to that area. My mother's place was an hour and half from the police station.

My mother lived in closer to the Grand Rapids area, so I paroled to her. My whole family except my daughter moved from Detroit. I could not wait to see my daughter. I wondered what she looked like. I had not seen her since she was 14 years old. She was 22 now. I was nervous and did not know what to say.

That would have to come later because I had things to do before I was able to see her.

My family went out, bought food, brought me flowers and made me feel very welcomed. My sister Nivea and her husband kinda met me for the first time. Nivea was a baby when I left home. She really only saw me once in a blue moon. She was very supportive. The evening was great and I was exhausted.

I lay in my bed at night with **fear** that someone would knock on the door. I felt like they would tell me I had to go back. That it was a mistake they let me out.

I went through a lot of emotional and psychological stress, something akin to Post Traumatic Stress Disorder (PTSD). To cross a street and determine how fast the cars were going was a challenge. To deal with the fast pace and loud noises were exhausting. The reality of my youth being gone, when I went in just turning 23 and coming home at the age of 43, bore down on me.

Just to drive again was freedom, letting the air blow in my face and feel others driving next to me was awesome.

I was like a new born child able to rebirth myself back into society. I was ready and willing to show the world a new me and somehow put back what I took so many years ago.

I did have one man I was writing that I liked and wanted to meet but he did not understand my parole stipulations. I could not just get up and leave. I had to get things together with my daughter and other obligations I had. Soon he stopped calling and writing me.

My parole agent was a woman from the rural area and a bit of a square. She was a bit too much. She stated she never had anyone who spent as much time as me in prison. She did not know what to do with me. She had me drop a couple times a week. She commented about how I was a heroin user. I told her the last time I used was in 1979.

She read in her books once a heroin user always a heroin user. I tried to tell her that was not true. You could tell, she did not have any life experience and her knowledge came from a text book.

Then she sent me to a psychologist. She felt I had many psychological issues from being locked up for so long.

I do believe I had PTSD, from being locked up so long.

I was given a test with 680 questions on it. When those test results came out okay she wanted him to give me another one. She felt since I had psychology classes in college I knew how to pass the test. Anyone with brains would know how to pass it.

Come on, it had questions like: "Have you killed animals?"; "Do you hate your father?"; "Do you ever think what it would be like to kill someone?". Anyone with common sense could pass it.

She was looking to see if I had issues with killing. She thought I was a psychopath. I had issues with integrating, social skills, anxiety with noise, movement, trust issues, basic socializing abilities.

She lost my respect after that. I felt like she was not a good fit for me. I could not wait to find a job and move away from her as my agent. I wanted to be close to an inter-city where they had experience with returnees. I did not want to be anyone's lab rat.

I bought my first car. My agent wanted to know who and how I got the funds to purchase it. She wanted all my family to write letters stating they gave me the funds to purchase it.

Then, I got a job as a Substance Abuse Counselor. My agent wanted to know how I received a Bachelor's Degree. When I told her I went to college while incarcerated she was not pleased.

Then she started complaining to me about her having to paying for her college degree. I felt like this was so unprofessional. What did this have to do with the price in China? She should be glad I was able to get a J.O.B.

I got mad and told her, "You could have gotten it free in prison."

My family begged me to keep my mouth shut. They could see she was bringing the worst out of my personality. I knew I had to get away from her before I got sent back. She was on a power trip.

I was released in September. I got a job at Wal-Mart in November within two months. I know people can get employment with a felony.

The manager came out after I filled out the application and said, "Ms. Giuliano, you forgot to mark the box on felony."

I told him, "No I did not, I left it open so when you asked me about it. I could explain to you in person about my felony."

After I told him I just got out of prison and I was a hard worker plus I needed a job, he hired me. I was willing to use my Warden for a reference.

He wanted me to stay on the day shift. I wanted afternoon shifts but they were not comfortable with me yet. I worked any shifts they gave me. I put all my checks into stock. My boss at Wal-Mart's liked my work so much that when he moved his family into his new condo, he asked me to come to his home and help him move.

I left in December after Christmas because I had the job at a substance abuse rehab in Battle Creek. It took a month for my paper work to come back. I rented an apartment near the Robert Colon Police Department. Lynn, who I worked with at the police department, co-signed for the apartment that my character was good. She knew me and wanted to help me. Some apartment complexes do not rent to felons like this one. I paid about three months' worth of rent. They would not allow me to pay any more in advance than that.

My parole agent would not allow me to go to the apartment. She warned me if I slept one night there before my paperwork came in she would violate me.

I cried, "Oh please, give me a break. I found two jobs and got an apartment and you will not allow me to go unpack my stuff?"

It was Christmas. I wanted to stay in my apartment. I had been waiting for three weeks for my paperwork and still nothing came through. My apartment had sat for three weeks without anyone living in it.

My family helped me move all my furniture in the house. My brother had nice furniture in his garage that he gave to me. It was a dining room set, coach, love seat, marble table, and bedroom bed set.

I also had saved up things while inside. I saved dishes, pots and pans, glasses, all kinds of sheets, blankets, nick-knacks, towels television sets (two). I was ready to keep house.

So on Christmas I went to the apartment. I did not care what the agent had to say. I sat in my own living room. I cleaned up my home. I put all the dishes away and hung up my clothes & pictures on the wall.

I was so happy and pleased with life that I stepped out on the terrace looking up at the sky watching the stars thanking my Heavenly Father. I was not much of a church going person but I knew somehow that God was the reason. I decided I was going to find a church and start going.

I was packing up to return to Wayland and the phone rang. My mom told me my transfer papers came through. I was allowed to stay in my apartment. I was so happy. I knew now it was time to go find my daughter and bring her out of Detroit.

I went to Detroit to get my baby except she was not a baby any longer. Sabrina was twenty-three years old with two children. I felt so guilty not being there for her. I talked Sabrina into moving out of Detroit and being closer to me. Sabrina and I went through our issues.

She was hurt from the past, for the things I put her through when she was younger. We went through our ups and downs but kept working at our relationship. My daughter is beautiful inside and out. She is a Peer Counselor for mental health program. We went through a lot of stuff together but I promised her I would not place it in the book. Through the grace of the Lord we are making it through all of it.

I started work as a substance abuse counselor and at first, everything was great. I looked around at a few churches but nothing really caught my eye. At work, my co-worker Deena asked me to come to her church so I went. I liked her church and I liked Deena a lot.

I had met a man named ZaKeith and we were getting fairly tight. He asked me to marry him and I did before he changed his mind. He and I got married in Deena's church that was the first church Deena took me to. ZaKeith liked that church. Our marriage had its moments and sometimes it was a nightmare.

We went on vacations every year had parties and get-to-gathers. Everyone wanted to be like ZaKeith and me. We were the couple of the year. Soon after three-in-half years ZaKeith and I started to grow apart. I was out of prison with my own psychological issues and ZaKeith had his drinking issues. My marriage was going bad.

ZaKeith and I separated but did not divorce until seven years later.

At first we were angry with each other but as time went on we became the best of friends. Years later, he stopped drinking and has continued with his education as a counselor. He will make a great one.

I had been writing a program for ex-offenders and putting together many things to assist them with transition to society. I had been working on it for a year. I ran the workshops and received a lot of support from others. I developed a website with assistance and wrote a manual.

I filed out a DBA and made the name of it. I conducted this program for two years with great results. It is a one of its kind in this area. I started running it independently at a Baptist Church in the Southwest area. They were my fiduciary. I conducted it for a year and until it was black-balled by many individuals who will be nameless. They did not like that I was a returnee conducting this program. They also wanted me to do the program for them, and when the program got up and running, they, then, would get rid of me.

I received a grant from a foundation for 10,000.00 dollars. We conducted groups every week and made some progress. I wanted more.

I was teaching social skills. The shortest words get you through prison life. for example: "Give me that" and "Move" etc. I realized that when returnee's come home, we are unable to fit in. We don't even realize we are speaking this way. It is a way of life in there with its own culture and values. It is so common and when we are released we continue speaking the same way out here.

We have problems with employment because when we spot someone making scrubby moves inside the joint, we will call them on it. Out here in society, people do not take kindly to you for calling them out. So they use information on you to get you out of the picture.

So I taught offenders how to fit in socially and keep their employment.

Of course, most of my teachings were by "Trial and error". (Smile)

If you have been in for a few years, one would be lost by all the technology changes. I would take them to Best Buy and have an associate there explain the technology to them, so they had some knowledge on how to use the new gadgets.

Even crossing the streets and judging how fast they had to move was a challenge to get across the street. The normal person would not realize that noise, and exposure to many colors would be a factor.

Inside, things move slowly and there is noise but not as loud as the stores, many people going at one time. Inside prison you usually went by groups or housing unit / sections.

Sitting at the table eating was a challenge. In there you have 15 minutes to eat.

You learn to huddle over your plate and eat fast. I assisted ex-cons on how to eat proper and regain their social skills.

When you correct an offender, they become very offended by the correction. They are used to being on the defensive. I would bring it to their awareness and help them not to take criticism negatively but as positive constructive feedback. Because of the hostile environment offenders have to live in, they are always on the defensive; they do not trust anyone.

I opened a half-way house for D-47 parolees, meaning individuals that have mental health issues. I started running it under my Billy Joe Consultant LLC but realized as time went on I would have to pay the taxes. I would not make a profit and did not want to pay taxes on something I was not making any money on. So I contacted a friend of mine named Jude. I met her at a MPRI program for prisoners. (MPRI stands for Michigan Prisoner Reentry Initiative)

She was working on a committee in the neighborhood. She started a 501c3 for employment for offenders. I wanted to invest in transitional housing for ex-offenders, when I met this woman Jude who was an advocate for offenders. We hit it off right away. We integrated our programs together and Jude became my fiduciary.

With this new backing and support from Jude, I was able to win a contract with MPRI, Mental Health, Psychological Counseling. We also gained a contract with DHS.

It was just my luck that an officer who worked inside the prison during my incarceration was now a parole agent . . . (What was the chance of that happening?) At first she went against everything I was trying to achieve.

Finally Agent Valerie and I talked and she gave me advice and helped me to become more professional with my project.

The university allowed me to do my internship at the half way house that I designed and started. I was personally working on a private project that expressed my desire to give back. I have been conducting this program since 2005 and do not receive any money for my work. I wanted to make that clear. Every bit of funds that comes my way goes into the program. Nothing goes in my pocket. Matter of fact, a lot of my own paycheck goes to this program.

Our program is called: **<u>Starting Over for Success</u>** www.startingoverforsuccess.org

My life has changed a great deal. I live in recovery every day doing the right thing. My spiritual aspect has developed in many directions. My program was inspired by God my Lord and Savior.

My life is not totally where I want it to be. I would love to end this book with my program running very successfully and with my book published and my master's degree but I have now achieved my Bachelors in Social Work and received a limited license through the State of Michigan. I am also working as a substance abuse counselor at a residential health clinic.

I don't have my Masters in Social Work yet but I am waiting to get accepted at Michigan State. My paperwork was not completed last year when I applied.

While attending school, I was on Facebook and got in touch with an old friend, Denver from my younger years growing up. I have not seen or heard from him in 30 years. I was so excited that I got in contact also with my old friend Lena my best friend from the past and now Denver. I can't express in mere words what that has done for me. It allowed me to have some connection with my past that was good, positive and pure.

Everyone had grown up and changed for the better. I almost felt complete.

I went upstate to visit Lena. I had a great time with her and her kids. The kids stated that we acted just like two school girls. My life was turning around. I felt so happy and full of life. Going back to school and taking vacations. It was the life I always wanted and now it even stepped up a pace.

After I came back from seeing Lena, Denver gave my phone number to Alan and he called me on the phone. I could not go see Denver, he was in Florida but Alan was outside of Detroit.

I was at the doctor's office and did not answer the call but after I got out of the doctors, I listened to my voice mail. Wow, it was Alan. Through a mutual friend Denver on Facebook, Alan and I got in touch with each other again after 30 years. We started seeing each other. Soon we started dating and it was not long before we got back together after all these years.

It is nice being with someone I knew since I was 11 years old. Who knew the changes I went through and understood me better? It is a missing link in my life that knitted me back to the past as if nothing ever happened with this nightmare.

I looked for employment around Alan's house as requested by him and found employment. I live my life in total recovery. I work as a Substance Abuse Counselor for this company. I am doing well and very happy in my life.

People may do bad things but it does not mean they are bad people. My life and book ends here, where my life is positive and it is great to be alive and free.

# CHAPTER EIGHT

# IT IS A NEW BEGINNING, A NEW LIFE, AND A NEW FREEDOM.

I hate the street life; I believe this is my calling to save our youth and adults from the lies of the streets. I am dedicated to sobriety and recovery. I have dedicated my life to Christ and a faith-based philosophy.

Others may boast of standards of academia, years of experience in social service organizations, even considerable time spent ministering to both prisoners and ex-offenders but I am unprecedented in my knowledge of life behind prison walls, its code of conduct, stress, economy, danger and opportunity for redemption.

I continue to walk the path the Lord set forward for me and successfully reach out to those who suffer, especially to those who society has cast aside and will not hire for employment or continue to ask if they have a felony 10 and 20 years later, when they have changed their lives. I follow my own resources, do my own research, while moving through "trial and error" and "failure and success".

I have a wonderful job and a great boss that believes in me despite my past. He feels I have done my time and have earned the right to pursue a little happiness now. All I have left now to make me complete is when I take that final leap into the next dimension when my Savior takes me by the hand.

It is almost like that poster of Jesus carrying me in the sand and only one set of footsteps are showing.

I am in great hope this book will help someone in life to understand our choices can cause avenues and tunnels through life that lead to hurt, pain and long term discomfort. I understood as a young girl what the consequences were but I did not know what the greater outcome of that concept was, in the long term. What we do as young adults can dictate one's whole future. I prayed a blessing comes to anyone that reads this book and learns from my choices.

The street life is a lie and we have to beware of the spirits (the streets is a spirit) in this world, our real inner self desires happiness for us. The street life can be enticing. It will pull you in. You start off by having a good time feeling the high, and then the other part of your personality comes out. It will suck the life out of you until you lose everything that matters around you. You spouse, your children and your life. It will not stop until you are dead or in prison. It will take your soul.

I am a proud mother and grandmother. I love my daughter with all my heart and am glad to have a relationship with her once again. God has both of us in his arms and heart. I am a part of my daughter's and grandchildren's lives. I love each day God has given me.

My brother Rip and I are still very close, more than anyone else in my family.

Thank you my Lord. I dedicate this book to my father, my daughter and my lovely grandchildren.

I thank my work for believing in me. Read this book and know you are all in my heart and soul.

Live in Recovery and don't let the street life take you.

The End!!